Free Spirit

Free Spirit

A Biography of Mason Welch Gross

Thomas W. Gross

RUTGERS UNIVERSITY PRESS
NEW BRUNSWICK, CAMDEN, AND NEWARK,
NEW JERSEY, AND LONDON

Library of Congress Cataloging-in-Publication Data
Names: Gross, Thomas W., author.
Title: Free spirit: a biography of Mason Welch Gross / by Thomas W. Gross.
Description: New Brunswick, New Jersey: Rutgers University Press, [2021] |
    Includes bibliographical references and index.
Identifiers: LCCN 2020057874 | ISBN 9781978808331 (hardcover) |
    ISBN 9781978808348 (epub) | ISBN 9781978808355 (mobi) |
    ISBN 9781978808362 (pdf)
Subjects: LCSH: Gross, Mason Welch, 1911–1977. | Rutgers University—Presidents—
    Biography. | Rutgers University—History—20th century.
Classification: LCC LD4752.7.G76 G76 2021 | DDC 378.1/11092 [B]—dc23
LC record available at https://lccn.loc.gov/2020057874

A British Cataloging-in-Publication record for this book is available from the British
Library.

♾ The paper used in this publication meets the requirements of the American National Standard for Information Sciences—Permanence of Paper for Printed Library Materials, ANSI Z39.48-1992.

www.rutgersuniversitypress.org

Manufactured in the United States of America

*Dedicated to the memory of anyone
who ever drew a line in the sand and fought for
what they believed in*

Tell me of the man
Who walks in wisdom;
How does he talk,
How does he sit,
How does he move about?
   —Bhagavad Gita 2: 54

Contents

Author's Note

The study of individuals, what their aspirations were, their struggles, and their difficulties, is a source of endless fascination. In a well-done biography, one can enter into the very soul of great individuals and expand one's own soul along with them. . . . The identification of one's self with the great men and women of history is the surest way of arousing the imagination to a sense of the possibilities of one's spiritual growth and to a . . . realization of one's own potentialities. —MWG, 1953

Mason W. Gross, philosopher, educator, athlete, musician, and the president of Rutgers University during the turbulent 1960s, was my father. Writing his biography was never on my bucket list. I was content to let the story of his life drift slowly out of focus, just as had my memory of my life under his roof and just as will my own son's memory of me. However, circumstances conspired that I would be the one to tell his story.

As Mason's biographer but also as his son, and in the interests of full disclosure, I will admit to the reader that, putting it mildly, Mason Gross and I never really got along. We didn't argue; one did not argue with Mason Gross. Arguing with Mason Gross was like bringing a knife to a gunfight. Our conversations were sometimes cordial, often not, but we never spoke about anything of value. The reader will sense my emotional distance from my subject. But, as credible witness to many climactic events in Mason's life, in this biography I must appear at times as both author and source. As a result, the completely objective and scholarly viewpoint to which a biographer should aspire may be impossible to achieve. With this excuse I also ask the forgiveness of others who did know him and saw him through differently colored lenses and who will counter me with statements such as "Oh, he wasn't like that at all."

A biography that is a mere chronology of a person's life would be a huge bore.

Biography, well written, is less about one's actions than it is a reflection on the motivation behind those actions. I have tried to build this biography using the best source that I have, namely Mason himself, whose own words I have emphasized throughout the book.

Admittedly, researching this biography has become an exploration of my own, a study of who I am in direct relation to who he was. It has been a voyage finally to meet the man I never knew, the man whom so many saw as a great mentor, colleague, and friend but who for me was both colossus and enigma. I'd say that I am not so much telling his story as I am also discovering it. But this is wholly his story and not mine. On those brief occasions when I appear in his biography, it is only to clarify his story, not to tell my own.

What can the life of a philosophy professor and university president from fifty years ago offer to us today? Not only is this a biography of a wonderful mind, but it has also evolved into a practical handbook for the twenty-first century. Mason's life shows students how never to settle for less than their best effort every day; it shows teachers how, hands-on, to inspire excellence in their students and to "never allow them to be satisfied with inadequate or shoddy performance."[1] His story shows us how music, theater, the visual arts, and the humanities are as important to our way of life as are engineering, clean water, and good plumbing. It shows us what excellence feels like. It reminds parents never to isolate themselves from the families who want only to love them, and it reminds children that their parents are only human. Mason's experiences reveal how "government secrecy benefits nobody except the government"[2] and that democracy is ever fragile and quick to descend into the depths of autocracy. This biography shows how to take your beliefs and turn them, confidently, into action in service to your community. Mason's story reminds us that the study of philosophy is not solely for the intellectuals in the ivory tower but instead is for everyone, for each, "to attempt to re-examine the principles upon which you have based your entire life. Philosophy in all its history has never gone beyond Socrates' classic phrase, the motto of all philosophers, that 'the unexamined life is not worth living.'"[3] Mason's story reminds us all that education, real education, is not something that you can pay an institution to do to you but instead is a personal and lifelong "habit of an individual pursuit of truth,"[4] which each of us must perform for ourselves.

For all the reasons to read Mason's biography, one stands out above the rest, namely that all the things that he stood for, all the issues upon which he refused to compromise, still resonate and remain unresolved in the twenty-first century, almost fifty years after he retired. Some of them have become worse. This biography shows how Mason cherished the ideal of free speech, which is now being trampled nationwide, even on college campuses such as at my own alma mater, UC Berkeley, where the Free Speech Movement originated in 1964, and how he abhorred the pernicious racism that underlies so many aspects of our culture. The biography also shows how public respect and support for the value of higher education, once seen as the salvation of our way of life, has sunk to a new low as our citizens have become generally disdainful of facts, expertise, reason, and intellect.

I have explored the experiences that made Mason into the man he had become when it came time to draw a line in the sand and stand up, like Socrates himself, for those absolute principles against which there can be no compromise. Maybe that is the lesson for me and for us in our twenty-first century. This is my reason for writing this book and hopefully is a good enough reason for you to pick it up and read it.

Free Spirit

CHAPTER 1

Prologue:
The Inauguration, 1959

The fundamental aim of education is, simply, freedom . . . , the freedom which results from a knowledge of how to organize ourselves politically, economically and socially, and which minimizes the danger of our collapsing, through incompetence, into the power of a tyrant . . . , the freedom which comes about from the increasing understanding of the forces of nature, and that freedom of spirit which Spinoza identified as the power of the intellect and which comes about when ignorance, superstition, hatred and fear yield to clear and adequate ideas. —MWG, May 6, 1959

Spring had arrived in New Brunswick, on the banks of New Jersey's fetid and fouled Raritan River, purported at the time to be one of the most grossly polluted rivers in the nation. Chestnut trees were in bloom. The New Brunswick *Daily Home News* forecasted for May 6, 1959, "sunny weather and seasonably warm."[1]

On this day, Rutgers University inaugurated its new president, Mason W. Gross, my father. The audience, both on the raised speaker's platform and those shifting uncomfortably in folding metal chairs on the green, represented the very old and, like myself, the very young, Rutgers's past and its future. For Rutgers University, this day was both an end and a beginning.

This day marked the end of Rutgers's vestiges as a private college, the end of the era when a faculty member's refusal to testify before the McCarthy hearings resulted in automatic summary dismissal, and the end of the era when the American Association of University Professors had officially censured this university for its failure to support academic freedom.

But, this day also represented the high-water mark of an era when higher education was seen "as the foundation of America's future—a golden age for public universities."[2] At Rutgers, this era marked the beginning of an intensive capital expansion plan to make room for the thousands of baby-boomer students, children of World War II veterans, who were soon to come knocking at the state university's doors. It was the beginning of a fevered national funding for higher education under the National Defense Education Act, which Congress had passed the previous autumn thanks to a national hysteria stirred up by Sputnik, the Soviet's first successful satellite; the unchallenged fiction of a missile gap between the United States and the Soviet Union; and the national epiphany that the majority of America's mathematicians, scientists, and rocket engineers were former Nazi European-born war prizes.[3]

Nationally, there were other new beginnings. Lorraine Hansberry's astounding *Raisin in the Sun*, the first play written by a Black woman to debut on Broadway, starred Sidney Poitier, further breaking the color barrier. The relatively ineffective Civil Rights Act of 1957, the first civil rights act passed by Congress since 1875, had established the toothless United States Commission on Civil Rights. Despite NASA's record of glaringly public missile launch failures, the Mercury astronauts, the first Americans to be launched into space, were introduced in April.

Within ten years, universities would no longer be seen as America's salvation and instead would be seen as seedbeds of communism, treason, and discord. The previously nonviolent lunch counter sit-ins and peace marches seeking to end racial segregation would evolve into riotous and chaotic unrest, breeding a violent reaction, a white backlash that would impact attempts to improve opportunities for minorities to obtain a college education.

In July 1959 in yet another beginning, the first two Americans soldiers would die in Vietnam. Within ten years thirty thousand more would die, and later over twenty thousand more would die once the peace talks started. American universities would become a major focal point of antiwar activity, setting the stage for a conservative backlash and a national delusion that the universities were the source of everything that is wrong in America.

During the next ten years, Mason repeatedly would have to defend free speech, academic freedom, and equal opportunity for all in pursuit of higher education. His actions would make him a target for all the pent-up conflicts of race, class, ideology, and politics that would develop by 1970 and lead to his consummate defeat.

But in the quiet spring of 1959, none of this was evident as several thousand guests sat in steel folding chairs that settled unequally into the soft spring soil. The guests included Mason's mother, brother, and sister from Hartford, his father having passed away only two years previously. Seated in the front row were Mason's wife, Julia, and their four children, the oldest of whom was graduating high school that spring and was knocking at the door for her college education. As their youngest, I was finishing second grade.

Standing at the dais to take the oath of his new office, at 6'3" Mason was taller than most men of his generation. Once extremely slender and narrow-shouldered in his adolescence, as photographs from high school and college reveal, he had gained weight in the ten years since becoming a full professor but for the time being carried it well, hidden in his large frame.

In 1959 very few American men sported facial hair, but Mason wore an understated black mustache that he had grown as an undergraduate at Cambridge, in keeping with British custom. It was mysterious, continental, professional, and worldly, reminiscent of a generation of British cabinet ministers. The mustache gave Mason an air of credibility similar to that of Walt Disney or journalist and CBS anchor Walter Cronkite.

Mason never wore a hat, not once, in the sun, the rain, or bitter cold. Showing no sign of impending baldness, his black hair, graying at the temples, was cut short on the sides and slightly longer on the top, combed through the arc of a cowlick, and parted on the right. He had dark, arching eyebrows that moved independently of each other, like those of a border collie. When with one raised eyebrow he looked over the top of his tortoiseshell bifocals, which he referred to as his "spectacles," his eyebrows could silently corroborate his full range of emotion, from playful inquiry to arctic glare.

At age forty-seven, Mason was not a career bureaucrat. Unlike many university administrators, he had never been a college president somewhere else. He was a thirteen-year member of the Rutgers faculty, hired in 1946 as an assistant professor and an assistant dean. Unlike his predecessor, Lewis Jones, Mason was not an import from a different university, brought in to clean things up. He was a local boy. He knew everyone and called them by their first names, from the deans to the groundskeepers. He was homegrown.

In 1946 Mason, recently discharged from the U.S. Army Air Force, had arrived as a junior faculty member just as Rutgers was transitioning from a sleepy private college, whose students were predominantly well-to-do, white, and male, to a state university, its doors thrown open to veterans, also predominantly white and male, who had walked across Europe or steamed across the Pacific Ocean to islands whose names, such as Guadalcanal, Peleliu, and Iwo Jima, now household words, had fifteen years previously been unknown to all but a handful of Americans.

In 1959, the public recognized Mason as the onstage mediator of a popular 1950s television quiz show. After his five years on camera as the credible face of authority on CBS's hit show *Two for the Money*, newspapers across the United States would herald his inauguration at Rutgers, referring not to his academic qualifications but instead to his presence on the TV program.

The governor and the university's Board of Governors knew him well and for many years as a gifted administrator who on several occasions had performed as temporary president during both previous presidents' prolonged absences. Archie Alexander, chairman of the Board of Governors, called Mason "mercurial by temperament, moving in a moment from anger to laughter."[4] The faculty knew Mason as an able advisor, advocate, and defender of their rights. University historian Richard P. McCormick called him "dynamic and charismatic." Provost Richard "Dick" Schlatter, Mason's colleague and best friend, saw in Mason the gift of genuine courtesy in that nobody ever left his office feeling belittled or dismissed, even when there was disagreement. Mason's students knew him as a dynamic teacher. His undergraduate class, titled "The Traditions of Western Religious Thought," which he cotaught with Schlatter, was extremely well attended and has since been described by former students as "the best class that I ever had in college."

To his late father, a Connecticut lawyer, Mason had been the rebellious son who refused to follow the family tradition of going to Yale and entering an uneventful and, for Mason, unchallenging insurance law practice. To his friends, Mason was an engaging but opinionated colleague and a gifted pianist who could play almost any song upon request. To his children, he was the Colossus of Rhodes; typically generous and kind, he was also mercurial, often distant, curt, impatient, and cruelly dismissive.

Schlatter recalled that Mason preferred Socratic dialogue to all other forms of discourse and called him "the philosopher-teacher of Rutgers,"[5] an American Socrates. With more than just a single raised eyebrow, Mason would vigorously protest any comparison between himself and Socrates, but some similarities are just too obvious to overlook, not so much to offer praise to his intellect but rather to note how completely Mason had absorbed the teachings of Socrates into his own heart.

Both Mason and Socrates were combat veterans. The Rutgers student newspaper *Daily Targum* referred to Mason as the university's "gadfly," a term once also used to describe Socrates himself as one whose persistent and annoying buzzing, like that of a large horsefly, could stampede a horse with just a small bite. Mason kept neither a diary nor a journal and never wrote a memoir. Socrates also wrote nothing and valued only the spoken word. Mason refused to permit publication of his speeches, claiming that once printed and not spoken, they would lose their vitality.* Both Mason and Socrates vigorously opposed moral relativism, that poison of the spirit that permits any injustice when deemed malleable for the occasion. When asked to compromise their principles, both would draw a line in the sand. Both Mason and Socrates eventually were accused of corrupting the minds of

---

*In 1980, three years after Mason passed away, Rutgers University Press published *The Selected Speeches of Mason Welch Gross*, edited by Richard P. McCormick and Richard Schlatter.

youths by a conservative and reactionary government in a world grown weary and disdainful of intellect. But mostly, they both loved discussion and dialectics, the asking of questions, and the pursuit of absolute truth, absolute justice, and absolute beauty in whatever form they might appear.

On this day, May 6, 1959, the turbulence of the following decade was unimaginable. We will see how Mason's optimistic inaugural address was about the future of Rutgers and the changing role of higher education. But first, we must see how Mason's early life brought him to this moment.

His story begins decades previously.

CHAPTER 2

Postmark:
Willcox, Arizona, 1928

*Alone in the desert, there is absolutely no more exhilarating experience in the
whole wide world than to read Shakespeare at the top of your lungs. I wasn't
reading Hamlet. I wasn't studying Hamlet. I wasn't analyzing Hamlet. I was
Hamlet, or the next day King Lear, or Othello, or Antony. This is what an
artist can do to you, he just absolutely grabs hold of the whole of you.*

—*MWG, April 23, 1964*

The black fingers of a thirty-foot-tall saguaro cactus reached into the cold
starlit stillness. Arizona's night sky was ablaze with more stars than this
lanky sixteen-year-old boy from humid and hazy Hartford, Connecticut, had
ever imagined. The nearest full-time electric light was in Tucson, fifty miles
to the west. A waning half moon, rising over the Galiuro Mountains, scattered its diamonds along the silvery shallows of the San Pedro River, whose
clear waters flowed north out of Mexico to join the Gila River somewhere
near Phoenix.

Mason was a novice in the saddle and rocked stiffly to the horse's slow
and steady gait. He was new to Arizona and had never ridden alone through
the desert, much less at night, to another ranch that he had never seen. No,
it was not actually a ranch; it was a well and a corral. Fortunately, the trail
was wide and well worn by cattle. Mason's horse was a veteran of the cattle
drives and knew the way. Together they followed the cattle trail south along
the San Pedro River.

Mason patted the folded telegram in his shirt pocket. Coralyn, the cattle
boss's wife, had given him the telegram and told him to follow the river south

five miles until he got to Poole Canyon, the entrance of which he would recognize because the San Pedro takes a sharp bend to the west at that point.
Climbing east into the canyon, he would reach the well at Coyote Springs.

Turning east into the straight and narrow Poole Canyon, Mason saw the
campfires ahead of him, with the silhouettes of the tall saguaro dancing in
the firelight's orange radiance. The large shadows gathering around him were
not desert spirits but rather scores of cud-chewing Herefords, milling about
in the dark. He dismounted at the corral.

When Mason asked for his cousin Deming, one of the vaqueros glanced
over his shoulder and pointed. Mason walked stiffly over to Deming, the
ranch owner and boss of the spring roundup.

Deming held the telegram up to the campfire light. It seemed that the
spring roundup was being delayed by a few days, as the buyer was still in
El Paso. Mason looked about for a place where he could throw down his
bedroll and go to sleep. Instead, Deming took out a pencil and scribbled a
short note on the back of the telegram. He stuck the note into the Western
Union envelope and gave it back to Mason.

"Take this to the postmaster in Cascabel," Deming must have said. "You
can spend the night there and ride back to the ranch in the morning."

Deming told him that Cascabel was a mile or so just over the ridge, but
he was welcome to take the much longer yet safer route back down Poole
Canyon and several miles south along the gleaming shallows of the San
Pedro River. Mason eased his sore thighs once again into the saddle.

Not an Arizona native, at the time of this first night ride Mason had been
in Arizona only three weeks. He had come to Arizona on the recommendation of a physician, a specialist in rheumatologic illnesses, in order to recover
from a medical treatment that had gone south. Back home in Hartford, Connecticut, Mason had lived under the shadow of his father's many expectations. Mason's father had already decided that Mason would go to Yale and
study law, just like his older brother Spencer was doing, in order to return
to Hartford and join the family firm, which specialized in insurance.

Here in Arizona, Mason had already learned that like Hamlet, he was
expected to make his own decisions. His father's unwelcome wishes were

irrelevant here. Mason looked down Poole Canyon, back along the well-worn path that he had just traveled. Then, he turned his horse and headed up the ridge. This would become the next pattern in his young life, that is, finally to listen to his own untested heart, to find his own destiny, and to become his own man in spite of his father's looming authority.

That night the Milky Way, and not his father's expectation, became Mason's compass. He was free. He guided his horse up a narrow deer path. Resting alone at the crest of the ridge, he saw the vaqueros' campfires behind him at Coyote Springs. Ahead in the valley below, the moonlight still glittered in the shallows of the lazy San Pedro River. The desert was in bloom. The cool night air was thick with sweet aromas, mixed with old sage and saddle leather. The deer path faded into the sage. Finding his own way in the moonlight, Mason eased his horse down the gentle slope. Turning south, he followed the river to Cascabel (population five), which consisted of two huts and the postmaster's one-room adobe.

The postmaster was awake. Mason handed him the telegram with Deming's note. After caring for his horse, Mason unbuckled his chaps and rolled out his bedroll in the corner. He fell asleep quickly to the crisp staccato of the postmaster's telegraph key.

————

Mason's ancestors were as Yankee as possible, having flourished in New England for almost three hundred years. Isaac Gross had arrived in 1636 from Cornwall, in England's wet and stormy southwest, and settled in wet and stormy Wellfleet, Massachusetts, on that slender forearm of Cape Cod that reaches out into the wet and stormy north Atlantic. Isaac's grandson Simon, born in Massachusetts, turned his back on the seafaring life and headed west, away from the salt air, eventually to Hartford, Connecticut.[1]

One of Mason's ancestors, Freeman Gross, married Suzanne Bunce, a descendant of Plymouth Colony's William Brewster, a marriage that entitled Mason's family one day to claim *Mayflower* ancestry, a dubious distinction now claimed by millions of New Englanders that Mason would someday dismiss offhandedly as utterly meaningless.

Another of Mason's forebears was credited with hiding the Connecticut colonial charter from British troops in a hollow tree trunk, an icon later infamous as the "charter oak." Later, other ancestors fought for independence, one as an officer in the Continental Army, but it is not recorded whether their zeal was motivated by liberal ideology or simple fiscal opportunity. Mason's great-grandfather, born Thomas Mason Gross in 1809,[2] became a prominent Hartford merchant, importing cotton and wool for New England's burgeoning textile industry.

In 1848 Hartford was a crucible of abolitionist sentiment, the home of Lyman Beecher, antislavery minister and father of Harriet Beecher Stowe. Thomas Mason Gross, preferring to use the first name Mason, was a Democrat and an abolitionist. Disagreeing with the more moderate members of his party who were willing to compromise and allow the extension of slavery into the newly opened western territories, he campaigned unsuccessfully for Congress in opposition to the 1854 Kansas-Nebraska Act.

The youngest of his five children, Charles Edward, was born in 1847. Charles completed secondary school at the end of the American Civil War and later graduated from Yale. As a new attorney, he prospered along with the postwar boom in insurance, which had overtaken weapons manufacturing to become Hartford's main industry. His only son, Charles W., also attended Yale as an undergraduate and then Yale Law School and joined the family law practice, having married Hilda Welch, the daughter of a prominent New Haven banker.

Mason Welch Gross, Hilda and Charles W.'s second son, was born in Hartford on June 3, 1911.

In the era before television or even radio, Mason quickly developed a zeal for reading. Additionally, by age fourteen he was an accomplished pianist, daily practicing one block down Asylum Avenue on his grandmother's 1895 Steinway, as his own parents were not musical and did not own a piano. At Hartford Public High School, Mason finished the tenth grade at age fourteen, receiving honors in both Greek and Latin, which were required courses for all Hartford students at that time. Advancing rapidly through the high school curriculum, he was scheduled to graduate from high school early, at age

From an early age, Mason enjoyed being on the water. He is shown here with his younger sister Cornelia on the beach at Hatchett's Point, near Old Lyme, Connecticut, 1916. (Gross family photo)

sixteen, which his father felt was too young. The Hartford High School principal did not agree and insisted on skipping Mason ahead, as he had already completed more credits than students who were one year ahead of him.[3]

As a result, Charles pulled Mason out of the public school system and enrolled him, repeating tenth grade, in the Taft Preparatory School in Watertown, thirty miles to the west. This school had been started recently by U.S. president William Howard Taft's younger brother Horace and had developed a reputation for preparing students to enter Yale University, which was Charles's intent all along. Charles had already chosen Yale for both of his sons. Mason's older brother, Spencer, was already in Yale Law School, primed to follow as the third generation in the family law practice. Mason seemed destined to the same fate. He was charismatic and brilliant, with the sharp and agile mind of a debater. Charles knew that his younger son would be a brilliant attorney and an asset to the family firm. Mason's wishes were not clear at the time; it is still not certain whether Charles ever took that into account.

Living apart from his family, away from his father's constant oversight, Mason prospered at Taft. He achieved one of the highest grade point averages in the school, with honor grades in Greek, Latin, French, and English. He struggled with Algebra, getting only an A-minus.[4] Mason worked on the school newspaper, the yearbook, and the literary magazine. He discovered that he could avoid football, not his favorite sport, by playing varsity tennis four days per week. He played the piano for a five-man school dance band.

Mason became "the only tenth-grader selected for the school's debating team." Here he honed his argumentative skills. The Taft headmaster noted in a letter that Mason was "prone to hyperbole" and seemed to present an argument intended to incite conflict, after which he would sit back and "watch the fur fly."[5] Supporting a repeal of Prohibition, a position considered radical at the time, Mason became an avowed Democrat, which he would remain for his entire adult life.

Meanwhile, Mason's father prepared for Mason's eventual admission to Yale by contacting the director of admissions while Mason still had over two years remaining until graduation.[6]

In the winter of 1926 during Mason's tenth-grade year at Taft, a scarlet fever epidemic swept New England. Scarlet fever is a systemic infection that results from *Streptococcus pyogenes*, the same bacteria that causes strep throat. In addition to a throat infection and fever, the strep bacterium secretes an endotoxin that spreads throughout a patient's body.[7] Prior to the development of antibiotics, a bacterial infection had to run its course. Scarlet fever resulted in mortality as high as 25 percent. Some patients would develop rheumatic fever, which could kill by destroying one's heart valves. Affecting mostly children and young adults, scarlet fever epidemics struck terror into parents. During that winter's epidemic, two students at Taft School came down with scarlet fever.

Only a few years earlier, medical researchers at the University of Chicago had developed a skin test to check for a person's immunity against strep. This test involved injecting a small titer of strep antitoxin under the skin. The presence of a raised welt after one to two days signaled the presence of immunity. Horace Taft, the school headmaster, declared that all students would be tested. In order to prevent the spread of scarlet fever in a closed community, such as a boarding school, those students who were not immune to scarlet fever would receive the new scarlet fever vaccine.

Mason's test was negative; he was not immune. His parents consented to the vaccine. He received five weekly injections of strep antitoxin, which had been derived by injecting horses with the strep toxin itself, a recently developed process that soon fell out of practice due to a combination of poor efficacy and high incidence of side effects.

Mason experienced no side effects from his first two doses, but the increasing antitoxin titers in the subsequent injections resulted in fever and extreme prostration, from which he slowly recovered. His immunizations did not contain the strep bacteria itself, so he did not come down with scarlet fever. Instead, the increasing doses of the marginally purified antitoxin afflicted him with the sequelae of scarlet fever, including shortness of breath; poststreptococcal arthritis in his knees, ankles, shoulders, and wrists; and swelling of his legs known in those medical dark ages as idiopathic dropsy.

Over the course of the next few months, Mason became unable to walk due to the inflammation and knife-like pain in his knees. He gradually recovered and was able to finish the year with his class. His symptoms had resolved sufficiently to allow him to take a trip to Europe with his family, visiting France, Switzerland, and Italy's Lakes region.

Throughout the junior year that followed Mason was able to stay at school, but the pain and swelling of his knees and ankles continued to burden him. Although he lost little study time and did not require hospitalization, his mobility was progressively hampered. His physician suggested that he spend the summer in a dry climate. Mason joined a classmate and his family at the Hilman dude ranch along the Little Big Horn River in Wyoming but was unable to learn to ride. His legs were still very weak, and although they improved somewhat during his vacation, his activity was quite limited.

When Mason returned to Taft for his senior year, his arthritis and dropsy worsened as his joints gradually succumbed to the chronic inflammation that had been initiated by the rudimentary immunizations over a year earlier. He was sent home for several weeks and later in the fall was sent to a rheumatology specialist in Boston. Mason then entered the Devereux Rehabilitation Hospital in Marblehead, Massachusetts, for twice-daily physical therapy to prevent both joint contractures and any permanent limitation of motion in his legs. As the antistrep vaccine was only a few years old and its side effects were not well described in large studies, there was significant disagreement among his physicians as to his eventual prognosis.

Mason grew frustrated over the endless debate between the physicians and his father over what would be the best course of treatment. At Devereux, Mason became bored and depressed. "Stir crazy," he called it.

By the early winter of 1927–1928, it was clear that Mason would not be able to catch up with his studies and graduate with his class. His father withdrew him from school, intending that he would return in the following fall and graduate with the class of 1929.

The Boston rheumatologist suggested a change in climate from damp and cold New England. In the era before antibiotics, the physicians could only recommend that a patient go somewhere else. Arid climates had worked for other illness such as tuberculosis, so why not scarlet fever?

Mason's mother Hilda contacted her first cousin Deming Welch Isaacson, who, with his wife Coralyn, owned a cattle ranch southeast of Tucson.[8] Deming had been born in 1886 and raised in New Haven. His mother, nee Zelinda Welch, had died when Deming was very young. As an adolescent Deming was, like Mason, already headstrong and rebellious, possibly a Welch family trait. Deming resented his father's early remarriage to his late wife's cousin Annie Mitchell and did not get along with his new stepmother. His father consented to send him to the new Thacher School, a boarding school in Ojai, California, just up from the Pacific Ocean in Ventura County.[9] The school had been started in 1889 by Sherman Thacher, the son of a Yale professor and friend of Deming's family. Not intending to start a school, Sherman had moved west to care for his brother, who was severely ill with tuberculosis. Sherman started the school as a favor to New Haven friends whose sons needed private tutoring in order to qualify for admission to Yale.

Mason's mother, nee Hilda Welch, reached out to her first cousin Deming in Arizona so Mason could recover from his crippling illness and free himself from his overbearing father. This experience, which Mason called "a blessing," came to overshadow in his mind many other major periods of his life. (Gross family archives)

Deming had needed distance from his family and first went west to attend Thacher. He was delighted to find that the school emphasized outdoor activity, to the degree that each student was assigned to care for his own horse and learn to ride.

When Deming turned twenty-one, he inherited some money from his late mother's estate. Having no intention to return to New Haven, he purchased the Hooker's Hot Springs Ranch near Willcox. In 1910 he married Helen Baine,* formerly of Cleveland, Ohio.

Mason's mother Hilda had not seen her cousin Deming since before he went west during their adolescence. But when she contacted Deming early in 1928, describing Mason's condition and treatment plan, Deming willingly agreed to host Mason for the remainder of the winter and through the following summer. Deming might have seen in the headstrong and rebellious young Mason his own struggles with an overbearing father.

Deming decided that Mason was not there to rest. This was a working cattle ranch and not a health spa. Soon after Mason arrived in Arizona, Cousin Deming put him to work. The spring roundup was imminent, and every hand was needed. At first Mason learned to drive the lunch truck, a 1920 Chevy flatbed. It broke down a lot.

One day when the truck was inoperative, Deming assigned Mason to take a horse and ride out to a camp to deliver a message. Having only ridden briefly the summer before in Wyoming, Mason confessed that he was not much of a rider. Deming took care of that, assigning one of his ranch hands to teach Mason as quickly as possible so he could be of some use.

Within a few weeks Mason was spending fourteen hours per day in the saddle, patrolling and repairing barbed-wire fences and roping stray dogies that had wondered off from the main herd. He wrote every week to his family:

April 12, 1928.
Monday, a Mexican and I "rode the fence" at the big Double Wells pasture about five miles from here, that is to say we rode along the side of the

---

* Helen Baine died secondary to surgery in 1914. Deming later married Coralyn Benton.

barbed wire fence to see if it was down or if any wire needed refastening. The fence was about fourteen miles long. It took us all day to fix it. Of course, we got caught in a thundershower.

Tuesday I rose at 3:45 and went out with the cowboys to a round-up in N.O. Canyon. We drove the cattle to Double Wells to the pasture where I had mended the fences. Wednesday I got up at 3:50 and assisted in the round up this side of Double Wells. Yesterday I helped mend the fence at Antelope Wells.[10]

Occasionally Mason got to go into town, not Tucson, which was a lifetime away, but rather the metropolis of Willcox (population fifty), where he could mail his weekly letters to his parents, his brother Spencer at Yale Law School, and his grandmother Nana, who had passed on to Mason her love of music.

Despite this intense physical activity, Mason's arthritis healed quickly, as did his mood. Mason was no longer "stir crazy" as he had been in New England. On some days he still drove the flatbed Chevy truck with the cattle feed. He often arrived at the rendezvous point early and waited for the herd to catch up to him. Always with a book at hand, he stood on the flatbed and "read Shakespeare aloud" to the desert sky, the cattle, and the cactus, noting many years later:

Some words are just too beautiful to be read sitting down. . . . I would sit up on the top of this truck—nobody in sight for miles and miles around, with the tremendous Arizona landscape, the mountains off in the distance, with thunder clouds building up, so that this was one of the most exciting bits of natural scenery one could possibly imagine; and the whole thing was mine alone. I would sit on top of the truck reading Shakespeare. And if you're out in the desert you just can't read Shakespeare. You've got to measure up to your surroundings. So I would shout it at the top of my lungs![11]

Writing from Hartford, his parents continued to pester him over his arthritis, cautioning him to be careful and not work too hard. Their letters expressed hope that since he was feeling better, he would come home to Hartford soon and maybe spend some of the summer with them at their beach house on Long Island Sound at Hatchett's Point near South Lyme.

But Mason wrote home that Hartford was a trap. It made his knees hurt and his head ache. He blamed it on the humidity, but there was more to it. Unlike in Hartford, where he was constantly subject to his father's plans for him, here in the desert Mason was his own man, now seventeen, free of his father's expectations.

Mason wrote home to his mother that, concerned over the risk of relapse, he did not wish to return to Hartford. "After two months in Arizona, I am feeling better than I have in years. This outdoor life is just the right thing for me. I am imbibing the Isaacson's distrust of the Eastern climate and the habits of living. If I came back to Hartford now, I'd fall back into that old rut of spending almost all my time indoors reading." He added forcefully that he'd "rather dig ditches in L.A." if he had to. "Why would I want to go back to the east with its rain, and cold, and damp, and fog, and chills, and wind and snow? The fact is, I don't."[12]

The spring roundups ended in late June. Deming and Coralyn were closing down the ranch. After twenty years raising cattle, they had profited only a few hundred dollars. In the last few years southern Arizona, already arid, had been plagued with a considerable drought. They sold the ranch to Jessica Wakem McMurray, a divorcee from Cleveland who waited to take possession until after the spring roundup and intended to turn Hooker's Hot Springs into a spa and dude ranch.

Mason reported to his parents that he had earned $450 and had spent none of it since his arrival. Unable to stay in Arizona, he agreed to return home in September to start his senior year at Taft. However, he delayed his trip east as long as possible by taking a side trip to San Diego and then north to San Francisco. There he visited a colleague of his father's from Aetna, who drove him to Palo Alto to visit "Leland Stanford Junior University," later to be known simply as Stanford University. Mason also visited the campus of the University of California across the bay in Berkeley.

While Mason traveled on his own in the American West, his father Charles had insisted that Mason keep strict accounting of the money he had spent on trains, hotels, cabs, meals, and so on. Charles was shocked to see on one monthly expense report an entry from San Francisco, whose raw and savage Barbary Coast was then one of the most infamous ports in the world. There was a single line item marked "Paid five dollars, cash, for miscellaneous." Charles assumed that his son, on his own in San Francisco, had succumbed to a temptation that any young man might find difficult to resist.

It was true. Mason had paid five dollars cash for a service that his father would have withdrawn from in horror. But Mason had not paid for the company of an escort. No, even more outrageous. Mason refused to tell his father that he had frivolously paid five whole dollars for his first airplane ride, in 1928, one hour in a battered open-cockpit Curtiss Jenny flying over San Francisco and the Bay Area. It never occurred to Mason that his Yankee father would misinterpret the meaning of "miscellaneous" and would assume the worst.

Captivated by the West and perhaps subsequent to some prompting by Deming, Mason attempted to transfer to the Thacher School in Ojai. Clearly he was hoping to finish high school out from under his father's shadow. As the school was already full and the start of the school year was imminent, Mason's application was denied.

With his extra cash from working the ranch and time to spare before starting school in September, Mason boarded a train to Seattle. From there he bought a passage on a steamer to Alaska, stopping in Ketchikan and Juneau and then Sitka on its return voyage. He then took a train to Bozeman and spent a week in the company of friends fly-fishing on the headwaters of the Gallatin River and riding the high country into the Valley of the Yellowstone.

Mason returned to Connecticut to complete his senior year. His knees would ache occasionally but would never plague him severely again. Something besides his knees had matured.

Mason's spine had stiffened. He had escaped his father's reach.

In the far distant future, an interviewer will ask Mason, on the eve of his retirement, if he would characterize his illness and his subsequent months working on a ranch in Arizona as a "blessing in disguise."

Mason will answer, "Drop the phrase 'in disguise.' It was a blessing."[13] This period came to overshadow in his mind many other major periods in his life. Yet oddly, as to the Arizona desert after he returned to Connecticut to complete high school at Taft, he rarely if ever spoke of it again. He never spoke of the desert sky, of his fourteen-hour days in the saddle, or of his dreams to return to the West. He never spoke of roping cattle, mending fences, or driving a Chevy flatbed with a nasty clutch. Occasionally in a speech, he would refer to reading Shakespeare aloud in the desert. Mason never spoke of San Francisco or of his voyage to Alaska.

Here is the irony. I mentioned earlier that Mason and I never spoke. Long after he retired and I was in the military, I was once stationed for a year near Ketchikan, Alaska. When I transferred home and spoke of my experiences in southeast Alaska, he never once mentioned that he had been there fifty years earlier. How fascinating that story would have been for me to hear. In a similar episode, in 1969 when I told him that I had visited the campus at the University of California at Berkeley with an eye to attending in the future, he never mentioned that he had done the same. As would become a significant pattern throughout his life, for unknown reasons he rarely alluded to his own personal history, and then only tangentially. The details of this entire formative year, which culminated in a declaration of independence from his father's intrusion, would remain a secret until 2017, ninety years after these events and forty years after Mason's death, when his weekly letters to his family, still in their envelopes and saved by his mother for decades, carefully bundled in twine, were discovered in long-neglected boxes stashed under the four-poster beds in my sister's Atlanta guest room. His time in Arizona had been a life-altering experience that he had described to a journalist as "a blessing" and yet never told us about.

One might dismiss Mason's silence as a classic characteristic of the stereotypical taciturn Yankee WASP, a class of men excused for their emotional distance from their children. This excuse would be too easy and likely incorrect. There seemed to be something more mysterious in his secrecy and in his reluctance to engage with those who were closest to him.

What Mason's year in Arizona did initiate was the pattern that he would forever push back against his father's continuing will to engineer his life, to bring him back to Hartford to join the family firm like his older brother Spencer. A rift developed between father and son. This did not keep them from treating each other warmly and respectfully, yet there would remain a fracture in their relationship that would rip open during card games or political discussions. Somewhere deep in his heart, Mason vowed never to treat his own children's dreams with such disrespect or to interfere with the arc of our lives as his own father had done. As such, he would deliberately maintain a considerable distance from the important decisions of our lives. Unfortunately, he let the pendulum swing too far, by misunderstanding that there is a difference between interest and interference. In the far distant future, I grew to misinterpret the distance that he created between us as either disinterest, indifference, or even antipathy. In his lopsided desire to avoid interfering, this brilliant and charismatic public educator would fail to get to know his own children.

———

In the fall of 1928, Mason returned to Taft. He refused to apply to Yale. His father agreed to pay for any university education as long as it was not at Princeton, which he considered a party school.

In June 1929, Mason graduated from Taft School at the top of his class. As valedictorian, he was selected to address the graduation ceremonies.

Mason's father had planned his vacation in New Hampshire for the same week and so did not attend.

CHAPTER 3

Postmark:
Cambridge, England, 1930

Man's inhumanity to man has never been more vividly revealed. Much of what is being so brutally disclosed to us today in the newspapers has been all too clear to the wisest of our forebears: poets, philosophers and dramatists. Gibbon will help you understand what happens when a ruling class permits greed and licentiousness to determine its policies, and many other classical writers will give you an account of things you would have preferred to ignore.
—*MWG, June 5, 1963*

For the next five years after graduating from Taft, Mason lived overseas, first for a year at the University of Aberdeen, Scotland, and then at Jesus College at Cambridge University, including five months in Munich in 1933 during the first year of Adolf Hitler's Nazi regime. Clearly this was a formative period in the life of any young adult, and Mason's experience there established those patterns of thought and values that helped to further solidify the foundation of his moral compass. The arc of his adult life was cast during this period. He transitioned from merely a great student to an academic "wunderkind," calling himself an "eccentric philosopher." He transitioned from a gangly youth with arthritic knees and shoulders secondary to scarlet fever to a competitive athlete and coach. He advanced from a skillful piano player in a high school dance band to a virtuoso pianist, expressing a love of music as deep as his own soul. Most importantly, in this next period, having considered various career choices from Christian minister to professional musician, toward the end of his time overseas he discovered his lifelong calling:

to be a teacher and, in his own words, to become "an interpreter and expounder of the culture, thought and civilization of the ancient world."[1]

Mason Gross was born with the gift of focus. He was inclined from an early age to excel at whatever he pursued. As valedictorian of the Taft class of 1929, he could have chosen any college. Lost to history is why he chose to attend Cambridge University. Clearly, he was pushing back against his father Charles and his family's three generations of Yale Law School graduates. Mason once stated that he had considered going to Princeton, which to his father had a reputation as a party school, just because he knew it would anger his father. But Mason knew what he wanted to study, and he had learned to stand up for himself. He was interested in the classics and not in Yale. He said that he was "disgusted with the Yale social state of affairs and its pseudo-sophistication."[2] Mason had to argue with his father in order to go to England. Interestingly, Mason's high school yearbook,[3] of which he was an editor, states that he was headed to Yale. Records show that he was admitted to the Yale class of 1933, but no record exists that he had submitted any application materials. There does remain an extensive correspondence between Mason's father and the Yale director of admissions in which Charles (1) thanked the director for providing a place for Mason in the fall class, (2) informed the director that Mason would not be attending, and (3) then asked the director to hold a place for Mason in the future on the assumption that the boy would eventually "come to his senses."[4]

Mason's father was well known in Hartford and in addition to his law practice served as chairman of the Board of Trustees of the Hartford Theological Seminary. Dr. William Douglas MacKenzie, who with Charles was a member of the Asylum Hill Congregational Church, was the director of the seminary and himself had graduated from Cambridge University. Mason had expressed great respect for Dr. MacKenzie and no doubt had engaged him in discussion about his own future. In the closing weeks of his senior year at Taft, Mason actively pursued admission to Cambridge, first with letters and then followed up with a trip to England for an interview in July 1929.

Although Mason and his siblings would later claim that Charles was vehe-mently opposed to any college except Yale, family correspondence reveals Charles's full support for Mason's decision. Charles even traveled with Mason to England for the interview and assisted with the logistics of the applica-tion, such as obtaining results from the college entrance examinations. Charles also ensured that Mason's application to Cambridge was helped immeasurably by a glowing letter from Mr. Horace Taft, the founder and then headmaster of Taft School, who stated that "Mason stands among a few of the very ablest in the history of this school, being exceptional in ability, in acquiring knowledge, in the logical use of it, and in intellectual interest."[5] It would not have gone unnoticed at Cambridge that Headmaster Taft was the younger brother of the former president of the United States and cur-rent chief justice of the United States Supreme Court. Mason was clearly a gifted and serious student whose drive and ability had been clear to see.

However, in another private letter to Charles, Taft did suggest propheti-cally that Mason was a "radical" and should "moderate the strength of his opinions and especially the emphasis which he uses in statement."[6]

In the summer of 1929, it was too late for acceptance to Cambridge for that fall. But Mason was admitted to Jesus College, Cambridge, to matricu-late, or in British terminology to "go up to Cambridge," in the fall of 1930, with the intent to major in the program known as Classical Tripos, which emphasized the language, philosophy, archaeology, and culture of ancient Greece and Rome.

Meanwhile, the bursar, or dean, of Jesus College recognized that despite Mason's skill in Greek and Latin, he was not as well prepared as his future classmates. He had read only one-tenth of the classics his fellow students had read. Charles's colleague in Hartford, Dr. MacKenzie, came to their assis-tance. Dr. MacKenzie knew Professor Alexander Souter, a classics professor at the University of Aberdeen who had once lectured at the Hartford Semi-nary. Through another colleague, Professor Gibbons of Philadelphia, Souter agreed to not only tutor Mason for a year at Aberdeen but also host him in his own home.

Mason arrived in Aberdeen in September 1929 in the middle of a violent thunderstorm that shook the ground, with thunder that sounded like "pulling sheets of iron into pieces." He wrote that it was "as thrilling as Montana." Scotland was "perpetually gray," yet he remained healthy despite his parents' concerns due to the harsh Scottish climate.[7]

Mason immediately began his studies with Professor Souter, which involved two hours of tutoring and six hours per day of independent study. Souter was immediately impressed with Mason's diligence and enthusiasm. Mason's letters during this year describe his extensive study of Latin and Greek, not only reading and translation but also composition in both languages. He read the *Iliad* and the *Odyssey* in Greek as well as the New Testament and the works of Aeschylus, Euripides, Plato, and Aristotle. In Latin, Mason read Cicero, Ovid, and Virgil, stating that Latin had become "second nature."

Mason took a class at the University of Aberdeen in epigraphy, the reading of ancient manuscripts.[8] The value of this entire experience is inescapable. Instead of reading translations of these classics, which would inevitably involve an author's own interpretations, Mason was able to interpret these words himself, poring over each sentence, each phrase, culminating in an intimate and personal understanding of Socrates, Plato, Aristotle, and Leviticus and of the literature and philosophy of that era, untainted by the opinions of others. In his graduate studies later on, Mason would discover that this experience was very rare among students of ancient philosophy who had relied on translations for their reading. Most important to his own spiritual growth, he read the New Testament in the original Greek and found that the translations available to him in English had widely misinterpreted key passages.*

While living in Aberdeen Mason took long walks every day, often with Professor Souter, for several hours in the afternoon over the moors of

---

* The evolution of translations of the New Testament over two millennia is a fascinating subject, well summarized in Michael Massing's *Fatal Discord*, published in 2018 by HarperCollins.

Mason traveled home from Scotland in the summer of 1930, now smoking cigarettes and sporting a new mustache that he would have until his last days.

Scotland. Souter did not encourage vacation, as it would distract Mason from his studies, but he agreed to Mason's occasional weekend travels to London or short vacations across the English Channel to France. Souter also agreed that Mason could go home for a few weeks in the summer of 1930 to visit his family in Hartford, provided he continued to study those items that did not require Souter's constant tutoring.[9]

Politically, Mason remained an antiprohibitionist, chiding his "Hoover-loving father" for his support of an administration that was doing nothing while the U.S. economy plunged into chaos. Although the global economic depression did not limit his own financial support from his father, Mason was deeply affected by the poverty that he saw in England. Having witnessed the infamous hunger marches, he later expressed support for the Socialist Party in Great Britain.

In his letters home Mason began to reveal another side of himself, namely his impatience with late trains, delayed Western Union telegrams, slow mail, and an occasional self-described "difficulty being civil."

In October 1930, Mason "went up" to Jesus College, Cambridge. Soon after his arrival, he entered the social milieu by joining several clubs, including the Music Society, the Choral Society, and the Jesus College Boat Club.

At Cambridge, Mason purchased a piano for fifty-two pounds. He had enthusiastically studied music from an early age, likely encouraged by his paternal grandmother. His own parents did not own a piano and seemed to have no interest in music, so Mason had practiced on his grandmother's 1895 Steinway grand at her house only several blocks away on Asylum Avenue in Hartford. At Taft he sang second bass in the Glee Club, was voted by his classmates as "most musical," and played piano in the dance orchestra.[10]

In Aberdeen, Mason did play piano at some dances and noted playing for a small audience the overture to Richard Wagner's *Tannhäuser*. Shortly after "going up" to Cambridge, Mason reported playing his piano two hours per day and within a year noted that he was developing a more "mature touch." He was playing less Chopin and more Beethoven and wrote his parents requesting that they send him the sheet music for George Gershwin's latest hit, "Rhapsody in Blue." Later from Cambridge, Mason wrote home that "my playing means more to me now than I can describe." He adds the following in a later correspondence: "When my heart is full of love, or when I am feeling most religious and most close to what I believe to be God, my piano is my friend and confidant, inspiring me to work, to please you and to thank God for his blessing."[11]

Mason later denied any aspiration of a musical career, dismissing the allegation as "Bunk!"[12] But in April 1931 he wrote home just the opposite, stating that "the idea has occurred to me." During this period he attended concerts by Vladimir Horowitz, "one of the greatest living musicians," and Artur Rubenstein, whom Mason would meet many decades later when he handed the maestro an honorary degree from Rutgers. Mason heard a solo concert by a very young Yehudi Menuhin and saw the famous tenor Beniamino Gigli.

A colleague, Samuel McCollough, later exaggerated that Mason was "the greatest pianist in England. He could play any tune, or any variation of a tune, known to the memory of those around."[13]

Mason gave a solo piano concert in London and experienced his own first encore and ovation. In the late summer of 1932 on RMS *Mauretania* bound from New York to Southampton, England, he was featured on the ship's evening entertainment roster playing two of Franz Schubert's Impromptus.[14]

Very protective of his own personal history, hiding the details of his life from others, in later years Mason claimed dismissively that he reached his musical peak at age fourteen. I have already noted that he was "prone to hyperbole." This style of evasive and dismissive understatement was a feature of his character that would become even more pronounced with time.

Faith and Reason

Mason's studies in the Classical Tripos took him deeper into the literature of the ancient world. Ever secretive, in his later life Mason never revealed to anyone that in 1931 as a result of his studies, he had considered a career in the ministry.

As a child, Mason had attended weekly services and Sunday school at Hartford's Asylum Hill Congregational Church. In October 1930, only weeks after his matriculation at Cambridge, he learned of the sudden death from pneumonia of Reverend Willis Howard Butler, the pastor at Asylum Hill. It is clear from Mason's letters home that Butler had highly influenced Mason when he was a young parishioner.

Reverend Butler had been selected pastor of the Asylum Hill Church after the previous pastor, Reverend John Brownlee Voorhees (MA, Rutgers College, class of 1896), had died on January 8, 1919, from recurrent infection secondary to a leg-shattering explosive wound that he had received while serving as a chaplain for American soldiers in France in 1918. Reverend Butler was originally from Maine and had graduated from Princeton University and the Union Theological Seminary. He was not only a gifted minister but also a widely respected theologian, a protégé of Woodrow Wilson, whom he had first met when Wilson was president of Princeton. Formerly the associate pastor of the Old South Church in Boston, Butler had chosen to become the minister at Asylum Hill after also being offered simultaneously a full professorship at the nearby Hartford Theological Seminary.[15]

Asylum Hill archives record that Butler's sermons "were earnest, deep, fearless . . . with what we all need to hear; namely, the truth." Butler renovated the Sunday school, which Mason recalled attending weekly. The school included a youth group "which met on Sunday evenings for fireside discussions on such subjects as 'the Idea of God' and 'How to Do the Will of God.'" At Butler's memorial service, Dr. MacKenzie described Butler's sermons as "addressed to a world in doubt and sorrow, struggling with the mysteries and difficulties of life." A *Hartford Times* editorial had noted Butler as "a man of culture, whose influence was at once spiritual and educational."[16]

Mason's studies in Aberdeen had taken him ever deeper into Greek philosophy and the writings of the early Christian theologists who relied so heavily on Greek culture and whose "thinking and preaching constantly revolved around the two poles of Faith and Reason."[17] At Cambridge, he was becoming aware of how extensive throughout history had been the clash between the warring adherents of faith versus reason and their polarity as two separate sources of knowledge. In both ancient and modern philosophy, Mason struggled with the roles of theology and philosophy and how each contributed to knowledge. He had first heard this from Reverend Butler, who also strongly advocated practical action:

> Suppose you live in a place where injustice flourishes; where ignorance or indifference or inertia make the prospect for better things almost hopeless; suppose you meet with others every Sunday and pray "Thy Will Be Done," and then never lift your voice in protest against existing conditions, nor lift a finger to remedy them, is it fair to expect that your prayer will be answered? . . . The Kingdom of God comes . . . only by the doing of His will by those who are clear-eyed enough to see it. . . . We are the means by which the will of God is accomplished.[18]

Butler's sermons are highly reminiscent of similar addresses that Mason gave decades later, decrying inaction in the face of the injustice of "abject, miserable poverty amidst such abundant plenty" and the "apparently invincible forces of racism."[19] Butler's sermons also reflected Mason's nascent view of the role of religion and philosophy in one's life and his abhorrence of moral relativism, that is, the shifting of morality to suit fashionable trends. Moral relativism was one of Socrates's major indictments of the Sophists' philosophy, and Butler's discussion of it is as much Socratic as it is religious: "In the realm of morals there are laws which are not of human manufacture, and which in an age of changing standards and customs are as authoritative as they ever were. . . . There is such a thing as a moral law which is as real and immutable as natural law."[20]

During this first year overseas, Mason had initially entertained the thought of studying at a seminary. He had been reading early Christian texts. Professor Souter encouraged Mason to read Saint Augustine in the original Latin, which may have contributed to his interest in the controversy between faith and reason.

Following the news of Butler's untimely death, Mason speculated more heavily about ministry as a possible career. He was attracted to the New Testament, having read it in Greek, noting that as a result of this experience he was able to discern the "truth of the matter" and "able to see it without hypocrisy or ritualistic red tape."

Meanwhile, the Asylum Hill Church was searching for a replacement for Reverend Butler. The search committee, which included his own father and Dr. Mackenzie, asked Mason to look into an applicant from Britain. In Mason's opinion, the applicant did not come close to meeting the standard that Mason had known under Butler. Mason concluded quickly that the applicant was a "condescending and pompous ass." The interview did not go well.

Disappointed with the candidate for Hartford, Mason began to rail against religion that was "tinged with emotional hysteria." At the same time that he was discovering that his own reading of the Gospels differed markedly from that of published versions, he began to notice what a career in ministry might be like. He added in one letter home:

> How disheartening to me on my first close inquiry of the religious world to find how cheap and unworldly it can be. For one who has of late more seriously than ever been contemplating the ministry, it is most revolting to find all is not sweetness and light but political intrigue and wrangling prevails.
>
> Until I can decide what Christ means to my own mind, I don't want to have anything to do with interpreters. . . . I came here to study Socrates, Plato, Aristotle and Cicero without interpretive translations. Shall I then accept someone else's interpretation of Christ who spoke for me and to me as much as for the St. Pauls of the world?

Mason spoke no more about a possible career in the ministry, but for many years into the future he would continue to address the polarity of faith versus reason in Western philosophy and theology.

Rowing for Jesus

The bursar of Jesus College had asked Mason what type of athletics he intended to participate in. Football (i.e., soccer) was out due to his knees. The bursar recommended rowing, which he said was less hard on the knees. The bursar was clearly not much of a rower, as rowing is all about the knees.

In October of this first year Mason, on a lark, joined the Jesus College Boat Club and became instantly enthralled with the sport of competitive rowing.

In Mason's weekly letters home from Jesus College, even though he briefly mentioned his work in the classics the predominant topic in each letter is his rowing. He described in great detail each race, the preparation, the weather, the opponents, and most of all not his own performance but rather that of his crew.

Mason recounted how he had never been athletic, in part due to his illness, but was never on the same level with other athletes. Here at the Jesus College Boat Club everyone was a novice learning together in the "tubs," a small stable rowing barge anchored securely to the dock, which allowed the coach easy access to each crew member.

By November Mason was rowing stroke in the D Boat, partially due to his sense of rhythm. The stroke oar, the rower in the stern of the boat directly facing the coxswain, is responsible for maintaining a steady cadence. Mason's letters detailed every race, including their times, such as "7 minutes, 52 seconds over a mile and a quarter, in a high wind, with waves breaking over the boat." He added, "I never dreamed that I would enjoy really hard exercise so much. Having never been an athlete at all, I can hold my own with my contemporaries in a strenuous form of exercise. I have never been physically stronger."

Mason typically rowed in an eight-man shell, called an "eight," plus a coxswain but also competed in fours, pairs, and single scull. His closest friends were not his academic classmates, whom he never mentions in his letters home, but instead were his fellow oarsmen, Arthur "Harry" Fraser, Archie Hamilton, Colin Cotteril ("a crazy, hard-drinking Irishman"), Lambert Shepard, and Bill Melish, an American theology student whose father was the pastor of the Trinity Episcopal Church in Brooklyn, New York.

Due to the narrowness of English waterways, the British style of racing involves the boats starting in brief intervals in a single line and then trying to catch each other, as the rivers are not wide enough to allow the boats to pass each other. When the bow of one boat overtakes the stern of the boat ahead, this is called "bumping," although the boats never actually touch. In

Mason's love for rowing would transform him. His coach, Steve Fairbairn, inspired him to become a teacher. (Photo credit: Stearn and Sons, Ltd., Cambridge, UK.)

this way, a faster boat that starts farther back may, in successive races, slowly advance to the first boat in line and is then referred to as the "Head of the River." This nomenclature, although not this "bumping" style of racing, exists in the United States today in such races as the "Head of the Charles" (Boston) and the "Head of the Schuylkill" (Philadelphia). Mason described races in the rain or in high wind. At one time his eight took on so much water that it sank from beneath them just past the finish line.

In June 1931, a slender and stooped elderly figure in a long dark wool coat appeared at the boathouse. The revered seventy-year-old Coach Steve Fairbairn had come out of retirement. Raised in Melbourne, Australia, he had rowed at Jesus College fifty years earlier and had coached rowing ever since. He had developed his own style of rowing, which differed from the British orthodox style. First, Fairbairn had proven the value of the sliding seat, allowing the oarsmen to push with their legs (and knees) and put more power into their stroke. The stiffly orthodox British style had emphasized that the oarsmen needed to remain rigidly in the center of the boat but then reach way out and "drop the oar" perpendicularly into the water at the "catch," or start of the stroke, in order to achieve to maximum time that the blade of the oar is immersed. Fairbairn instructed his oarsmen to concentrate less on their position in the boat and more on the movement of the oar in the water, on the catch, and on the release, when they lift the blade back up out of the water. Critics of this method described Fairbairn's crews as swaying all over, looking very sloppy, undisciplined, and decidedly un-British as they came up the river. Criticism notwithstanding, Fairbairn's sloppy and undisciplined crews consistently won. The Fairbairn method was adopted by crews throughout Europe, Australia, Japan, and the United States and is still taught at some institutions.

Fairbairn's key point was that rowing is not just a brutish exercise. A rower has to concentrate but not just on the sweaty neck of the guy thirty inches away from him. Fairbairn instructed his crews to read frequently from books on rowing, mostly his own. He urged his oarsmen to forget about the previous stroke, to ignore where the boat is in the race, and to concentrate only on the next stroke, seeking to make it perfect.

With the power of each stroke, the shell actually lifts partially out of the water and then settles back down during the reset. Excellence in rowing is found in a rare and elusive experience called "the swing." This occurs when all eight rowers are pulling in perfect unison, with each blade entering and leaving the water exactly at the same time and each rower pushing against the blocks at the exact same moment. "Each minute action, each subtle turning of the wrist, must be mirrored exactly by each oarsman. Only then will the boat continue to run, unchecked, fluidly and gracefully between each pull of the oars. . . . Only then will it feel like the boat is part of each of them, moving as if on its own. Only then does pain give way to exultation. Rowing then becomes a kind of perfect language. Poetry. That's what a good swing feels like."[21]

On this occasion, the shell rises up in the water and does not resettle between strokes. With the boat riding higher in the water, the actual wetted surface of the boat decreases, thereby minimizing its resistance through the water due to drag and dramatically increasing its speed. Mason provided his own description: "I shall never forget one particular four-mile race When everything went absolutely perfectly . . . the crew as a unit rowed better than it knew how, with an incredible sense of ease and rhythm, so that . . . we felt that we could keep going forever."[22] Each rower, focusing only on his own effort, feels like he is pulling against air rather than water. Some rowers now describe it as being "in the zone." It is a surreal experience, and when it occurs everyone in the boat feels it.

By November 1931, Fairbairn was coaching full-time. Mason recalled one of Fairbairn's lectures, noting that it was "perfectly clear and lucid, with a gift of vivid explanation." Fairbairn took interest in Mason, noting that Mason had good style but needed more strength.

Fairbairn was not a young man and was often too weak to attend all practices. He assigned Mason to coach the Jesus Lent Boat, the most junior crew of all. Mason traveled with the crew to races when Fairbairn was too ill to attend. By 1933 Fairbairn had assigned Mason to help coach more oarsmen and asked him to edit and assist in the publication of his newest book, *Chats on Rowing*. He even convinced Mason to pose for photographs illustrating proper technique.

Mason wrote how he had become "intoxicated by teaching" and was certain that he had discovered his calling. "I now coach better than I row. I am quite sure that my vocation will be teaching. I have been able to communicate my ideas to the crew, and they are continually improving. . . . I feel certain that teaching is what I am best fitted for."

By April 1934 with his graduation from Cambridge looming, Mason was coaching the first Jesus boat and rowing with Archie Hamilton and Art "Harry" Fraser in the first four (the varsity four-man shell). As graduation approached Mason wrote, "Rowing is in my blood, and I cannot bear to think that my rowing and coaching career may soon be finished."

Mason later recalled a moment when his father was visiting England that spring and came to watch his son rowing in the Jesus I Boat in a fiercely competitive regatta. The highly proper British crowd sat still, hushed, and

Mason helped to edit Coach Steve Fairbairn's book *Chats on Rowing* and served as a model for Fairbairn's technique, which is used to this day. (Photo credit: Stearn and Sons, Ltd., Cambridge, UK)

clapped politely as each boat rowed by. But the sole American visitor, a proud father, would have none of this. More accustomed to shouting over the raucous cheers of a Yale-Harvard football game, Charles stood up as the Jesus Boat went past. Mason heard the familiar voice of his father, the only voice that carried across the quiet water above the muted applause, the voice of this normally silent and subdued New Englander caught up in the moment enthusiastically bellowing at the top of his lungs, to the consternation of the well-behaved Brits looking up at him from their seats. Charles called out loudly, "Row, Jesus! Row! Goddammit, Jesus! Row!"[23]

INTO THE REICH

When Mason had arrived in Aberdeen in 1929, there had already been some rumblings that world economies were becoming unstable, with crop failures and large fluctuations in prices. Three weeks after his arrival at Professor Souter's house the New York stock market crumbled, reported in London's *Daily Mail* as a "Wall Street slump," sending repercussions throughout the world economy. For example, much of Europe's recent financial improvement had occurred secondary to loans from British and American banks. As the American banks tottered precipitously, they called these loans in. The Brits were unable to pay and called their loans in from Germany as well. Financial crisis erupted, with massive inflation wiping out the assets of so many German families who had already been struggling.

Mason supported the socialist cause in England, perhaps after watching the hunger marches. He had always opposed prohibition, not necessarily for personal reasons but mostly because it was ineffective. He chided his father, stating "Hoover is a tremendous failure," and voiced his early support for Franklin Delano Roosevelt for president in 1932.

On a summer vacation to the continent, Mason and his older brother Spencer drove in Mason's 1924 Morris through the World War I battlefields, noting the shards of barbed wire left to rust from fifteen years earlier. Writing from Germany, Mason noted that Hamburg had been hit hard by the economic depression and that he had seen ships "laid up at Hamburg for want of trade." He described the old German families, "literally penniless," who had to sell their homes: "previously wealthy they had not a pfennig to spare." He added, "I was so blue that there could be no relief from this ghastly depression." He noted how far the Deutschmark had fallen and wondered if the American dollar was "about to crash" as well.

Additionally, tensions were building in Europe. The Franco-Italian border was bristling. Announcing that he was "becoming blatantly pacifist and anti-debt," Mason wrote that he "wouldn't give a penny for world peace right now."

In Germany, former field marshal President Paul von Hindenburg, who at age eighty-four and in poor health had hoped to retire after one term, was convinced to run for reelection in order to prevent his succession by Adolf Hitler, whom he despised. In the 1932 election the Nazi Party, to their leaders' disappointment, polled fewer votes than in previous elections, but no party achieved a majority. In a runoff election, Hindenburg achieved a majority and was reelected. The German economy was in free fall. In local and regional elections in November 1932, the Nazi Party won a plurality in many districts and became the largest party in the Reichstag, albeit without a true majority.

Due to the failing British economy, in the fall of 1932 there were fewer freshmen at Cambridge. Expressing his concern over the Great Depression at home, Mason wondered how his father was dealing with bank failures in Hartford and, having celebrated his twenty-first birthday, planned to vote for Roosevelt.

In late 1932 Mason expressed his desire to spend a year in Germany, first in Munich and then studying at the University of Berlin, partly to immerse himself in German and study the German philosophers but mostly to study under Professor Werner Jaeger, a classicist whom Mason had learned was the "greatest living teacher of Aristotle." In January 1933, Jesus College agreed to allow Mason to complete a fourth year in Germany.

On January 30 Adolf Hitler was appointed chancellor of Germany, having convinced President Hindenburg that due to the Nazi success in the November elections and the Nazi plurality in the Reichstag, the Nazis deserved a role in a coalition government.

In March 1933 a fire devastated the Reichstag, the seat of Germany's parliament. Reichstag president Hermann Goering claimed that the fire was caused by communist arsonists. Hindenburg agreed to the suspension of civil rights and detention without trial, both authorized as emergency actions under Article 48 of the Weimar Constitution. In the March elections the Nazis again failed to achieve a majority, requiring a coalition government. In order to achieve total control, the Nazis proposed an emergency powers act, called the Enabling Act, that could allow Hitler's government to bypass the constitution. This act, in accordance with the Weimar Constitution, required a two-thirds majority vote of the Reichstag. The Nazis did not have enough votes. In order to ensure victory of the Enabling Act, Nazi squads, through arrests or physical violence, kept the liberal Social Democrats and a few communists from attending critical votes in the Reichstag, thus allowing the Nazis to achieve a quorum for a two-thirds majority in the critical vote and consolidate their power legally.

In a letter home in March 1933 Mason, still at Cambridge and noting his pleasure at Roosevelt's inauguration, described his understanding of events in Germany as "disturbed" and "the very opposite of peaceful." Mason called it a "bad month for weather, politics, war and finance." He suggested in a following letter how the international press was giving an inaccurate ("disturbed") picture of Germany and that perhaps "we should reserve judgment."

Hitler soon banned the Social Democrat Party and all trade unions. He purged his own party leadership in the Night of the Long Knives in July 1934. In August 1934, the cabinet passed a law that upon the death of the president all power would be transferred to the chancellor.

Oddly enough Hindenburg died the following day, and Hitler claimed full power as dictator, or führer.

Mason left England for Munich in August 1933, driving again through Bastogne and the "beautiful Ardennes Forest," which would a decade later become the setting for one of the most costly tactical blunders of World War II. He visited the Bavarian resort of Garmisch before reporting to his host, Herr Strive, who was a German foreign minister. Mason studied German intensely, finding it easier than French, and appeared to pick it up readily, as its grammatical construction is so similar to Latin.

In October 1933 Mason sympathized "most heartily" with Germany's withdrawal from the League of Nations, declaring that England and France were "seeking trouble with Hitler." Mason's father Charles wrote to him, describing Germany as a "total failure." Mason vehemently wrote back that his father was dismissive of his opinions, indicating a "complete lack of confidence and distrust of my judgment." Mason wrote, "The government has the support of the people and is here to stay." He did not "approve of the present regime" but sympathized that the economy was already improving. He saw that Germans had to be either "violently in favor of the Party and blind to its weakness or violently opposed and blind to its good points," upon which he did not elaborate.

Mason would later become an ardent hawk, advocating firm resistance against Nazi aggression in Europe. But at this point, still an undergraduate, he offered some justification and tacit support for Hitler's regime, a position also then supported by many British politicians.

On Saturday October 21, 1933, Mason, already facile with the German language, heard Hitler speak in Munich and then went to the Braunes Haus, the Nazi Party headquarters and command center at which they also commemorated the 1923 Putsch. Mason described the ubiquitous "banners, posters, bands, and parades of Brown Shirts shouting 'Heil Hitler.'"

At the Braunes Haus, Mason heard Hitler speak again and noted that on two occasions Hitler had walked by him so close "that I could have touched him." At such proximity of Hitler's physical presence, Mason wrote, "I was impressed. The atmosphere was charged with emotion. Storm troopers out in the streets. A fear of talking politics. You could feel what was coming."[24]

By December, it was clear that Mason would not be able to cut through the red tape to attend the University in Berlin. Already the academics were supporting the Nazi regime, often starting their classes with a Nazi salute and a loud "Heil Hitler." Mason remarked, "Who would have believed that in six months Hitler would have the whole country behind him?"*

Mason's parents were concerned that he was in danger in Germany. He wrote that the country was "very hectic," that "everything about Berlin is a mess right now," adding also that "the constant propaganda got on my nerves." He stated clearly that he "felt no danger from physical violence." Noting that several of his colleagues had been beaten, Mason later said, "I was never attacked but I just did not trust German crowds after that. When the crowd roared I got scared and got the hell out of there as quickly as possible." His account differs from a later version, certainly apocryphal, from his younger sister Cornelia that he had been "roughed up," having been identified as a foreigner and perhaps Jewish, an episode that then precipitated his departure from Germany but never made it into his letters to his parents.

---

* Professor Werner Jaeger, the classicist with whom Mason had hoped to study, was vehemently opposed to the Nazis and would immigrate to the United States in 1936, first to teach at the University of Chicago and then later at Harvard.

At the start of 1934, Mason described Europe as "excitable," with riots in Paris, trouble in Spain, and an early threat of Nazi invasion into Austria. Unable to pursue his studies in Berlin, he returned to England in time to spend the holidays with his closest friend Lambert Shepard and his family and to consider where, upon graduation in the spring, his life would take him next.

Mason had read a review of Alfred North Whitehead's *Nature and Life*, which the reviewer described as the "greatest book in contemporary philosophy." By now, Whitehead was at Harvard. Mason decided that to be a teacher of philosophy he could not concentrate only on the ancient Greeks. Having already studied Saint Augustine and Saint Thomas Aquinas, Mason knew that he had to study more modern philosophy as well.

At the suggestion of his father, Mason decided that Harvard offered the best program. The Harvard philosophy department accepted him immediately upon his application, and in August 1934, after the races at Henley and after five years living overseas, Mason sailed west for home.

CHAPTER 4

The Blind Date, 1939

I am very much in love, although I do everything to avoid showing it.
—MWG, April 1940

"Well, he certainly is full of himself, isn't he?"[1] Julia Kernan said of Mason, laughing while she and Dolly washed the supper dishes. The value of first impressions is generally well established.

It was a blind date.

In 1939, Phil and Dolly Minis had been recently married. Phil had known Mason in high school. Dolly was a friend of Julia's from college. In New York money was tight, and disposable income was rare. Instead of going out to dinner, people often entertained in their own apartments. Phil and Dolly thought that Mason and Julia would make a good couple. In early autumn 1939, they all met at the Minises' minuscule one-bedroom New York apartment, the four of them sharing a home-cooked meatloaf and mashed potatoes around a small folding card table in the living room.

Julia Kernan was twenty-six years old, slender, brunette, and Irish. She denied that she was six feet tall, preferring to state her height at "five eleven and seventh-eighths." She had been born in Savannah, Georgia, on October 26, 1912.

Not a native southerner, her father, Reginald Devereux Kernan, also known as Dev, was originally from Utica, New York. He was temporarily working on the Savannah streetcar system and had moved there with his wife Jessie for the duration of the project. Dev was the grandson of Francis Kernan, abolitionist and former U.S. congressman from Utica during the American Civil War from 1862 to 1866 and U.S. senator from 1874 to 1880,

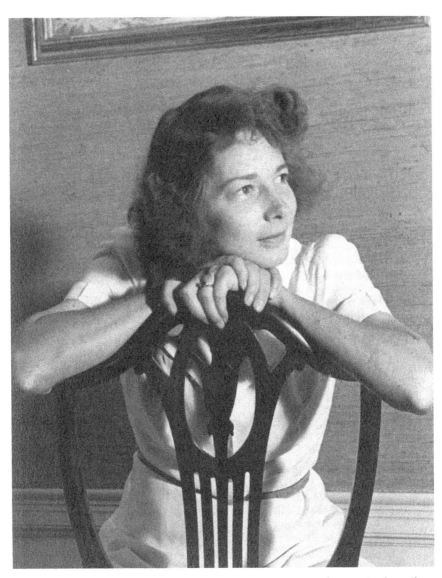

Julia Kernan, a jazz enthusiast who loved to dance, was working two jobs and living in Greenwich Village. Revealing her honest and soft-spoken Irish wit, she first found Mason to be quite "full of himself." She is shown here wearing her emerald engagement ring, which she continued to wear for decades after Mason had passed away. (Photo credit: Cornelia Gross)

most well-known for his calm leadership during the constitutional crisis that had plagued the Tilden versus Hayes presidential election of 1876.[2]

Julia's mother, Jessie Clark Wood, also from Utica, was the daughter of Thomas Clark Wood and Julia Anna Rudd. Thomas Wood was an 1876 graduate of the U.S. Naval Academy at Annapolis. At that time, Annapolis graduation did not necessarily result in a commission aboard a vessel. He returned to Utica to start a business in cotton and wool importing, supplying the busy New England textile industry. In 1898, after the sinking of the battleship *Maine* in Havana Harbor, he was recalled to the U.S. Navy for the Spanish-American War. He served under Lieutenant Commander Richard Wainwright as the chief gunnery officer aboard the 240-foot USS *Gloucester*, formerly the yacht of J. P. Morgan that upon donation to the navy had been turned into a gunboat. Lieutenant Wood's courage under fire was cited, as the accuracy of the *Gloucester*'s gunnery was instrumental in turning back the Spanish fleet that attempted to run the blockade and break out during the 1898 Battle of Santiago in Cuba.[3]

———

Julia Kernan was three years old when her father's job in Savannah was complete. Dev relocated the family back to the Northeast so that Julia grew up in Germantown, Pennsylvania. When she was fifteen, her father died suddenly of streptococcal pneumonia while away on a weekend business trip to Providence, Rhode Island. In the era before antibiotics, strep pneumonia struck quickly and, in healthy individuals, still resulted in a mortality rate of greater than 50 percent. Julia's mother, Jessie, was now penniless and moved back to her family home in Utica. Jessie's sister Kitty (Katharine Wood Crocker) stepped up to pay for Julia's education as well as that of Julia's two younger brothers, Reginald (RDK Jr.) and Walter. Thanks to Aunt Kitty, Julia attended Milton Academy, in Milton, Massachusetts, which she later described as "liberating." She graduated from Vassar College in 1934 but found little opportunity for employment with a BA in economics as the world wallowed in the depths of a global economic depression. For her education Julia remained ever grateful to her Aunt Kitty, later naming her second child for her. The value of a good education to provide liberating opportunities for young women would remain a touchstone throughout Julia's life.[4]

After graduation Julia moved to New York City, into an apartment on West 4th Street in the West Village, with a friend from Vassar. Julia obtained employment in the circulation department of the *New York Times*, earning a minimum wage of twenty-five cents per hour, or $500 per year. Later in her life she expressed some twinges of guilt that her job had been to hawk newspaper subscriptions to people, many of whom had very little money due to the Great Depression. Elegantly tall and slender in a time when tall women were uncommon, Julia supplemented her income working part-time modeling clothing—mostly overcoats, hats, and scarves—for department stores.

Prohibition had been repealed only a year before. Greenwich Village teemed with bohemian culture, including some of the first openly integrated jazz clubs in New York City. Julia recalled listening to Billie Holliday and Count Basie when she lived in New York and may have developed her lifelong love of Ella Fitzgerald by listening to the young singer at one of these New York venues.

While Julia was enjoying the single life in New York City her college roommate, Mary deSchweinitz from Dorset, Vermont, had married Yale graduate William Parrish. Together the couple had moved to the tiny village of Peru, Vermont, up the mountain from Manchester. In partnership with Mary's brother Lewis deSchweinitz, they were busily renovating a broken-down mountaintop speakeasy, previously owned by a Russian immigrant bootlegger named Ivan Sesow. Whether Sesow was dissuaded by his competitors in the illegal liquor import business prior to the repeal of Prohibition or whether the business folded simply as a casualty of the Great Depression, in 1932 he moved on with his family and left the property to the investors.[5] When Mary and Bill obtained Sesow's foreclosed property in 1938, it had four log walls, a bar, and a dance floor. As the property was adjacent to the newly opened Bromley Ski Area, the Parrishes turned it into a ski lodge, which they renamed Johnny Seesaw's in honor of the missing Russian.[6]

Julia visited Mary frequently, taking the night train from New York to Manchester, Vermont. Julia later described the renovations, supported by "sweat equity," that included digging ditches for water and septic systems, installing electrical wires, using a blowtorch on frozen pipes in the winter, and building a kitchen. Sesoff's mountain speakeasy hadn't needed a kitchen; people came to drink and dance, not to eat.

Johnny Seesaw's opened in December 1938. Julia learned to ski in the era when Bromley Mountain had installed its first rope tow. Skis were made of wood with wooden edges, which required resharpening with a flat file after each run. Safety release bindings did not exist. Steel braces, cable, and leather bindings served only to secure the skier via a heavy leather boot. In the presence of a guide, usually William or Lewis, guests of Johnny Seesaw's strapped strips of sealskin to the bottom of their skis for traction in order to climb straight up Bromley Mountain. After a long climb and a picnic at the summit, they tied their sealskins around their waists and skied downhill back to Seesaw's, arriving dog-tired and thirsty by mid to late afternoon, ready to enjoy an evening of drinking and dancing. They skied one run per day.

Summers at Johnny Seesaw's included hikes along the newly established Appalachian Trail, which to this day skirts over the top of Bromley Mountain. Julia recalled fly-fishing for brook trout along the Batten Kill long before it became fashionable, usually necessitating a brief stop at the small family-run Orvis fishing supply shop in Manchester.

Regular visitors to Seesaw's included Julia's youngest brother Walter, who was an undergraduate at Harvard. As a cadet in the Civilian Pilot Training Program, in 1938 he flew to Manchester's Equinox Airport in a borrowed Piper J-3 Cub. On a cool, gusty Vermont morning he took Julia for her first airplane ride. She recalled later that her little brother was no longer just her little brother. Walter had changed. As a pilot he was now all business, telling her precisely where to put her feet and what buttons not to touch. Today in an era when aircraft travel is so taken for granted, it is interesting to imagine what one's first view of the planet from the air would have been like.

Julia was in no hurry to get married. But at some point, Mary's brother Lewis deSchweinitz proposed. It is not clear that Julia ever accepted his proposal, although Lewis once insisted to me that they had actually been engaged. Years later Julia admitted to having seen a lot of Lewis, but neither confirmed nor denied the engagement. Recalling that her own brother Walter was also seriously involved with Lewis's sister Patty, Julia only smiled, possibly blushing, and answered, "Yes, those were very incestuous times."

Julia, raised in Utica and educated just outside of Boston and New York, had become a city girl. She did not want to "spend the rest of her life on the top of a mountain in Vermont." She loved New York's active lifestyle. She never mentioned going to the Metropolitan Opera or to the Philharmonic, but she often later reminisced about taking the subway uptown to the Apollo in Harlem and recalled several trips to the Glen Island Casino in New Rochelle, a popular big band–era dance venue that featured the Dorsey brothers, Benny Goodman, and the Ozzie Nelson Orchestra.

Julia was already living and working two jobs in New York City's Greenwich Village, while Mason was still living in Boston, a graduate student in philosophy at Harvard.

In the autumn of 1934 as Julia settled into Greenwich Village, Mason moved into Leverett House on the Harvard campus. He found the campus excessively noisy compared to Cambridge University. Mason noted radios blaring in the dormitory and an excess of banjo music, apparently not his favorite instrument. He wrote home wishing that "Harvard could only cultivate the same academic calm as Aberdeen."

Mason's reputation as a classicist who could read and write in both Greek and Latin had preceded him. At a department reception for new graduate students, a faculty member said to him, "Oh, you're the one we're afraid of."[7] Mason's first two years were busy with lectures and seminars; he mentioned specifically his classes in logic, epistemology, ethics, metaphysics, Immanuel Kant, René Descartes, and George Santayana, including more German so he could read the German philosophers in their own language. Mason expressed some concern over his exams, stating that he had "some rather unorthodox ideas that have not been widely accepted." During this period he mentions his fascination with the intersection of philosophy and Christian theology, of faith and reason, having read *The Mediator: Religion in Life* by Swiss theologian Emil Brunner, who had by then captured the imagination of American theologians.

By 1936, Mason had finished his coursework. He noted that he had come "a long way since September 1934" and expressed his confidence that he was "on the right track." He was interviewed in 1937 for employment by three Harvard senior fellows, John Livingston Lowes, naval historian Samuel Eliot Morrison, and A. L. Lowell, the former president of Harvard. Mason accepted a lecturer position and in 1937 began teaching five classes per week of undergraduate "Philosophy A."

Mason's correspondence during this period does not reveal any detail about his personal life, which he clearly meant to keep from his family. Aside from occasional discussion of his courses and the subject of his dissertation, mostly he describes concerts, sports, weather, and family matters. Every summer he returned to England and Scotland to see his best friends and to coach crew at Cambridge, but he did also spend a great deal of time studying.

Describing a "desperate train journey from New York to Boston," Mason became less interested in rail travel and more impatient because the trains never seemed to run on time. He borrowed his parents' car and drove often, encouraging them to allow him to use it as long as possible. He once told his parents that on his next drive home to Hartford, he intended to stop at "one of those new Howard Johnson's Restaurants."

Professor Alfred North Whitehead had come to Harvard from England in 1924. Before matriculating at Harvard, Mason had not communicated that he intended to study Whitehead's philosophy. Yet soon after his arrival, Mason wrote that he and Bill Melish, his American colleague and rowing buddy from England who was now enrolled at the Episcopal Divinity School in Cambridge,* attended all of Whitehead's lectures. Mason took Whitehead's course "Philosophy III" for three straight years and later stated, "I studied under Whitehead in the sense that I attended every lecture that I could, and sought out every other occasion for talking with him. I did not realize how great was my debt to Whitehead until I reached Columbia."[8]

---

* Bill Melish graduated and was ordained in 1935, moving first to Cincinnati and later back to Brooklyn, destined to take over from his retiring father as pastor of the Holy Trinity Episcopal Church.

Whitehead did not direct Mason's dissertation. However, it is clear that Alfred North Whitehead figured prominently in Mason's graduate experience at Harvard.

In early 1938 Mason's major concerns were preparing for his orals and writing his dissertation. Mason kept his parents apprised of his progress but never once told them what was its subject, which was itself a critique of the Viennese Circle of logical positivists. While awaiting its evaluation by his dissertation committee, he struggled with self-doubt, writing to his parents that "the more I think about this thesis the more inadequate it seems."

By early May, Mason's dissertation was approved. The committee rushed through his defense, as they were all watching the clock, hoping to go down to the Charles River in time for the Harvard-Yale crew regatta. There were very few questions, mostly for clarification. Mason was informed immediately that he had passed, whereas most candidates had to wait for formal notification after the committee members had discussed and written their comments.

Mason expressed concern to his parents that their physician had not sent him refills of medication for his "indigestion." He expressed his impatience, being "fed up to the teeth" as to why Dr. Ritter could "not take the time to write ten words on a piece of paper." Mason continued to use the antacid Bisodol on a daily basis, finding it marginally better than bicarbonate of soda. He was a steady cigarette smoker by this time, and his letters refer to gatherings where alcohol was plentiful. There is no suggestion that he drank more than socially, but the combination of tobacco and hard alcohol was much later linked to severe gastric reflux and eventually to esophageal cancer, and no doubt these two habits contributed to his stomach distress.

In April 1938, Mason received notice of selection as an instructor in philosophy at Columbia University for an annual salary of $2,400. In June, he traveled to New York City and, after a prolonged search, found a suitable apartment for $75 per month, more than he wanted to pay. It was a third-floor walk-up at 552 West 114th Street, just across the street from the Columbia campus.

Mason candidly mentioned to his father that the salary of a new Columbia instructor was barely enough to live on but not enough to participate as fully as he wished in New York and certainly not enough to travel. His father agreed to continue to send $150 per month to him.

Prior to starting at Columbia, in June 1938 Mason traveled to England to attend the annual races at Henley, where a crew from his alma mater, Jesus College of Cambridge University, had qualified. For a former oarsman, Henley was "four days of pure joy." After Henley, the Jesus College crew traveled to race in Norway, at the invitation of Bergen's Fana Roklubb (Fana Rowing Club). When the Jesus coach withdrew due to illness, Mason was invited along as coach, in part due to his reputation as a former student of Cambridge rowing icon Steve Fairbairn. Mason admitted that the Jesus College crew did not need coaching but went along as a proponent of the Fairbairn method.

The members of the Fana Roklubb had read Fairbairn's 1934 guide *Chats on Rowing* and, noting that photos of Mason had been used in the book to demonstrate rowing technique, recognized him immediately. After the regatta, the Fana Roklubb invited Mason to return the following summer to coach them.

Mason returned to New York on RMS *Aquitania* and into his new job. His weekly letters home describe the life of this young instructor, with a heavy teaching load of undergraduate classes and a graduate seminar. He regularly attended Columbia's football games. He clearly enjoyed the city life, frequenting the Philharmonic, where he saw Maestro Arturo Toscanini conduct Beethoven's Fifth Symphony, and also going to Carnegie Hall, on different occasions hearing Rudolph Serkin, Yehudi Menuhin and Vladimir Horowitz. Mason wrote home that he had been to the New York Metropolitan Opera where, among other performances, he again saw Beniamino Gigli perform in *Tosca*. Mason mentioned a few occasions when he was asked to dine at the Rainbow Room, high atop 30 Rockefeller Plaza.

In October Mason's parents shipped to him his late grandmother's 1895 Steinway piano, which he had played in her house as a boy. The movers struggled bringing the piano up the steep and narrow stairway and promised the nervous landlord that they would find a better way when it came time to move it out.* A technician came over from the Steinway factory in Astoria where the piano had been built. He tuned it and repaired a squeaking damper pedal.

Mason's letters home from 1938 to 1940 describe a busy nightlife of music, philosophy, and going out with old friends, especially Hartford friends Jack and Patsy Huntington, Jack's sister Sally and her husband Martin, and Bill Melish, Mason's former rowing buddy from Cambridge and Harvard, now a newly ordained Episcopalian minister. These evenings out were interspersed with evenings home grading examinations. On one occasion when assigned to teach a class about Baruch Spinoza, Mason was not satisfied with available translations of Spinoza's work, which was originally written in Latin. Consequently, Mason translated the necessary documents himself. It came to sixty typed pages. Invited to join the Columbia Philosophical Club and the New York Philosophical Circle, he was seen as a rising star in his profession.

During his first years at Columbia, Mason expressed how philosophy as a discipline was losing much of its relevance and cultural power, as "philosophers increasingly wrote not for the public but for each other."[9]

In an essay for *Columbia Quarterly*, Mason described the difficulty in presenting "a clear picture of contemporary philosophy." Noting that there seemed to be as many schools of modern philosophy "as there were individual philosophers," he added that traditional methods of classifying them were no longer applicable. He felt that modern philosophy had become too cautious, as philosophers spent "time trying to justify the existence of philosophy itself." Mason believed that this reticence was "largely due to the brilliant and rapid advance of science into the very fields which had been the traditional province of philosophy."[10]

Mason wrote to his parents of his travails in the philosophy department at Columbia. He described how "speculative metaphysics," a method of

---

* It would later exit through the front window, to the delight of the neighbors who gathered to watch, hoping that the block and tackle would break and the piano would crash to earth like in a scene from a Charlie Chaplin movie.

philosophical inquiry based on intuition and a popular school of thought at the time, was leading nowhere. In other words, as summarized later by philosopher Richard Tarnas, "unverifiable and untestable metaphysical propositions concerning the world as a whole were without genuine meaning."[11]

More than two centuries of scientific discovery had tended to support rational and logical methods in the approach to understanding the human experience. However, due to the more recent progress of natural sciences, including the work of William James and Sigmund Freud, human thought was found to be governed and "distorted by nonrational factors, and . . . the mind's conclusions were neither ubiquitous nor universally verifiable,"[12] such that speculative metaphysics was becoming more and more subjective and less universally applicable. Mason stated that this speculative metaphysics "has brought philosophy itself into disrepute, open to criticisms by logical positivists," who argued that all philosophy must be grounded in science and observable empirical data and that "all philosophical propositions which are not verifiable are meaningless."[13] Their opponents, many of them Thomists, whose original sources of inspiration included Saint Thomas Aquinas and Saint Augustine, countered that there were elements of philosophy, issues reflecting "states of being" such as ethics, sin, death, and the meaning of existence, that "transcended the boundaries of logical analysis and empirical science." Mason wrote that most contemporary philosophy was "cautious and diffident, capitulating for the most part either to science or to religion."[14]

Mason asserted that most attempts to reconcile this controversy of religion versus science, of faith versus reason, were "either halfhearted or extremely biased." In an article for the *American Scholar*,[15] he argued that Whitehead's philosophy, unlike that of other modern philosophers, was strongly applicable to, relevant to, and dependent upon the many unquantifiable aspects of human experience. Mason strongly advocated Whitehead's "bold and imaginative" construction, which he summarized as follows: "Whitehead is fully aware of the contradictions in much dogmatic religion but is unwilling to abandon religion for science alone. . . . It [philosophy] must not be afraid to employ the results of science and it must not ignore the claims of religious experience."[16]

Not a supporter of the logical positivists, Mason hoped to mount a defense of John Dewey and Whitehead, who had attempted to mediate a position between the two extremes. Although stating that he was an "avowed disciple of Whitehead," in a moment of candor to his parents Mason humbly admitted that his difficulty resulted in part because he didn't really "understand it all."

In the summer of 1939 Mason returned to England, departing New York on May 31 on SS *Normandie* and arriving at Southampton on the morning of June 5. Taking the train to London, he arrived by noon. He crossed the North Sea to Norway to coach the Fana Roklubb again and reported home that as the club's American coach, he "was treated like royalty." In late June he left Norway, back to England with the Fana Roklubb, as they had entered the Henley crew regatta at Mason's suggestion. They actually reached the semifinals and returned home to Norway with much fanfare.

Before departing west for New York, again on SS *Normandie*,* he visited old college friend Colin Cotteril's farm and had dinner with Lambert Shepherd and his new wife Iris, who had married in early June. Mason wrote to his parents that "England isn't very pleasant now. The whole country is thinking about the possibility of war." There was little "news about what was really going on." He wrote prophetically that "August will be a critical month."

Critical, indeed.

Following his appointment as chancellor of Germany on January 30, 1933, Adolf Hitler consolidated absolute power, leading to the rapid rise of Nazism in Germany. The repossession of the Rhineland and the Ruhr in 1936, Germany's role in the Spanish Civil War, and the Austrian Anschluss of March 1938 bespoke of Germany's rebirth as an aggressive European power.

While in Munich in the fall of 1934, Mason clearly had witnessed enough personally threatening behavior of the fascist mob to conclude that Nazi

---

* These were the *Normandie*'s last days. The ship was interned in New York City by the U.S. Navy when the war began. While being outfitted as a troopship, the *Normandie* caught fire and capsized at the pier on February 9, 1942.

Germany would be a threat to European peace. Later back in the United States as public debate became polarized between interventionists and isolationists, Mason began vehemently to advocate that war would come and that the United States would have to intervene.

In 1938 Czechoslovakia had existed as its own country for only twenty years, carved out of the carcass of the Austro-Hungarian Empire. Western Czechoslovakia, also known as the Sudetenland, was ethnically German rather than Czech. Hitler claimed that at least three million Germans wanted to belong to the Reich. He insisted that the Sudetenland should return to German control, as he had already accomplished with his seizure of the Rhineland from British and French authority and with the Austrian Anschluss* earlier that year.

In retrospect, the tension is difficult to imagine. War was imminent. For the British, the memory of the last war's unspeakable savagery was still an open wound. Hitler had already announced his plans to solve this situation in his own way by invading Czechoslovakia. In September, British prime minister Neville Chamberlain flew on several occasions to Munich to meet with Hitler. Along with Prime Ministers Edouard Daladier of France and Benito Mussolini of Italy, they held a summit meeting in Munich whose outcome would live in infamy. Interestingly, representatives of the Czech government were not invited to the meeting, and yet the subsequent Munich Agreement sold the Czechs down the river. The agreement handed the Sudetenland of western Czechoslovakia to the Nazis. In October Chamberlain flew home to England in triumph, waving a document that he declared would assure "peace for our time." Within a year, Britain would be at war with Germany.

In accordance with the Munich Agreement, the German Army soon occupied the Sudetenland. Then early in 1939, the Nazis forcefully invaded the remainder of Czechoslovakia. The term "appeasement," as it applied to Chamberlain's Munich Agreement, became a four-letter word, forever commemorating and thus connoting the ultimate sellout.

---

* "Anschluss," best translated as "union," refers to Germany's annexation of Austria.

Having lived in Great Britain for five years and having seen the incipient Nazi horrors up close in their infant stage, Mason clearly recognized the dangerous developments in Europe. He did not applaud Chamberlain's appeasement of the Nazis. With his first cousin William "Bill" Welch (Yale class of 1935), a political scientist two years younger than him, Mason engaged in a two-year correspondence, arguing over the future of Nazism and fascism and the best means to stop them.

The record of their correspondence between 1938 and 1940 reveals the depth of their debate.[17] Mason was a hawk. Having personally witnessed Hitler's speeches, Mason predicted that the autocracies of fascism and Nazism would spread throughout the countries of Europe, especially those whose populations were suffering the extreme scourge of economic depression. He urged immediate pushback against the Nazis by the combined might of Britain, France, and Russia, up to and including the threat of war.

Cousin Bill was an isolationist. Admitting to Mason that he favored appeasement over war, Bill disagreed with Mason's tripartite defense plan, noting that fascism if allowed to spread would likely burn itself out. Bill argued first that the Brits so hated the communist Russians that they would never cooperate with each other and that the Brits themselves had become adamantly pacifist as a result of their catastrophe in the Great War (World War I), ironically once misnamed as the "war to end all wars." Bill also argued that the French were fundamentally powerless, despite having the most numerically superior army in Europe, larger than the Germans and with better tanks. He predicted that these countries would never agree to cooperate against the German forces. Hitler had reoccupied the Rhineland in 1936 with a token force, and historian William Manchester notes that the French Army, outnumbering by tenfold the "half-trained and inadequately equipped Wehrmacht" and "supported by tanks and the finest artillery in the world," could have retaken "the Rhineland in a matter of hours."[18]

Mason argued that the situation would eventually require American intervention, the sooner the better. Mason and Bill's debate echoed the larger controversy that was engulfing the United States at the time, whether or not to get involved again in another European war. Having seen the destructive potential of the Nazi ideals and having witnessed the sting of their fists in Munich, Mason insisted that war was inevitable unless early action was taken to stand up to Hitler.

As Mason predicted, August was indeed "a critical month." In August 1939 diplomats from Britain, France, and the Soviet Union were secretly negotiating for a tripartite alliance for mutual defense in case of German attack. The Soviets wanted the agreement to include permission to counterattack Germany through Poland, but the Polish foreign minister would not agree, knowing that once inside Poland, the Red Army would never leave.

Germany was gearing up for inevitable war. The German Wehrmacht amassed on the Polish border. On August 21 Hitler ordered ships of the Reichsmarine, including the pocket battleship *Admiral Graf Spee*, to put to sea in order to be ready to raid British merchant shipping once war inevitably broke out.

Secretly, the Soviet Union and Germany were simultaneously negotiating a trade agreement. When this German-Soviet Commercial Agreement was signed on August 19, 1939, the Soviets broke off the tripartite defense negotiations with France and Britain, citing other reasons. Then on August 24, Hitler and Joseph Stalin announced the Molotov-Ribbentrop Pact, also known as the German-Soviet Non-Aggression Pact. A secret provision of this agreement, long suspected but not fully verified until 1989, allowed for the creation of "spheres of influence" in Eastern Europe, which included the Russian occupation of eastern Poland in case of German attack from the west. Poland was destined to be partitioned, in other words, carved in half and obliterated.

If August was indeed a critical month, September was even more so.

Hitler was emboldened by the easy acquiescence of the other European powers. On September 1, 1939, the Nazi invasion of Poland finally triggered Britain's declaration of war against Germany. Mason's British college friends immediately volunteered for military service.

———

In the fall of 1939 while building his career, Mason first met Julia at Phil and Dolly's small New York apartment. Mason later wrote to her how he had

immediately fallen in love with her "green dress, her sweet and gentle disposition, her soft voice and her freckles."[19]

———

Through the winter of 1939–1940, Europe engaged in the so-called Phony War.
Few shots were fired. In contrast to the blitzkrieg (lightning war) that had
characterized Germany's ferocious assault on Poland, the sarcastic humor of
the British press referred to this period as the "Sitz Krieg," or "Sitting War."

By late winter of 1940, Mason's cousin Bill Welch had experienced a
change of heart subsequent to the German invasion of Poland and the British and French declarations of war. Bill wrote to Mason in February 1940:
"The march of events has gone so that our discussions of last winter would
now rank as purely academic. A new line of argument must be developed."[20]

———

After several months of dating, in January 1940 Mason first mentioned Julia
in a letter to his parents, who were planning a visit to New York City. He
wrote, "I should like to invite my friend Julia Kernan to dinner. I have been
seeing quite a bit of her lately here in the city and I should like very much to
have you meet her." He noted to his parents that Miss Kernan was a Vassar
graduate, as were Mason's mother and sister and their close friends from
Hartford, Sally and Patsy Huntington.

By April in his correspondence Mason had stopped referring to Julia so
formally by her full name, although he did refer to her affectionately as his
"good pal." His letters home mentioned the word "we" often. He and Julia
enjoyed the opera together and saw Vladimir Horowitz with the New York
Philharmonic. Mason occasionally asked his parents if he could invite Julia
to come home with him for the weekend or to come with him to their beach
house at Hatchett's Point, near Lyme, Connecticut. In May they drove twice,
once to Princeton and once to Philadelphia, to watch Julia's brother Walter
rowing in the Harvard crew.

Julia clearly warmed quickly to Mason's constant attention despite her
first impression, which in retrospect had been a fairly accurate observation.

No correspondence exists as to her feelings about him, but her best friends were already married. She later confessed to me that at this point in her life, at age twenty-eight, the timing was right. But that would not have been the sole basis for her decision to stay with Mason. Yes, he was successful and driven and clearly going places in his career. He had boundless energy and enthusiasm. She must have seen the side of him that he kept hidden from the world, the playful piano player capable of enjoying either a drive through the country with the top down or an evening at the Met. It couldn't hurt that he was three inches taller than Julia and was a great dancer. As she later stated, "Everything about him just felt right."

In the spring of 1940 while Mason and Julia were getting to know each other, Europe's Phony War heated up. The Western Front, quiet since the previous autumn, came alive with Germany's invasion of Denmark, Norway, and the Low Countries. Mason wrote home that he was especially disheartened by the underplanned and poorly supported British attacks in northern Norway and the British troops' subsequent calamitous withdrawal. Mason's friend Harry Fraser, who had rowed in the same shell with him at Cambridge, participated in the Norway debacle.

The German invasion of France quickly ensued. The British Expeditionary Force (BEF) rushed to the continent and moved northeastward into Belgium. Letters to Mason from England mentioned that "Johnny, Derek and Shrew are serving with the BEF somewhere in France." A German tank corps, spearheaded by a previously unknown but aggressive commander named Erwin Rommel, rushed through Belgium's "impassable" Ardennes forest and outflanked the BEF, circling behind and trapping the entire British army with its back to the English Channel near the French city of Dunkirk.

Lambert Shepherd had been an undergraduate Jesus College rowing colleague of Mason's. On June 9, Lambert wrote to Mason describing his involvement rowing a small boat to the beach at Dunkirk. Lambert had been "trying to get into the Navy since the war broke out." Still waiting for a navy commission, he had received a request to assist. With only one hour's notice, he boarded a ship's lifeboat that was one of many being towed behind tugs to Dunkirk. "It was an unbelievable sight," Lambert wrote, with "every type of craft imaginable, fishing boats, drifters, trawlers, lifeboats, and even a Thames River fire barge." He added that they had been "bombed a bit on the way over." Lambert stated that they repeatedly rowed their lifeboat to the beach; loaded up with soldiers, many of them badly wounded; and rowed back out to the waiting tugs while under fire from German aircraft and artillery, partly shrouded by clouds of heavy black smoke.[21]

Mason kept his private life very private. He did not announce his intentions to his parents until June. By July, he corresponded regularly with his parents about wedding plans. He and Julia had agreed on a small wedding to take place in New York City rather than in her home in Utica.

The Utica Kernans were Irish Catholic. Julia's mother Jessie was Episcopalian but upon her marriage to Dev Kernan had agreed to raise her children in the Catholic faith. Julia recalled attending Sunday mass with her father, who was worldly, outgoing, and popular with his peers, in retrospect quite similar to her future husband Mason. Dev's presence made Sunday mornings more festive than they might otherwise have been. Julia enjoyed conversing with his colleagues and their family members. Attending church with him was stimulating but not necessarily from a religious standpoint. When informed by a priest that all babies are born in sin, young Julia had countered boldly that "anyone who believes that has never actually held a newborn baby."[22] When Julia's father died in 1928, Julia's mother, Jessie, did not continue to take her children to Catholic mass, and Julia no longer wished to attend in her father's absence.

When Julia told her mother that she wanted to marry Mason, Jessie approved, and, for her, religion was not a factor. However, Mason's correspondence to his parents reveals that Jessie's other Kernan relatives were less than pleased. They criticized Julia's mother heavily for failing to live up to their view of her sacred obligation to raise her children in her late husband's Catholic faith.

Through July while making wedding plans, Mason cautioned his parents not to bring up the subject of religion. He wrote, "For heaven's sake, don't mention it!" He added that Julia did not "wish to flaunt her apostasy in front of her family." Noting that his and Julia's ideas of religion "really do coincide," he told his father, "back me up." Although he appeared nonchalant and all business, he told his parents of his "deep private joy and unexpected happiness."

Money was also an issue. Jessie could not afford to contribute to the wedding. Mason was impressed with Julia's mother, stating that she "is the stuff that heroes are made of, for she has lived on almost no money since Mr. Kernan died" twelve years before.

Mason and Julia decided to get married quietly, without announcing their engagement, in order to take the family pressure off of Julia's mother. Mason's mother agreed to address the envelopes for the announcements, which would be mailed after the wedding. Julia wrote to Mrs. Gross thanking her for the warmth and sweetness with which she was being welcomed into the family. Julia said that she would not be wearing a wedding dress and that her younger brother Dev (Jr.) would "give me away" while wearing a simple gray suit. Julia asked Mason's family to wear whatever would be most comfortable.

———

The infamous Battle of Britain escalated through the summer of 1940. The climactic battle began in early September 1940 as the German Luftwaffe prepared to deliver on Reichsmarschall Hermann Goering's promise to destroy the Royal Air Force prior to the invasion of England. Mason was paying close attention.

———

By September 1940 Mason Gross was a busy philosophy instructor, the newest faculty member in a very large department. As expected of new faculty, in addition to teaching he was also publishing and attending meetings of philosophical societies. Professionally, he focused on the philosophical arguments of the times, including the battles between the speculative philosophers, the metaphysicists, and the logical positivists. He relished the philosophical controversies that swirled in the ivory towers, which may have had little or no interest to the guys from Steinway who had lugged his five-hundred-pound grand piano up three flights of stairs. He frequented the Metropolitan Opera and Carnegie Hall, attended Columbia football games, and played his Steinway in his small New York apartment. A scion of Yankee aristocracy, he now owned his own Ford convertible and drove frequently on weekends to see his family in Hartford or friends in New England. He was tall (6'3"), trim, and athletic. If at this point in his life he appeared to be "full of himself," he may have had good reason.

Julia Kernan was a bohemian, having lived in the West Village since 1934. She shared a one-bedroom apartment and was grateful to be working in the *New York Times* subscription department. More liberal than Mason, she had joined local marches in support of the republican antifascists in the Spanish Civil War. She walked to local jazz clubs and listened to Billie Holiday and Ella Fitzgerald. Julia occasionally took the train either home to Utica to see her mother or up to Vermont to visit the Parrishes at Johnny Seesaw's.

The world was ablaze in a war that would shake civilization to its core. The German Luftwaffe, based in occupied France, was bombing England daily. Mason's college friends had already heard shots fired in anger and were "in it up to our necks."[23] Archie Hamilton had survived with the BEF in France and was rescued at Dunkirk; Lambert Shepard, after Dunkirk, was awaiting a commission in the Royal Navy; and Colin Cotteril was a pilot cadet in the Royal Air Force.

Julia and Mason had known each other less than one year. They chose to marry in a small ceremony in the Holy Trinity Episcopal Church in Brooklyn, New York, where Mason's college friend Bill Melish had just taken over from his father as pastor. In the presence of only a few family members, with Mason's brother Spencer serving as best man and Julia's younger brother Dev standing by her, on September 6, 1940, Columbia University philosophy instructor Mason W. Gross, age twenty-nine, and West Village bohemian jazz enthusiast Julia Kernan, age twenty-seven, were married.

The next day, September 7, 1940, as Mason and Julia departed for their honeymoon, the German Luftwaffe began an indiscriminate bombing of British cities that would become known forever as the Blitz.

As Mason and Julia began their life together, the world war threatened to rip everything apart.

CHAPTER 5

Postmark:
Somewhere in Italy, 1944

I am furious on the point of making sure that a war like this never happens again. —MWG, October 1944

In March 1944, Julia had no idea where on Earth her husband had gone, only that he had departed five weeks earlier for an overseas combat zone, destination unknown. She was coping with two young daughters, one a newborn, and was residing with Mason's parents in Hartford, Connecticut. Except for a telegram received on March 5 and briefly stating, "All well and safe," she had not heard from him since January 30, when he had sent a "hasty note" from Gowen Field in Boise, Idaho, stating, "Goodbye for now," adding that his squadron would be departing soon and that she would not hear from him "for a while."

It was the winter of 1944, and Mason had a lot of company. Waves of American soldiers were boarding ships and moving overseas to staging areas in the Pacific and in Europe. Mason may have gone to Guadalcanal, an island that one year previously had been all but unknown to most Americans but by 1944 reflected a struggle that would live forever in that generation's collective memory. The troops now on Guadalcanal were preparing for upcoming battles in the jungles of Guam, Saipan, and Peleliu and on the beaches of Iwo Jima, names that once were unrecognizable to many people but were soon to become as familiar as Chicago and Los Angeles.

Mason may have gone to Great Britain, one of millions preparing for the long-anticipated invasion of France, which everyone, including the Germans, knew was coming. Only a very select few in Supreme Allied Headquarters were discussing exactly when, where, or how.

If in Britain, Mason would have been assigned to the U.S. 8th Air Force. Already fighting in an attempt to disrupt German industrial power, the 8th Air Force was suffering catastrophic casualty rates. In October 1943 on a day henceforth known as Black Thursday, 229 B-17 bombers had attacked the ball-bearing factories in Schweinfurt, resulting in a loss of 60 aircraft and the death of 690 out of 2,900 airmen participating in the raid.

Mason may have gone to the Mediterranean theater, where the battle for North Africa was completed and Sicily had fallen after a fierce struggle. The invasion of Italy had begun in late summer of 1943. By January 1944 after the liberation of Naples, the advance of General Mark W. Clark's Fifth Army northward through Italy had stalled. This was partly due to two factors. First, there was the winter in the Apennine Mountains, which brought cold, rain, and knee-deep mud, the latter of which inevitably resulted when heavy machinery moved over wet ground. Second, the advance had also slowed because Italy's rugged mountainous terrain provided the German Wehrmacht with ideal defensive positions on the high ground. Italy's fast rivers pouring out of the steep mountains, the Volturno, the Garigliano, and the Rapido, now swollen with rain and dark with mud, each had to be crossed against withering firepower that decimated Allied troops. In January 1944 an Allied amphibious force landed at Anzio, forty miles south of Rome, hoping to outflank the Germans defending their mountain positions farther to the south near Cassino in the Liri Valley. This assault also bogged down and remained in place for months under heavy German artillery from the high ground surrounding the beachhead.

On March 25, 1944, almost two months after Mason's last letter had arrived, Julia received several letters at once, as the mail from soldiers overseas typically arrived in bundles. In the right upper corner of one letter, dated March 8, Mason listed his return address as "415th Bomb Squadron,

98th Bomb Group, APO 520, c/o Postmaster, N.Y." Having already documented the "polite fiction that officers censor their own mail," on his return address Mason surreptitiously added the subscript "Somewhere in Italy."

———

Two years previously in 1941, Mason and Julia were still living in New York City. Soon after the December 7 Japanese attack on Pearl Harbor, millions of Americans, both men and women, had descended upon armed forces' recruiting offices to enlist. Mason was no different. He was already thirty years old, married, and with one daughter, Ellen Clarissa Gross, born in New York City on July 28, 1941. Mason had been classified by the Selective Service on November 19, 1941 as 3A, exempt due to "dependent spouse and child." Although this class of exemption would later be rescinded due to higher than anticipated American casualties, at age thirty, Mason would have been a low priority for the draft. He likely would never have been called at all. In a letter to Julia, Mason himself later wrote, "I could so easily have talked myself into waiting for the draft to catch up with me, with an armful of good excuses about the importance of teaching and bringing up one's family. But with a person of your honesty around, that just wouldn't do. . . . The necessity of doing the right thing in your eyes broke down all the possibilities of self-justification."

Mason's best friend from his undergraduate years at Cambridge University, Lambert Shepard, had written repeatedly to Mason early in the war about how eagerly he was awaiting a commission in the Royal Navy. Lambert got his wish. He enlisted as an "ordinary seaman," with a promise of a commission within a year. He was assigned to the battleship HMS *Hood*, the unsinkable pride and flagship of the Royal Navy.[1] Lambert, who had survived the 1940 evacuation at Dunkirk, perished violently in May 1941, along with 1,411 other Royal Navy shipmates, when the German pocket battleship *Bismarck* sank the *Hood* in a North Atlantic battle that lasted only eight minutes from the first salvo to the last. The *Bismarck*'s first shot bracketed the British battleship. The *Hood* fired only once in response. The *Bismarck*'s second salvo penetrated the *Hood*'s wooden deck and exploded in the powder magazine. Eyewitnesses from the nearby HMS *Exeter* stated that the *Hood* disappeared in a fireball and a cloud of black smoke. When the smoke cleared the *Hood* had vanished, having sunk in less than three minutes. Out of the entire crew there were only three survivors, who were blown off the stern when the ship exploded and were luckily rescued after two hours in the icy waters of the Denmark Strait. The sinking of the *Hood* was an unparalleled catastrophe that shook confidence among the British in their military and in Churchill's government.

For Mason, Lambert's death was shattering. Lambert's last letter to Mason, written when he was first assigned to the *Hood*, had reminded Mason "how much your friendship has meant to me." Lambert's widow, Iris, wrote to Mason in August describing "a link between you two that could never be broken."[2]

Then came more bad news. Mason had once described his great friend Colin Cotteril as a "hard-drinking Irishman" but the best oarsman at Cambridge. Colin was not much of a correspondent, but he had written to Mason in November that an Irish Republican Army bomb at King's Cross railroad station killed their friend Duncan Campbell and his wife. Colin added that he and his fiancée Peggy were finally getting married. But in March 1942 as disastrous news of continued Allied defeats poured in from around the globe, Mason received a letter from Peggy stating that Colin, a new pilot in the Royal Air Force, had perished on January 14. Colin had never known his own father, who had perished in World War I. Peggy wrote, "I have always been afraid that he wouldn't survive the war, because his reckless courage plus a bomber made a fatal combination."[3]

In 1942 as Mason argued to enlist in an army that did not want thirty-year-old philosophy professors, he cited among his reasons that "I have now lost the only true friends that I have ever had." Fortunately, the U.S. Army needed instructors. Mason's teaching skills were valuable.

Living in New York and teaching at Columbia, Mason corresponded weekly with his parents in Hartford. About the war, he wrote only that he was in training to become an air raid warden. Meanwhile, he wrote frequent letters to the War Department requesting an assignment.

At 11:30 P.M. on Sunday, July 12, 1942, Mason received a telegram ordering him to report immediately to Officers Training School in Miami Beach.
He and Julia rushed about on Monday with last-minute details. He boarded
a Pullman car at Pennsylvania Station and discovered that many of the men
in the car were going to the same destination.

Mason was commissioned in the U.S. Army Air Force (USAAF) on July 13,
1942. He reported first to the Officer Training School of the USAAF Technical Training Command in Miami. The students were lodged on the beach
at the Wofford Hotel, which like many hotels and apartment buildings had
been leased for use by the army to accommodate one hundred thousand new
air force officers in 1942 alone. He wrote his parents on Saturday, July 17, hoping that they were not dismayed at his decision to join up and noting his
certainty that he was doing the right thing.

Mason's six weeks in Miami included basic military drills, which he wrote
thinned his waistline and straightened his posture from the slumped shoulders of a philosophy professor. Classes in military law, military conduct,
and leadership were interspersed with calisthenics in the heat of the mid-
day Florida sun on a field with two thousand trainees exercising simultaneously. On one afternoon, the temperature was the highest recorded in
Miami for the previous thirty-one years. There were classes in public speaking, where each student had to prepare a two-minute discussion. It was
based on Dale Carnegie's course in salesmanship. Mason referred to it only
as "dreadful."

At 6'3", Mason was the tallest man in his class and was assigned to the
color guard, a team of four who marched in the front of the formation carrying the American flag and the school colors, with one man on each side
marching with a rifle. Formation occurred every day in midafternoon, usually at the precise moment when the Miami heat would generate a thunderstorm with lightning and high winds.

After six weeks of basic military indoctrination, on August 26, 1942,
Mason transferred to the USAAF training command at Ellington Field near
Houston, Texas, where Julia joined him, with Ellen now a toddler. There he
taught aircraft identification, physics, aerodynamics, and fundamentals of

aircraft maintenance to pilots. Often staying only one lesson ahead of the students, he wrote home to his parents that he "had only a few hours to learn the subject." At Ellington Field, Mason was offered a permanent position as a historian. He respectfully declined and sought orders to go overseas. He noted again to his superiors his personal motivation that several of his British colleagues from Cambridge, including Lambert and Colin, had perished early in the war.

Mason was selected for training to be an intelligence officer. Among other tasks, the purpose of the intelligence cadre was to evaluate the effectiveness of the bombing, determine the effectiveness of enemy fighter tactics and anti-aircraft artillery, and anticipate what defenses any bombing mission might come up against. Mason hoped to be sent to Intelligence Training School in Harrisburg, Pennsylvania, before receiving his specific assignment. He finally received orders first to combat training, at Gowen Field in Boise, Idaho, which had become a major training base for B-24 bomber crews. He departed Houston for Idaho. On July 28, 1943, Ellen's second birthday, Julia, now pregnant in her second trimester, with Ellen on one arm, departed for Hartford.

After Mason settled in at Boise with his training squadron, in October 1943 his orders came through for the air force's Intelligence School in Harrisburg, Pennsylvania. As in Houston, when his superior officers noticed his gift for teaching, they offered him a permanent stateside teaching assignment at Harrisburg, safe from the hazards of overseas duty. It was a plum assignment, close to home and out of harm's way, but he again respectfully declined, reiterating his reasons for joining up in the first place. Finishing his intelligence training at Harrisburg, he was granted two weeks' leave before heading back to Idaho. Leaving Harrisburg in December 1943, he arrived in Hartford in time to "pace the hospital floor" as Julia delivered their second daughter, Katharine (Kitty) Wood Gross, on December 13, 1943. A few days before Christmas, Mason departed for Idaho.

Historian William Manchester wrote, "One difficulty of re-creating the past is that the reader knows how it will turn out, so that events have an air of inevitability."[4] That was not true in 1943. Mason's last sight of Julia before departing for the war was her sitting up against pillows in her hospital bed, holding her newborn daughter, and "looking lovelier than ever." Later that day, Mason stood on the platform in downtown Hartford waiting for his train, with Christmas lights aglow in Hartford's store windows. Realizing that he would not see Julia and the girls again for several years or considering perhaps that a fate such as Lambert's or Colin's might await him, he later admitted to her that he had "burst into tears at the Hartford station."

Mason's next letters to Julia from Idaho follow a similar pattern. The first paragraph describes the January weather, predominantly beautiful, often "clear and bracing" (zero degrees Fahrenheit). Next, he describes his training and his tasks as he became more familiar with the duties of an intelligence officer. He then describes his correspondence from other family members, close friends, or their acquaintances from Ellington Field and reminds Julia how important her letters are to him, as they lifted his morale even if she wrote about mundane daily routines.

Rarely, Mason reflected on his current situation, awaiting orders for an overseas assignment, and their separation. He was not ashamed to write how much he missed Julia and loved her, referring to his own thoughts as "adolescent and obscene." He wrote frequently about the end of the war so they could "pick up the threads of courtship" and "settle down again and be normal."

Mason wrote that his commanding officer had asked him point-blank if he wanted an overseas assignment. Mason answered unequivocally "yes, definitely." Rumors swirled, and he tried not to put too much stock in them, noting that previous assignments had fallen through at the last minute. On January 11, 1944, he wrote that he had received "completely secret" orders, giving him "the best assignment I could get." Noting his own excitement of his pending departure to a combat zone, his letters reflected the thoughts of a man on the threshold of a life-altering episode.

"I am no hero," Mason wrote, "and have no desire to pose as one." He expressed doubts about his own self-sufficiency and realized how dependent he was on his own family. He wrote, "Having a loving wife and children makes certain values a lot clearer." He added, "You give me strength."

In one letter before his departure he wrote, "I would not have my present assignment if not for you. . . . You provide strength, honesty and clarity."

Sometime after his last letter to Julia on January 30, Mason departed for New York with orders to report overseas. In New York he was unable to break away to visit his family, only two hours away. On February 1, he boarded a Liberty Ship bound for Europe.

Having arrived in Naples on March 1, Mason describes that "we climbed into G.I. trucks" for the remainder of the trip, but he would not name the destination. Records show that he traveled across the boot of Italy, reporting in to the 15th Air Force Headquarters in Bari. On March 5, he reported to the 98th Bomb Group Headquarters near Cerignola, twenty miles southwest of Foggia. He stated that he and his colleagues from Boise had traveled together but were then assigned individually rather than as a single group.

———

Following World War I, proponents of military aviation had advocated that the next wars would involve large fleets of heavy bombers, which would take the fight to the enemy's homeland and relieve the combatant nations of the high cost of stagnated trench warfare that had from 1914 to 1918 decimated European youth. The U.S. 8th Air Force, based in England since the late summer of 1942, had gradually begun to bomb German targets but had suffered astronomical casualties.

Once southern Italy had been liberated by the British Eighth Army in late 1943, USAAF general Hap Arnold established the 15th Air Force, which opened its headquarters in Bari, Italy, on the shores of the Adriatic, on December 1, 1943. The 98th Bomb Group, of the 47th Bomb Wing, initially one of only six heavy bomb groups in the 15th Air Force, to which Mason was assigned, took up residence near Foggia at one of twenty-five Allied air bases that would eventually be developed on the table-flat ancient seabed of the twelve-hundred-square-mile Tavoliere Plain. The 98th Bomb Group consisted of four flying squadrons; each squadron flew seven B-24 Liberator bombers.

In the winter of 1944 the Italian campaign, described by its participants as "the forgotten war," was a slaughterhouse reminiscent of the trench warfare from the previous world war. The battle for the village of Cassino has been described as "little Stalingrad."[5] Mason described southern Italy in March as cold and damp. He spent all day in rubber boots and wool trousers caked with mud, the inevitable result of heavy rains and the movement of numerous military vehicles. He lived in a small tent with two other officers that had a dirt floor, a single electric light, and a hand-crank field telephone. They were issued either sleeping bags or two wool blankets to use on a folding metal cot. There was no running water; cold water for shaving or washing had to be carried to the tent in a bucket. Mason's tent had an oil stove. The most commonly described makeshift tent stove in Cerignola consisted of a fifty-five-gallon drum fed with a drop-by-drop plumbing device feeding waste aircraft engine oil from another drum outside the tent. The stoves were prone to malfunction. One rainy evening in late March when Mason had been "in-country" for only three weeks, the stove exploded. Fire consumed the entire tent in less than five minutes. Mason was unhurt, and one tentmate suffered a mild burn to one hand while rescuing some personal items. However, most of their clothes and the remainder of the 175 pounds of personal gear that Mason had been authorized to bring from Idaho were destroyed. He salvaged some undergarments in a footlocker, the clothes on his back, and a singed leather folder containing two photographs of his daughter Ellen at age two, all smiles with one hand digging deep into her Christmas stocking.

"Italy was in ruins," Mason wrote. Once the wheat basket of Europe, the granaries of southern Italy—some extant since Roman times—had been looted to support Benito Mussolini's military expeditions and never resupplied. Mason noted the "degradation to which the Italian people have sunk. The poverty is past description."

The population in Cerignola welcomed the American forces. Mason told of a young Italian boy who cleaned their tent, took laundry out for his mother to wash and fold, and brought him hot water in a bucket for shaving. Americans traded tins of chicken, Vienna sausage, and Spam for vegetables, pasta, and local wine, which Mason recorded as "atrocious."

Mason did not mention in his letters home about the malaria, tuberculosis, and cholera rampant in the area. Although his own health was generally good, he described colds and an occasional nondescript "flu," which actually could have been any febrile illness ranging from dysentery or food poisoning to actual influenza. His weight had fallen from 182 pounds ("in my prime") to 172 in Idaho and then dropped to 157 while in Italy. Mason experienced periodic sinus infections, treated with nasal rinses in the era prior to the development of antibiotics. He also remarked on a recurrent gastric reflux ("the old heartburn") that had plagued him since college and would continue to do so into his sixties. He continually requested that Julia send him Bisodol, a common antacid with magnesium and sodium bicarbonate that he would use daily for the rest of his life. Unfortunately, the medical profession would not realize for fifty years that prolonged gastric reflux, especially when exacerbated by tobacco and hard alcohol, would be the single greatest risk factor for esophageal cancer.

Mason's correspondence from Italy describes in some detail his collateral duties, noting the irony of his assignment as the squadron gunnery officer and admitting that he did not know "one end of a machine gun from another," having barely qualified on the pistol range himself. Fortunately, the master sergeants knew how to teach gunnery. Mason was assigned to be the squadron transportation officer, again ironic in that he was the only officer in the squadron without his own transportation. Later he was assigned his own jeep, the rattiest on the base.

With no legal training, Mason was assigned to be the prosecutor on several court-martial cases and relied on the U.S. Army manual to guide him. All officers rotated as the finance officer, handing out pay and arranging allotments or saving bond purchases, and as officer of the day, responsible for base security and emergencies.

Mason was briefly assigned as the 415th Bomb Squadron adjutant, reporting to the commanding officer. Usually an assignment reserved for those officers who had received special training, the adjutant was the commander's surrogate for all administrative matters, both personal, such as leave or

Mason later stated, "The war shook me up." It is not known how many of his squadron members shown here did not survive the war. (Photo credit: Unknown airman)

payroll, and also operational, pertaining to logistics and training. Describing his assignment as adjutant, Mason never informed Julia that his duties included seeing that a dead airman's personal effects were sent home with a letter from the squadron commander.

Intelligence officers had access to classified information from all theaters of war. Mason quickly realized that the 415th's morale was affected by not knowing what was going on anywhere in the world except in their small, wet, and muddy corner of it. He organized weekly briefings, with voluntary attendance, that would provide information on what was occurring elsewhere. He included information on the advance of the Russians in Eastern Europe and on the advances in the Pacific war as well. Word of these briefings spread rapidly, and Mason found himself giving the same briefing on several occasions to different groups who had not been able to attend the original meeting. Some of his fellow airmen stated that they had learned more from him in one hour than they had in the entire previous year.

Mason's letters rarely mention his primary assignment. As a first lieutenant, he was the 415th Bomb Squadron's assistant intelligence officer. The task of the "Intel" section was to evaluate a squadron's bombing results to determine if a target had been sufficiently destroyed or if a second mission on that target was indicated. Another task was to debrief every crew member after a mission for information concerning enemy fighter tactics and anti-aircraft effectiveness. Additionally, aircrews often witnessed other crews bailing out of disabled bombers and could estimate how many had parachuted and in what general location they had landed. It is no wonder that Mason wrote "after a mission, life is hectic." He added, "Naturally, I have to leave out all the details which would make it interesting, . . . details about getting the missions off and welcoming them back; sitting, in the jeep out on the line ticking them off as they land and then driving to meet them as they taxi in."

One significant detail is missing from Mason's correspondence; that is, he was not permitted to describe what was really happening in Italy in 1944. Mason could not write in any of his 120 letters to Julia from overseas that in the eighteen months that the 15th Air Force was in operation, 1,756 of the 15th Air Force's 3,544 four-engine B-24 bombers were shot down.[6] Mason's description of driving out to the flight line to meet the aircraft did not include his experience that many aircraft did not return. Those that did return often included severely wounded crewmen or were ablaze or so damaged that they crashed upon landing. Mason also could not mention those aircraft that caught fire on takeoff and crashed, killing an entire crew. He mentioned that he debriefed aircrews after each mission but did not include their descriptions of their severe frostbite from flying for hours in open aircraft with temperatures of thirty degrees below zero, where bare skin would stick to gunmetal and peel off, or their sights of bombers colliding or exploding in midflight, with wings falling off, or of crewmen badly injured by German attacks on their formation.

Many years in the future when I asked Mason about his war experience, as all sons did then, he only shook his head and answered "you'd find it boring." Like most veterans of his generation, they kept their war experiences private and in the past.

Mason noted to Julia his respect for his fellow airmen who were "incredibly modest" about their achievements. He wrote, "There are more heroes in this war than you could possibly imagine." Mason reports that during his aircrew debriefings, their stories needed "to be dragged from them."

Mason was not an aircrew member and would not have been assigned to a flight every day. He wrote briefly about his first operational mission "over enemy territory," which occurred in June 1944; he described it as "exciting for an old man of 33." He described the countryside and the view of the mountains as they crossed the Alps. He did not describe the head-on strafing attacks by enemy fighters or the black bursts of antiaircraft cannon fire, the black-and-white photographs of which he stowed away in his army footlocker, where they remained for years hidden in a dusty corner of our family's attic.

————

Mason would later claim that he flew only three combat missions. On another occasion he said six. Yet by the end of the war, he had been awarded the Bronze Star. His official U.S. Air Force photograph taken in late 1945 shows him wearing also the Air Medal with four oak leaf clusters, which signifies that he had completed at least twenty-five combat missions. His description of his flying as "rare" appears, in retrospect, equal to his observation of the humility of the other flight crews as "incredibly modest." We don't know exactly how much he flew, but we know he did fly combat missions. The total number is irrelevant. His experience would seem that whatever it was, unlike his future answer to me, it was not entirely "boring."

Julia did not record her own experience while Mason was gone. Except for a few anecdotes offered to family later in her life, her wartime experience is available now only through Mason's eyes in his letters home.

When Mason received his transfer orders from Houston to Idaho in 1943, Julia was in her second trimester with their second child. When Mason departed, Julia and Ellen were promptly evicted from married officers' housing in order to make room for the next family ordered inbound. Julia had to find her way home. Priority for transportation was given to soldiers traveling on active orders. Julia, the very pregnant wife of a very junior officer, with one child on her arm and also carrying luggage, food for the trip, and a crib, was not given high priority. She was able to leave Houston but experienced delays when changing trains en route. When she was finally able to obtain a seat for a train home, a conductor told her that her crib could not be transported, as there was no room for it in the coach and the baggage car was filled. Julia later described this as the only occasion in her life when, with her husband gone, no friends in sight, and now exhausted, she "pulled out her female card," sat down on her bags on the platform, and cried.[7]

Julia would forever recall the patient Red Cap who came to her rescue.* With the calm disposition of the Buddha himself, the Red Cap folded the crib and stashed it in the coach. Then, he lifted their bags and, carrying Ellen on one arm, ushered them aboard and assisted Julia to her seat.

With the help of Mason's younger sister Cornelia, who met her in Washington, D.C., Julia returned to Mason's parents' home at 229 Kenyon Street in Hartford. Mason's older brother Spencer, a bachelor, lived at home with his parents. At age thirty-six, Spencer was a successful partner in his father's law firm that specialized in insurance law. Sister Cornelia also lived at home. At age twenty-nine, graduated from Vassar, she was close to Julia and, as an accomplished photographer, had her own darkroom in the basement. Cornelia provided Mason with many photos of his children while he was overseas, but Julia self-consciously abhorred being photographed even though she had been a clothes model in New York City five years previously. Despite Mason's pleas for a photograph of Julia, all that she sent him were shots of the girls. Julia struggled with the polite rigidity of the Hartford household with specific mealtimes, even for breakfast, for which she always arrived late and uncombed, having dealt first with her children. As Mason pointed out in a letter, this household was "not conducive to childish hilarity." Mason

---

* Red Caps, originally identified by a red ribbon on their caps, were exclusively African American workers hired by railroads to assist passengers on the platform. They often worked for tips only. Interestingly enough, at least one-third of Red Caps were college educated, often with a master's degree, PhD, or even MD, but could only find work lifting bags.

consoled her once, also in correspondence, after she had "blown up at Spencer" for one of his typical offhanded platitudes. Julia was an ardent supporter of President Franklin Roosevelt, and the conservative Connecticut household never missed an occasion to berate the president. Mason's family was otherwise courteous and very supportive. His father provided Julia with an extra $150 per month, and his mother graciously understood, as perhaps all mothers do, that infants follow nobody's schedules but their own. However, soon after arriving in Hartford, Julia immediately sought a different living arrangement, with Mason's complete agreement. In May 1944 she moved to Dorset, Vermont, staying in the farmhouse of Mrs. deSchweinitz, the mother of her college roommate Mary who was living an hour away in the village of Peru, just up the mountain from Manchester. As the winter of 1944–1945 approached, Julia moved back to Connecticut into a house in Bloomfield with two other mothers of young children whose husbands were also overseas. They were able to share duties, such as childcare, while one of them went out on the predetermined days to try to buy meat or sugar or obtain gasoline ration cards.

———

Shortly after the liberation of Rome, Mason accompanied the group adjutant on a two-day jeep ride to Rome. The city itself was largely undamaged, since the German troops had vacated the city just before the Allies' arrival. However, in the remainder of Italy, signs of war were evident. Cassino, only months previously the site of a major battle, was "just a mass of rubble, with no house standing."

Driving to Rome they took several wrong turns, which led them to an area north of the city that they soon surmised was well behind enemy lines. Since the Wehrmacht was busily retreating to fortified positions to the north, somehow their jeep escaped notice, and they returned to Rome unharmed. They toured the Vatican and on a sunny afternoon were ushered into a spontaneous audience for Allied soldiers. Mason attended, finding himself seated only fifteen feet from Pope Pius XII.

At the end of 1944, Mason was offered ten days leave in the Holy Land when several of the group's officers flew a B-24 to Cairo for a conference. Mason toured Egypt and crossed the Suez Canal to Palestine. Visiting Jerusalem and Bethlehem, he noted that the locals knew what visiting Christians wanted to see and provided tours to sites alleged to be locations where Jesus had suffered or later risen. The sites seemed so conveniently accessible such that they actually "weakened rather than strengthened" one's credulity. He reported that seeing Jerusalem did not increase his own piety, of which we actually know very little. He did remark that despite the vacuity of the tourist sites, he did "prefer to be a believer."

By this time, Mason's letters home began to reflect more on his future and that of Julia and the children. He knew that he had changed and that an academic career would not be sufficiently rewarding. He noted also that Julia was not a true "city girl" and would prefer to live and raise a family in a more rural setting. He reflected that he and Julia, having "no geographical roots of our own," could never have a "real house in New York City." He did not want to raise his family in a small apartment in Manhattan and expressed disappointment that although he was still on a leave of absence from Columbia, his prospects for advancement there were hampered by the large size of the department and lack of funds to promote him.

Mason wrote to Julia that they would "pick up the threads of courtship, . . . settle down again and be normal." He expressed his gratitude for his family for allowing "little Mason to go off and be an eccentric philosopher or a soldier boy."

———

What was the effect of this war, this global catastrophe, on this young father, who had grown up in wealth, had been educated in the finest private schools, and had become, in his own eyes, a stooped "eccentric philosopher" at a prestigious Ivy League college?

One can hardly speculate on the many ways in which this war would have affected everyone, even those peripherally involved. For so many GIs it was

the first time they had ventured outside their own country or even their own
state. Over four hundred thousand young Americans died overseas. A larger
number were affected physically by disfiguring wounds, both large and small.
Some were emotionally traumatized, and many would remain so for the rest
of their lives, with a mental condition that, glibly labeled "combat fatigue,"
implied that the sufferer was congenitally lacking in some unnamed fundamental facet of masculinity and was subsequently ignored both by the medical profession and the Veterans Administration (VA). Combat fatigue has
only in recent decades been identified as the significantly disabling condition now known as post-traumatic stress disorder, which the VA (now the
Department of Veterans Affairs but to millions always simply the "VA")
admits can occur after a single incident. Veterans of Mason's war witnessed
these traumas daily for months or even years.

Many returned home wondering how there could have occurred such a
catastrophe for which they had a front-row seat, a true apocalypse with so
many faces of destruction, poverty, suffering, pestilence, and unimaginable
inhumanity. The details of what Mason actually saw are lost to history, but
we know that he was on the front lines of the air war. We know that he was
shot at; we know that he flew into frightening enemy antiaircraft artillery.
He never spoke about specific events that he may have seen, such as when
the disabled bombers limped home full of bleeding and eviscerated fellow
airmen, often his own tentmates who had shared a joke with him at breakfast that very morning.

———

To put it bluntly, Mason's debt to the U.S. Army was that he had developed
a low tolerance for bullshit. This intolerance would last him the rest of his
life and would surface when indicated. Reminiscent of Reverend Willis Howard Butler's sermons back in Hartford, which advocated taking action when
needed, Mason wrote periodically about his preference to be assigned to a
squadron with flyers who were putting their lives on the line rather than with
the "brass hats at Headquarters." He referred to headquarters staff often milling around with nothing to do except for "stabbing each other in the back."

He mentioned one officer who, having kept them standing in formation in the hot sun, seemed to be "growing stupider every day."

Mason's letters home also reflected his growing disillusion with his previous purely academic life. He speculated on possible careers in industry or business. In his correspondence, he described his reluctance to return to Columbia's academic environment after the war. Before leaving Columbia for basic training, he had turned down a graduate student's "Ph.D. thesis cold, on the grounds that it was wrong, incompetent and incoherent." He had referred it back to the thesis committee to be rewritten. After Mason left for the USAAF, another philosophy department professor actually bypassed the thesis committee, passed this same dissertation (as it had been "written under his direction"), and ensured that the student won the coveted Woodbridge prize, given by Columbia University for the most important work of philosophical analysis being done in the Columbia Graduate School. Mason's Columbia colleague and close friend Ernst Nagel cited this as "as an example of how the wind is blowing." Mason's "fighting blood was up." He concluded that he would return to Columbia with no priority for promotion to professor and that his years in military service would have no value to a university that was about to be flooded with veterans, his own fellow soldiers and airmen who were then risking their lives daily while the professors in the ivory tower were risking nothing, just playing their childish academic politics. Mason was "beginning to understand how a great many people in the Army feel about the people who have stayed on at their jobs at home and have decided what is to be done with" the returning soldiers. Like many combat veterans, his military experience was distancing him from the life that had so delighted him before the war.

———

In his weekly briefings on the global situation, Mason reported that he had become "well known in this area as a commentator in world affairs." In November 1944, he gave a talk titled "Prospects of Democracy in Postwar Germany." This topic is especially prophetic, as before the war he had witnessed firsthand the dangers of the Nazi autocracy. Although no text of this briefing remains, on the night before his address he wrote to Julia his thoughts. He believed that after the war, Germany would "either go communist or gradually slip back into its Nazi ways." He doubted that Germany would embrace democracy, which had already failed twenty years previously, in part because of his belief that "no democracy has ever succeeded that came about as a result of a defeat." He wrote that "democracy isn't really a political system at all—in a sense it is this absence of a political system and a conglomeration of compromises, hard to formulate and impossible to impose on an uncomprehending populace."

In March 1945 after hearing of the Yalta peace talks in February, Mason described an "argument" that he had with the 98th Bomb Group's chaplain, who felt that "any compromise or settlement with Russia was a compromise with our own basic national and religious faith." Mason agreed with the chaplain and also with his own father that the Russian communists presented "a direct threat to a Christian way of life" and "an evil force operating against civilization as we know it." However, Mason seemed not so concerned about the development of communist governments in the East European countries devastated by the war. He wrote to Julia the following:

> We are left with the choice of allowing people in these countries to fall under Russian influence or else propping up some thoroughly rotten regime which will fall prey to the next Hitler who comes along. Then arises the question in their minds whether Hitler is worse than communism. . . . I can't help feeling that it might be an important factor in the ultimate liberation of the peoples of central Europe. Something else would be more ideal, but somehow a government must be provided for these people now.
>
> I am not afraid of the spread of communism. I am definitely afraid of an incomplete settlement of the German problem, leaving a loophole open for the rebirth of German militarism. . . . I am furious on the point of making sure that a war like this never happens again.

In several letters Mason mentioned this "magnificent thing," namely the new GI Bill of Rights, officially the Servicemen's Readjustment Act of 1944, that would aid veterans in many ways, such as low-interest home loans and

medical care for those injured. The GI Bill also offered subsidy for education. Mason wanted to convince people of the idea of a good education not
just for vocational training but also for college education.

Mason wrote that he had "something to say" after the war but added "I
must find the correct method of expressing myself." He described an atmosphere of futility about the academic environment and how he had once
"built an academic wall" around himself. His correspondence revealed a
transition away from academic scholarly work and those controversies that
swirled through the ivory towers, where philosophers increasingly wrote not
for the public but instead only for each other. His studies under Alfred North
Whitehead at Harvard and analysis of contemporary philosophy published
in the *Columbia University Quarterly* before the outbreak of war reflected
Mason's previous self-assessment as the "eccentric philosopher" and not the
man that he had become, seeing his love of free and unrestricted dialectic
under attack from autocratic regimes. His experience saw the need for a practical application of these principles, the role of education in a democracy,
and the prevention of autocracy and the preservation of freedom, "the kind
of freedom that a democracy can bring that must be more valuable than anything else."

As a result of the war, Mason had learned that his world was no longer
just about him. He had a family, and he had a mission, the details of which
were still unclear.

———

On April 13 Mason wrote to Julia that he was in a "very very blue and despon-
dent mood," noting that the news of President Roosevelt's death had
reached him at breakfast. Recognizing that Roosevelt's record "had a few
blemishes," Mason added that the president was "so head and shoulders
above everyone else that his loss is irreparable." Mason compared this event
to "the obvious parallel; namely, the death of Lincoln at the close of another
war." Although admitting that he had not been in favor of Roosevelt's long
presidency, Mason did concede that Roosevelt had been the right man to lead
the country during the war and that none of his challengers would have been

suitable. Mason expressed hope that "Mr. Truman" would prove capable of the task.

Mason's correspondence ends in mid-April 1945. It picks up again back in the United States on June 10 when he arrived at the 47th Bomb Wing's new location at Sioux City, Iowa. There is no record of how or when he actually got home. Military records reveal that the 47th Bomb Wing returned to the United States in May 1945 in preparation to transfer to the Pacific to participate in the anticipated Allied invasion of Japan. Mason reported in a letter to Julia that having spent sixteen months overseas in Europe, "I have good reason to believe that I will have to go the Pacific."

The war in Europe was over, but the war in the Pacific was actually escalating, with each successive battle taking place closer to Japan and resulting in progressively greater American and Japanese casualties. Various estimates debated the eventual human cost of the invasion of Japan, but they were all dismal. The possibility of a million more American casualties in a war that over the previous four years had already cost four hundred thousand American lives was a sobering proposition. The anticipated cost to Japanese civilians, whom it was believed would fight to the death, was astronomical.

The 47th Bomb Wing was preparing to deploy to the Pacific. Mason felt a "great pressure being put on" him to go. He was due to be assigned as the chief intelligence officer (abbreviated "A-2") for the entire wing. Whereas in Italy he initially had been in a squadron with seven aircraft and then a group with twenty-four, to be the A-2 for an entire wing was a heavy responsibility. The wing commander lobbied heavily for Mason to accept the assignment. Mason was conflicted by the "duty to the Army and the duty to Julia and the kids." He stated that he did not want to "get out of the Army until Japan is beaten for the same reasons that I got in the first place." Eventually, he accepted the assignment to "go out with the 47th." On July 3, his orders came through. During July he traveled periodically from Sioux City to Colorado Springs, the headquarters for the 2nd Air Force, to which the 47th Bomb Wing had been reassigned.

Having not seen Mason since the day Kitty had been born eighteen months earlier, Julia realized that she would have little opportunity to see him before he departed for the Pacific theater. She left the children in Dorset in the care of Mrs. deSchweinitz and on July 29 arrived by train in Sioux City, Iowa.

There was a dance at the Officers' Club. Mason had strained his knee, but at almost six feet tall Julia was the "belle of the ball, with everybody from the General on down lining up to dance with her." Mason and Julia enjoyed their time together in Iowa, with picnics, dances, and time together alone.

Mason arranged for eight days' leave, anticipating that the 47th would depart for the Pacific theater soon after September 1. On August 6 he wrote home to his parents, "On Tuesday, we depart for the east." They were bound for Dorset, Vermont, so that Mason could see his girls once more before his departure on his second overseas assignment.

By the beginning of August 1945 the air was electric with the tension over the upcoming invasion of Japan, which we now know was scheduled for November 1, 1945, only three months away. Mason's letters do not mention the atomic bombs that were dropped on Hiroshima and Nagasaki on August 6 and 9, respectively.

The debate over the decision to drop these new weapons continues into the twenty-first century, but a few things are clear. Although predictions varied widely, the invasion would cost massive casualties, both American and Japanese. The majority of Japanese civilians who had died in the war had perished only in the previous three months after the crushing B-29 attacks on Japanese cities, most notably the mid-March low-level firebombing of Tokyo. The casualties in this attack, perhaps more than one hundred thousand dead after a firestorm from a single night's raid, paralleled those of the later atomic attacks upon Hiroshima and Nagasaki. Also, the atomic scientists and the U.S. military were unclear on how widespread the destruction would be or what would be the long-term effects of radiation, as witnessed by the American military's untested new policy that U.S. troops could be within two miles of an atomic blast and suffer no ill effects from radiation and that the blast zone itself would be safe to enter within twenty-four to forty-eight hours. Studies after the war would conclude that these estimates were criminally inaccurate.

The atomic bombs were dropped on the expectation that the horror of these new weapons and the threat to Japan of their own widespread devastation that would ensue would induce a Japanese surrender and prevent the need for invasion.

The debate over the wisdom versus the inhumanity of that decision may never end. However, the effect of that decision on the troops who were destined to invade Japan is crystal clear. They were overjoyed and believed forever that their lives had been saved because of it.

The tension over the pending invasion now included rumors of peace. With Julia now visiting in Sioux City, she and Mason were preparing for their train trip back to Vermont. On August 12, Mason wrote to his parents "we clustered around the radio wondering what the next bit of news is going to be."

At 11:40 A.M. on Tuesday, August 14, Mason and Julia departed Sioux City aboard the Chicago, Milwaukee, St. Paul, and Pacific Railroad's high-speed Midwest Hiawatha, due to arrive in Chicago at 9:10 that evening. But halfway through the journey to Chicago at Davenport, Iowa, on the banks of the Mississippi River, they disembarked briefly to stroll in the fresh air on the station platform while the train prepared for the next leg of the journey.

As they stepped onto the platform, they heard all the church bells in Davenport ringing loudly. There was no radio on the train. How could they have known? They stopped to ask a couple boarding the train.

It was official. The Japanese had surrendered.

It was over. It was all over.

Julia was not a diarist. She kept no journal. But she did keep a calendar to remind her on what days she had to get ration cards or buy gasoline or meat or eggs or sugar or milk for the kids. Amid all the notes for the tasks that she had to remember, on this calendar there is an entry of a different sort, written with the nonchalance of a grocery list. Her sparse words do not reveal the sometimes simultaneous sighs of joy and feelings of sadness, fatigue, and relief that echoed from a million families who suddenly had their futures back.

Julia's words carry an emotionality all their own. More than loud church bells or celebratory crowds in Times Square, this single phrase in her calendar for August 14 summarizes the four years of war at home for millions of spouses, parents, and children.

Julia's characteristically few words settle softly on one's heart, like a benediction: "On the train, Sioux City to Chicago. Peace."

CHAPTER 6

The Homecoming, 1945

I don't think that most of us realize what the word "future" means. It refers to a world which simply has not come into existence in any way. We think of time as a road already constructed, down which we are going to travel. But the road is not yet constructed. The exact character of that road will depend very much upon the efforts of the people who are going to travel down it. In short, the future isn't there to be looked into yet. —MWG, June 1950

After the war, millions of American servicemen remained overseas as military officials, and the Harry S. Truman administration, in a global postwar strategy that was fundamentally anticommunist but at the same time vague and undefined, struggled to bring some of them home but leave enough in place if needed. Tired of war, American servicemen still overseas were actually beginning to mutiny, impatient for their return home before all the jobs were gone. In November 1945 alone, one million men were discharged from the U.S. Army.[1]

On November 29, 1945, Mason Gross was one of them.

It is impossible to predict in what ways war will affect someone. There is the isolation and distance from everything that one recognizes as normal. Letters from home that describe washing diapers, going to a movie, or having supper with friends are invaluable because they describe a life somewhere on the planet that is still functioning normally. In war, everything is either too cold or too hot, too wet or too dry, too much or too little. There is boredom, uncertainty, and endless waiting punctuated with unspeakable and unforgettable horror. There is always enough chaos, a maelstrom of destruction for which neither metaphor nor memoir has ever proven sufficient to describe to the uninitiated what that hell is really like.

Mason witnessed up close the effects of not only his squadron's bombing raids but also the ground war in Italy, which was still going on near him until peace was signed. Having traveled to Italy on many occasions as a college student, in 1944 Mason drove in an open jeep to Rome, which itself had not been destroyed, but en route he saw all that close combat had done to Italy. There is more to war than rubble and individual catastrophe. The destruction that he felt was personal. Mason's own squadron had bombed the ancient Benedictine monastery at Monte Cassino. In Italy he saw the collapse of a whole civilization, resulting in unspeakable poverty, famine, and pestilence, and the destruction of an economy that some believe has still never recovered.

How did this affect Mason? On the one hand, he described how the "quick wit and individual ingenuity and daring" of his squadron mates had restored his faith in human nature. He did add, however, that "the war really shook me up." But most of all, he labored to understand how the world had fallen into the depths of such destruction and decided that part of it had to do with a people's inability to reoiot the tempting orations of demagogues such as Adolf Hitler and Benito Mussolini. Mason wrote to his parents that "I am more interested in education in general and in the state of the world than in the routine details of teaching philosophy."

While overseas in Italy, Mason had written to Julia repeatedly about "what to do after the war." He described how "the atmosphere of futility about the academic environment gets on my nerves." He was clearly looking for something else, but what?

During the war Mason had recognized that he no longer wanted to be a "mere philosophy professor," not "mere" in a derogatory sense but in that he sensed a need to pursue something different, something still undefined. He had recognized that the life of a pure academic, writing philosophy papers to be read only by other philosophers, the life he described as that of an "eccentric philosopher," had, as a result of his war experiences, lost its luster. "I couldn't go back to the ivory tower," he said. Without actually stating so, he was describing Socrates, who in ancient Athens had brought philosophy "down from the clouds" into the marketplace and into real life.

It is unlikely that in 1945 Mason would have predicted where the arc of his life would take him. A few years in the future, he would describe in a 1950 commencement speech to a graduation class at Bennett Junior College* that the future is not even a road that one can look down, because even the road is not there yet to be looked at. He told the graduates that "we ourselves are the building blocks of the future" and that "the shaping of a new world depends very largely upon us who have the ability and the knowledge, . . . but, despite very serious difficulties, . . . we must have faith in our ability to do it."[2] Reverend Willis Howard Butler of Hartford had stated it very similarly: "If you never lift your voice in protest against existing conditions, nor lift a finger to remedy them, is it fair to expect that your prayer will be answered? . . . The Kingdom of God comes . . . only by the doing of His will by those who are clear-eyed enough to see it. . . . We are the means by which the will of God is accomplished."[3]

In 1945 Mason was certainly a brilliant professor, classicist, musician, former athlete and a combat veteran, husband, and father. He was not an administrator, but in fourteen short years he would be selected as the youngest ever president of Rutgers University. What circumstances or events would occur between 1945 and his selection in 1959 that would most contribute to his success? Who was he in 1945, and who was he destined to become? The road to that future did not even exist in 1945.

* Bennett Junior College, in Millbrook, New York, northeast of Poughkeepsie, closed in 1978 due to bankruptcy.

CHAPTER 7

Goodbye to New York, 1946

I do feel that there is a certain amount of education and mental training which are prerequisites for citizenship in the postwar U.S. There are certain problems which will arise after the war and which will have to be understood thoroughly or else demagoguery will be able to run hog wild.

—*MWG, April 1945*

Mason returned to Columbia in December 1945 following his honorable discharge from the U.S. Army Air Force. He and Julia and their two children moved into an apartment at 401 West 108th Street. But like everything else during the war, New York had changed. Mason found it was harder, tougher, louder, dirtier, and more angry.

Common practice at the time ensured that returning soldiers could have their old jobs back, when possible. Mason was rehired at Columbia as an instructor at his previous annual salary of $2,400. He was not a professor. He was not in a tenure-track position. With typical hyperbole, Mason later claimed that he had been forty-seventh in line for promotion. Due to the controversy over his refusal to approve a substandard dissertation, he was not welcomed back to Columbia with open arms. Academic politics being what they are, Mason had clearly pissed somebody off. He was good at that.

Upon his return to Columbia University in January 1946, Mason was coldly welcomed with an office down a dark and dusty hallway. Across the hall was a darkened and unused office. The faded nameplate on the door read "Houston Peterson, Philosophy." In 1937, Professor Peterson had left Columbia to join the faculty of Rutgers College in New Brunswick, New Jersey, but his nameplate was still on the door in that dark hallway. In 1945 Peterson was the only philosophy professor at Rutgers; in other words, he was the entire Rutgers philosophy department. He lived at One Washington Square in Greenwich Village and commuted twice weekly by train to Rutgers, carrying the entire records of the department in his briefcase.

Peterson had been born in 1897 in Fresno, California, at the time a small whistle-stop in the fig orchards of California's Central Valley. Escaping from the farm to Pomona College, "Hugh," as he was known, met Mitzi Berrien, a musician and dancer who with her twin sister Kay toured the West with vaudeville shows. Peterson and Mitzi were soon married, and he joined the act. He would later state, not entirely tongue in cheek, that the best preparation for a career in academics was a few years on the boards of vaudeville learning how to hold an audience's attention, sometimes in spite of a dearth of stimulating material.

Having had enough of the vaudeville life, Peterson pursued a doctorate at Columbia University, awarded in 1929, and served on its faculty until 1937.[1]

In the 1930s Peterson also joined the faculty of the Cooper Union for the Advancement of Science and Art. Founded in 1859, Cooper Union was a unique educational institution. Its founder, Peter Cooper, had wanted this institution to play a large role in the political and cultural life of the United States. Tuition was free, and from its inception Cooper Union provided unqualified access for both minorities and women. Cooper wanted an arena for teaching students the skills of debate and democratic leadership. Recognizing that not all students could participate in full-time study, he opened a public reading room and a library that grew to more than one hundred thousand volumes. Cooper also provided for evening and adult education classes.

The Great Hall at Cooper Union quickly became one of the most important political and intellectual venues in the United States. Here on February 27, 1860, Abraham Lincoln, still a dark horse in his candidacy for the presidency, gave his famous "Right Makes Might" speech opposing slavery, which propelled him to national attention. Frederick Douglass spoke at Cooper Union in 1863 after the Emancipation Proclamation. Other speakers included Mark Twain, Susan B. Anthony, Chief Red Cloud of the Lakota Sioux, and seven U.S. presidents. Barack Obama has spoken there twice.[2]

In 1937 Houston Peterson started a lecture series at Cooper Union, which
he maintained through World War II. For Mason, just released from active
duty and finding his previous workplace more than slightly hostile, an evening in the company of like-minded individuals at Cooper Union was a
dream come true.

Professor Peterson claims that he brought Mason to Rutgers. Peterson first
briefly met Mason at an evening discussion at Cooper Union. One day at
Columbia, Mason had a knock on his office door. Peterson had come uptown
to Columbia to invite him to speak in his lecture series at Cooper Union.

In 1945, Rutgers had become a state university and braced for the increased
enrollment of a state university in the immediate postwar period, despite a
small faculty and inadequate facilities. Peterson needed another philosophy
professor, and Rutgers needed some more administrative assistance.

If Mason had ever been to Rutgers prior to 1946, he had never mentioned
it in any correspondence. On February 10, 1946, Peterson brought Harry
Owen, dean of the Rutgers College of Arts and Sciences, to his Greenwich
Village apartment, where he first met Mason. On February 24, Mason
traveled to New Brunswick for further discussion. He described to his father
that Rutgers was "expanding at a great rate and is now entirely a state
university."[3]

Rutgers College had been founded in 1766 as Queens College, primarily
to train clergy for the many New Jersey parishes of the locally predominant
Dutch Reformed Church. Financially always strapped, the college was rescued from oblivion by a gift from college trustee Henry Rutgers, for whom
it was later named. In 1864, tiny Rutgers College, financially struggling, was
also designated as New Jersey's Land Grant college in a sweeping federal legislation known as the Federal Land Grant Agricultural and Mechanical Act
of 1862. Also called the Morrill Act, it was initiated to support training in
agriculture, mechanical arts, and other practical disciplines. The Morrill Act
helped to found many state universities, such as the Universities of Iowa,
Wisconsin, Indiana and New Hampshire. The financial support and administrative oversight of many of these other institutions was thus secured at
their founding as state universities, written into their state constitutions, and

the position of these universities matured, as did each state's government. For example, the regents of the University of Michigan were set up by the state constitution as a fourth arm of the government, on par with the executive, legislative, and judicial branches. Under the federal Morrill Act, Rutgers, still a private institution, was given the Land Grant funding to start a state-supported agricultural school but otherwise did not have a secure place within the state's fiscal structure.

In 1945 when Rutgers College became designated as the state university of New Jersey, combining campuses in New Brunswick, Newark, and later Camden, the significance of this oversight would come to light. Unlike other state universities whose position within the state hierarchy was established at their inception, Rutgers had to transition from a small private college, step by step. Although the state had assumed some financial support for the new state university, there was no pathway in place for this funding to flow, and the administrative chain of command remained unclear and subject to the whim of the governor and the legislature.

At Rutgers, from here on out nothing would ever be easy.

———

In March 1946, Mason wrote to his parents that Rutgers had offered him a tenure-track position as assistant professor of philosophy and assistant to the dean, to commence July 1, 1946. Offered a three-year contract at an annual salary of $3,600 with 50 percent administrative time in the dean's office, Mason negotiated instead for only 25 percent administrative time and an annual salary of $4,600, which he described as an "exceptionally high salary for the rank, more than at most places." He also noted feeling "no sentiment over leaving my eight-year connection with Columbia."

In the summer of 1946, Mason and Julia began looking for a home in New Jersey. Julia was six months pregnant. She was in good company; several million other American wives whose husbands were now home from the war were also expecting.

Mason and Julia found a three-bedroom house at 25 Grant Avenue in Highland Park. Music professor Howard McKinney lived behind them on

Harrison Avenue. Next door to McKinney was University librarian Donald "Scottie" Cameron. Microbiologist Selman Waksman, who would receive the 1952 Nobel Prize for the discovery of streptomycin, lived up the street. Although it was an easy walk across the Raritan River to the Rutgers College Avenue campus, the war was over. Gasoline was cheap and no longer rationed. Nobody walked anymore.

American manufacturers had transitioned from war matériel to consumer products. Mason bought a push lawnmower. He had never owned one before. Having used only local laundromats in New York, Julia admitted a thrill over buying her own "precious Bendix washing machine." She had never owned one before. She hung the laundry to dry either in the basement near the furnace or, like everyone else on Grant Avenue, on lines in the backyard. The yards were small, and most of the neighborhood children played in the street. Mason bought an Ansley phonograph for $250 and began to buy records at the Rivoli Music Shop on George Street. Soon after he bought the phonograph, a modification was introduced that allowed long-playing (LP) records to be played at a lower speed. He wrote to his parents that he had purchased a record of Arturo Toscanini conducting Beethoven's Ninth Symphony. With "every instrument recorded faithfully," Mason wrote, he could now hear "a whole symphony on one record!"

Julia's physician in New York had referred her to an obstetrician in Plainfield, New Jersey, a half-hour drive from New Brunswick. In late October she went into labor, and Mason drove her to Muhlenberg Hospital in Plainfield. Julia later recalled that there were women everywhere, all in various stages of labor, mostly on army stretchers crammed into the hallways. The women, total strangers, were crawling on the floor, comforting each other, and alerting the few nurses as to who was most likely to deliver next. There was one obstetrician.

Later in her life, Julia reflected on that night when a friend suggested how horrible it must have been to be crawling on the floor with strangers.

Julia answered, "No, you misunderstand. It was joyous. The war was over and we had our futures back."[4] On October 30, 1946, my older brother was born, their first son, Charles Welles Gross, named for Mason's father.

Mason began teaching at Rutgers in September. He taught one large intro-
ductory class on philosophy, which he dreaded because he felt rusty. He
stood behind a podium and lectured but then realized he was not making
any "contact with the students." He also taught a small seminar on Platonism
from its origin in ancient Greece down through the present day.

But, according to Mason, "Rutgers was in bad shape." A campus that had
held 1,700 undergraduates before the war now in 1946 had 4,200. Housing
was nonexistent. Many students rented rooms in private homes. The old Raritan Arsenal, along the railroad tracks in Edison five miles from Rutgers,
was a storage and shipping terminal for military supplies, including a dump
for the unmonitored disposal of old explosive ordnance and chemical agents.
Another 450 veteran students were billeted there.

Consistent with his desire to be more than a philosophy professor, Mason
began promoting his views on education, speaking at local community
organizations, Rutgers alumni meetings, and back at Cooper Union, where
his audience often included public figures, business leaders, and university
faculty from around the country.

Mason was already being recruited to go elsewhere. Veterans on the GI
Bill were seeking an education; colleges were desperately searching for faculty. Mason was developing a reputation very quickly. In 1948, he was offered
an immediate full professorship at the University of North Carolina. There
was another opportunity at Harvard Law School and a tempting offer from
Oberlin College, with a "considerable salary increase." At one point, he wrote
to his family that he and Julia fully expected to move to Oberlin, as Rutgers
had not matched any of the other offers, and his three-year contract was near
completion. In May 1949, Rutgers came through with an appointment as
director of student life and professor of philosophy at an annual salary of
$10,000.

———

Mason once stated that the "G.I. Bill utterly changed the character and the
academic life of American universities."[5] In the Rutgers class of 1950, matric-

ulating in the autumn of 1946, 65 percent of the students were veterans.[6] Forrest Clark (Rutgers class of 1949) recalls that as veterans "we had many questions in the aftermath of war and the Depression, and many sought answers in philosophy."[7] Ed Vincz had spent three years with the U.S. Marine Corps in the Pacific, including "the annealing maturation of battle experiences such as D-Day at Iwo Jima."[8] Upon his return to Rutgers in 1946, Vincz enrolled in Mason's philosophy class and found that Mason taught about "philosophers Whitehead and Santayana with a casual familiarity as if he had breakfasted with them that morning."

Monte Gaffin (Rutgers class of 1945) recalls returning to Rutgers from his own experience as a navigator in the 98th Bomb Group, based in Italy. "Imagine my surprise," he wrote, "when I discovered that the Group Intelligence officer who had given our morning targeting and enemy air defense briefings was now my philosophy professor, none other than former Captain Mason Gross."[9]

Despite a full teaching load, Mason moved quickly into administrative matters as well. He was one of the few Rutgers faculty with recent military and actual combat experience, and the vets knew it. Consequently, the newly arrived veterans sought him out as one who might understand their difficulties. One veteran later noted how an archaic rule prohibited smoking on campus for freshmen. Most of the veterans had practically lived on cigarettes during their years overseas. Mason was able to change the rule. Another rule required freshman to wear a demeaning red-and-black beanie, known as a "dink." The veterans refused. One veteran, having been instructed that "no beer is allowed on campus," responded "Who says so?" Thanks to Mason, these rules soon disappeared as well.

Roland Winter (Rutgers class of 1949) reports that after "nearly three years of front-line infantry battles in the Pacific, transition back into civilian life was very tough for me. I was bitter and confused." Unable to "find myself," his family encouraged him to re-enter Rutgers, having completed almost two years before being drafted in 1943. Winter was directed to the dean's office. He wrote that Mason gave him two full hours of his time and "immediately made me feel like he and Rutgers were there for the sole purpose of welcoming me back. No single event in my post-war experience played a more significant role in helping me back into society. I have, and always will, revere that wonderful man."[10]

Marine Corps veteran and Rutgers undergraduate Robert Ochs (class of 1949), attending college on the GI Bill, later wrote that Mason, also a combat veteran, "understood the challenges of veterans at Rutgers." A combat veteran of the war in the Pacific, Ochs was referred to Mason by Dean Owen in 1948 for "counseling" as a result of his indecorous handling of a minor disagreement with a faculty member. Bob had entered into a political discussion with this professor, a discussion that rapidly deteriorated from a mere debate. Ochs openly admitted that he had mildly threatened this "draft-dodging part-time Communist professor with physical harm."[11] (Ochs later told me that he had threatened to throw him down a flight of stairs.) Mason tactfully illustrated that there was more than one way to solve a dispute, even for a marine combat veteran. Ochs later credited Mason's intervention with saving him from expulsion.

––––––––

Rutgers president Robert Clothier was a Princeton graduate and the former dean of men at the University of Pittsburgh. He had been appointed to the Rutgers presidency in 1932. During his tenure, the state legislature selected Rutgers to become the state university of New Jersey.

As Rutgers began to grow exponentially after World War II, partly due to its new status as the state university but also due to the large numbers of returning veterans entering college under auspices of the GI Bill, Clothier saw the increased administrative load in his office. The trustees, with the consent of the faculty, created the Office of the Provost, which would deal mostly with faculty and student issues, allowing the president to concentrate more on external issues, such as fund-raising and dealing with the public and the state government. On the advice of faculty and the deans, in 1949 Clothier put Mason in the new position. As provost, Mason now dealt with all departments and student issues of all kinds.

For example, music professor Howard McKinney (Rutgers class of 1913) came across the backyard in Highland Park to Mason with a special request.

McKinney was a friend of Erich Leinsdorf, the young conductor of the Rochester (New York) Symphony Orchestra. As a child, Leinsdorf had emigrated from his native Germany with his parents. Drafted into the U.S. Army during the war, he had been stationed at Camp Kilmer across the Raritan River in Piscataway Township. Already an accomplished musician and conductor, he sought out what music was available locally. George Huddleston, the choir director of Christ Church in downtown New Brunswick, had served briefly in the Army Reserve with Leinsdorf at Camp Kilmer and introduced him to Howard McKinney and to F. Austin Walter, the director of the Rutgers Glee Club.

After the war Leinsdorf, as director of the Rochester Symphony Orchestra, needed a mixed chorus* to perform Beethoven's Ninth Symphony. Not able to afford to bring in musicians from New York or Philadelphia, he contacted his friends at Rutgers. McKinney and Walter quickly assembled a mixed chorus from the Rutgers Glee Club and the women's choir from Douglass College† to become the University Chorus. Now they had a chorus but no way to get them to Rochester.

Leinsdorf arranged for the chorus members to stay with families in Rochester. Mason tapped into some available funds to pay for their transportation. The concert was an enormous success. Later when Leinsdorf became the director of the Boston Symphony Orchestra, he continued to call on the Rutgers singers.[12]

Mason later described the value of experiences such as this, even for students who were not majoring in music. "I have always felt that one of the important objectives in any complete educational program is to give the students an opportunity to take part in something that is obviously first class. At Rutgers, every year the University Chorus performs some significant piece with one of the major orchestras. . . . They are singing better than they ever

---

*A mixed chorus has both men and women, as opposed to an all-male or all-female chorus.
† At that time, Douglass College was still known as the New Jersey College for Women.

imagined that they could sing, and they are exceeding their best. Their actual emotion is one of high exultation, even to the point of sublimity."[13]

As busy as he was, Mason enjoyed his family life. Marine veteran Robert Ochs recalls, from one clear and very cold December day, the sight of Mason, without a hat, driving his 1940 black Ford convertible through Highland Park with the top down and a large Christmas tree sticking out over the trunk. His very young daughters Ellen and Kitty were standing up in the back seat, bundled against the cold and screaming with high-pitched delight. Ochs recalls that Mason wore the grin of a man who was very much pleased with his life.[14]

Houston and Mitzi Peterson owned a small cottage in Dennis, Massachusetts, on the north shore of Cape Cod. In the days before air-conditioning, they spent most of the summers there to escape the heat and humidity of New York City. The Petersons had become quite close to Mason's family, as the children all now called them "Uncle Pete" and "Aunt Mitzi."

Julia and the children traveled to Dennis every summer for more than just a few weeks to escape the still and humid air of New Brunswick but also to put some distance between themselves and the ever-present threat of polio epidemics that stalked through urban and suburban neighborhoods in those summers prior to the development of the Salk vaccine. (One of Julia's closest friends, Atreus Von Schrader, had been paralyzed with polio in the summer of 1948.) Mason, still at work in New Brunswick, on Friday nights took the sleeper train to Hyannis and returned to New Jersey on the Sunday night train.

Julia's younger brother Walter, former Harvard oarsman and army artillery officer who had been awarded the Silver Star at Okinawa, was now back at Harvard studying law but was divorced, with sole custody of his five-year-old daughter Wende. When Julia came to the Cape, Walter brought Wende, who was around the same age as Ellen and Kitty, to join them on the beach. Julia remembers watching Walter, Mason and Uncle Pete, three large men cramming themselves barefoot into a twelve-foot gaff-rigged Herreshoff sloop, reminding her of the children's rhyme "Rub a dub dub, three men in a tub." Off they sailed into the shallow waters of Cape Cod Bay, taking with them for their afternoon hydration only a bottle of blended scotch whisky.

Julia listened as their voices traveled low over the water, hearing their discussions of politics and current events but mostly philosophy. Over the course of the afternoon they exercised progressively diminished situational awareness of their surroundings, the state of the tide, or the buildup of cumulonimbus clouds in the afternoon sky. Then occasionally the sails would luff in the breeze, and the boat would lurch to a stop as it ran aground on one of the many sandbars of Cape Cod Bay. Julia watched as the men rolled up their pant legs above their knees, stepped barefoot out of the boat to lighten its load, turned the boat around, and climbed back in. Off they sailed, continuing their debates, until the boat lurched to a stop again on yet another sandbar farther up the beach, repeating the cycle during a lazy afternoon on Cape Cod. Running aground was only a minor annoyance. Even the threat of rain did not seem to interrupt their discussions.

One summer day in 1948, Julia heard a scream in their cottage. As the cottage had no washing machine and she had three children, she daily boiled water on the stove and poured it into a washtub to wash their clothes. It took several iterations for there to be enough hot water. When Julia had turned her back to get more hot water from the stove, young Charlie, not yet two years old, dropped a toy into the boiling water and reached in quickly to retrieve it. His high-pitched screams echoed through the neighborhood as the skin peeled off his right arm in sheets.

A rapid trip to a local general practitioner resulted in immediate referral to the small local hospital in Hyannis. In the era before ambulances and burn centers, this became a long day. Burn care has revolutionized since that time, minimizing the risk of death or permanent disability that resulted back then from similar second-degree burns. Charlie was hospitalized in Hyannis, and it soon became evident that he would survive despite the high risk for infection. To his good fortune, he received state-of-the-art attention for his burns from a local surgeon and nurses whose expertise in burn care had derived from their hands-on combat experience during the war, when they had taken care of severely burned soldiers on European battlefields.

Julia was beside herself with sadness and guilt. Mason tried to write to his parents about the whole episode but admitted that he was unable even to write about it because it distressed him so.[15] Mason had never been short of words until this moment.

As he grew older, Charlie underwent multiple surgeries attempting to restore full use of his right hand. He learned to write left-handed, but the thickened scars on his arm would always remain, reminding Mason and Julia of one of the most terrifying days of their lives.

CHAPTER 8

In the Second Chair, 1949

The "playing fields of Eton" theory of education died at Dunkirk, . . . and its successor is being cradled in the G.I. Bill. —MWG, November 1948

In July 1949, President Robert Clothier became ill and took a medical leave of absence, culminating in thyroid surgery a few months later. With the approval of the Board of Trustees, Clothier assigned to Mason the full duties and authority of acting president, issuing a directive that "the duties of the president shall be exercised by the Provost." Interestingly, the Office of the Provost had been created when Clothier realized that the president's tasks required more than one person. After three years at Rutgers and within one year of his appointment as provost, Mason was acting president as well. Although he reported by detailed letter weekly to Clothier, recuperating in Nova Scotia, the daily decisions were Mason's to make, such as the site for the Selman Waksman Institute of Microbiology and making voluntary any participation in the Reserve Officers' Training Corps (ROTC). The correspondence with Clothier, despite being courteous, does reveal that Mason pushed back on some issues. Still teaching several courses, he was not completely enamored with administrative duties and provided Clothier with an easy out if he disagreed with Mason's actions; that is, Mason wrote to Clothier a "standing request that I be permitted to resume my duties as professor of philosophy."[1]

—————

During his career in New York, Professor Houston "Hugh" Peterson had used his vaudeville experience to expand into radio and had hosted several radio shows pertaining to current events. He got Mason involved as well. Mason participated in a CBS radio show called *Invitation to Learning*, moderating discussions on topics such as William Shakespeare's sonnets, Baruch Spinoza's ethics, and Margaret Mead's *Coming of Age in Samoa*. As television exploded into prominence, Peterson was invited to move into this medium as well. In his self-effacing manner, he explained that he was neither young enough nor handsome enough for television and referred the television producers to Mason instead.

Mason's television career premiered in March 1949, when he served as the moderator for a quiz show titled *Think Fast*. The show ran on Friday evenings but lasted only eighteen months. Mason left the show early in its run for reasons that are unknown. His successor as moderator was Gypsy Rose Lee.

———

Stating that it was "time for a younger man to take over," President Clothier, not fully recovered from surgery, announced his retirement. Clearly, Mason was an experienced front runner. The *Daily Targum*, the Rutgers student newspaper, campaigned hard for Mason. Despite support from the faculty as well, enough of the trustees felt that Mason, at age forty, was too young for the job. Mason's outspoken political comments had also turned some of the trustees against him. Instead, the trustees chose the president of the University of Arkansas, Lewis Jones.

Mason was back "in the second chair." There is no record of how he really felt about it at the time. However, he did comment a few years later when he was being considered again for the position that "having once been mentioned prominently as a candidate for the presidency of this university, and having not been selected, I can assure you I have no intention of allowing myself to get into that position again."[2]

Subsequent to the success of Groucho Marx's NBC quiz show *You Bet Your Life*, the television industry was cashing in on the quiz show genre. Producer Mark Goodson premiered the show *Two for the Money* and chose Mason as his onscreen moderator. On the day before each live show, Mason

Mason was on live television as the onstage "professor" for the quiz show *Two for the Money*. He is shown here with the show's host, comedian and television personality Herb Shriner. While campaigning for state bond issues in support of higher education, Mason later stated of his audiences, "They knew me. I had been in their living rooms every week for five years." (Photo credit: Columbia Broadcasting System)

received a special-delivery envelope that contained the questions and sample answers.

Mason remained on this show for five years, driving every Saturday afternoon into midtown Manhattan from New Jersey in time for supper and then moderating a late-evening live broadcast before a live studio audience. For one evening per week and including a brief overview of the questions the day before, Goodson-Todman Productions paid Mason $225 per episode totaling $9,275 per year, almost equal his full-time salary as a professor and provost at Rutgers.

Mason was becoming more visible. In 1951 Governor Alfred E. Driscoll appointed him chairman of the New Jersey State Labor Mediation Board, which also paid Mason a $65 per diem, totaling about $4,000 per year. During his tenure, the board mediated an average of seventy labor strikes per year, which involved all-night negotiations and a lot of waiting, smoking, and playing cards while the opposing groups debated various proposed settlements. With typical hyperbole, Mason wrote an article about this experience, never published, titled "The Uses of Gin Rummy in Labor Mediation."*

Mason was becoming much busier, out many evenings giving talks in support of public education and working with the Mediation Board. He and Julia found less time to go to Cape Cod in the summers to visit the Petersons. However, to escape the heat of July's dog days in central Jersey, for several weeks each summer they rented a house on the beach in Mantaloking on the Jersey Shore.

Richard Scudder (Princeton class of 1935), publisher of the *Newark Evening News*, was a World War II U.S. Army veteran and a Rutgers trustee, which was unusual because most trustees were Rutgers graduates. Richard and his wife Elizabeth (Libby) became close friends of Mason and Julia and in the early 1950s frequently invited them to their home in Navesink, also on the Jersey Shore. In 1954 a run-down three-story Tudor-style house came on the market in the exclusive town of Rumson, the home of shipping magnates, stock brokers, and the movers and shakers who commuted daily by train to New York's financial district. The house, on a one-third-acre lot, was so overgrown with thickets that it was barely visible from the street only yards away. Having enjoyed their visits to the shore, Mason and Julia purchased the home, not on the water but close enough to feel the evening breezes off the ocean and the Shrewsbury River. They left Highland Park, and Mason traded a five-minute commute for a forty-five minute drive each way.

For the children, Rumson had three options for schools: the Catholic Holy Cross School, the private Rumson Country Day School, and the public Lafayette Street elementary school, a dilapidated old brick firetrap on a back

---

*I could find no copies of this article, only references to it by Mason's cohorts on the Mediation Board.

street in Rumson. Charlie and Kitty started school that fall at Lafayette; Ellen started at Rumson-Fair Haven Regional High School.

Mason strongly advocated for support of public schools. Ellen recalls that her teachers in Highland Park had been gifted and imaginative, and her classes were stimulating. She noted also that all of the children in our neighborhood had gone to the same schools, first Highland Park Elementary and then the local high school.

Kitty and Ellen noticed a change when they started school in Rumson. Unlike Highland Park, where there had been but one school, in Rumson few of our neighbors went to the public school, many going either to Holy Cross or Rumson Country Day. In Rumson, Ellen, already brilliant and outspoken at age twelve, got into an argument with her English teacher, who had insisted that Plymouth Rock was in Virginia. Ellen felt unchallenged and somewhat demoralized by the high school experience in Rumson, in the adversarial teeming social anthill that was a common high school experience for girls of that era. Julia suggested to Ellen the idea of going to a boarding school, specifically to Milton Academy, which had been so eye-opening to Julia compared to the 1920 gulags of upstate New York and her conservative Irish Catholic relatives.

––––––

Back in 1946, Mason had been at Rutgers for only two months when he received a letter from Mr. Charles P. Taft, chairman of the Board of Trustees at Taft School and brother of Mr. Horace Taft, the original Taft headmaster who had recently retired. Charles Taft was polling selected Taft graduates on their opinion of the future of Taft School and private boarding schools in general.[3]

Noting that his own son, Charlie, a potential Taft student, had just been born, Mason rephrased the question to "what contribution could a private school make to my son's education that a public school could not?" Mason did not sugarcoat his reply and proceeded to rip into the rarified atmosphere of Taft as a bastion of elitism, noting that "the 'playing fields of Eton' theory of education died at Dunkirk . . . and that its successor is being cradled in the G.I. Bill." He blasted private boarding schools as a "breeding ground of exactly the type of traditionalistic myopia" unsuitable for solving problems of a modern democracy. Mason noted from his experience that the "liveliest and most aggressive students do not usually come from private schools," adding that many private school students exhibit "a kind of smooth and affable dullness rarely found in a public school product."

In his response, Mason did equivocate and outline many of the advantages of private schools, such as small class size and, with the resources to provide higher salaries for faculty, the likelihood of attracting better teachers. But he closed his letter with the admonition that if Taft School could not surpass the public schools in the most important aspects, he "would feel bound to send my son only to public schools."[4]

Mason had not met many boarding school graduates in the muddy fields of Italy at war. In 1946, the value of the GI Bill and the role of education in democracy were much on his mind. He had gone to war not only to defend our democracy but also in memory of his closest friends. Now, Mason was seeing the influx of veterans eager for education, many of them with little previous education and seeking the causes of the great catastrophe that had stolen their youth.

Once in Rumson, Mason and Julia joined a public campaign to build a new elementary school and to modernize the public high school but found that many conservative Rumson voters, whose children all went to expensive private schools, were unwilling to support funding for either the local high school or a new elementary school that none of their children would ever attend. The public high school, short of adequate funding, appeared to offer less opportunity to Ellen and Kitty. They stayed at public school through the ninth grade but then both chose to go to Julia's alma mater, Milton Academy in suburban Boston, coincidentally two miles from where Julia's youngest brother Walter, now in law practice, was raising his family. Compared to small and conservative Rumson, Milton Academy right away seemed to open doors to them, with small classes, stimulating discussions with faculty, and frequent short trips to the cultural opportunities of Boston. Additionally, Kitty's Latin teacher was Frau Ruth Jaeger, the wife of philosopher Werner Jaeger, the Aristotle expert under whom Mason had hoped to study in Berlin in 1933. Having emigrated from Germany in 1936, the Jaegers had relocated to Boston, where Professor Jaeger had joined the Harvard faculty only a year after Mason had left. Despite Mason's advocacy for public education, he and Julia clearly agreed that this was the best choice at the time for their daughters.

By the time of his 1959 inauguration as Rutgers's president, Mason had tempered his vehemence against private schools somewhat and sent us all to one private school or another. It would be easy to accuse him of hypocrisy, but I maintain that it was just a father's prerogative to find the best education for his children. Later in 1966 when Mason informed me over the top of his bifocals that I was going to Taft, where Charlie had also graduated two years earlier, I gathered the will to suggest, as an alternative, that I could go to Piscataway High School, where a great many Rutgers faculty sent their children.* Mason raised one eyebrow and dismissed me with his usual one-word answer, "Ridiculous," and returned to his reading.

In Rumson, as Mason and Julia campaigned hard for the new public elementary school, which Charlie and I would later attend, they met Bill and Jane Robinson, who lived in a house on Waterman Avenue that flooded several times a year in the winter nor'easters that have plagued the Jersey Shore long before global climate change. The Robinsons exaggerated that aside from Mason and Julia, they were perhaps the only other Democrats in Rumson.

Bill Robinson (Princeton class of 1939) had grown up in Elizabeth, New Jersey. An experienced mariner since childhood, before the war started Bill joined the U.S. Navy and later served in the Pacific as the commanding officer of a 110-foot wooden subchaser, SC 743. A crew member called him "the best navigator in the whole damned Navy."[5] During the war Bill married Jane Dimmock, whom he had known since childhood. First a reporter for the *Newark Star Ledger*, Bill parlayed his love of the sea and boats into a position

---

* Dr. Richard L. McCormick, future president of Rutgers, graduated from Piscataway High in 1967.

with *Yachting Magazine*, rising to become the editor in chief, a position he held until his retirement. Living one block up the street in Rumson, Bill and Jane became Mason and Julia's closest friends. Mason had instantly loved sailing since his college friend Arthur Frazer had introduced him to it in 1932. As a graduate student at Harvard and afterward, Mason often slipped away to sail in Maine with his close friend John Cooley. Bill Robinson was an avid sailor; Mason never hesitated to go out on the Shrewsbury River with the Robinsons. He and Julia eventually took many sailing trips with Bill and Jane, to Maine, the Bahamas, and the Windward Islands.

Mason and Julia settled into their house in Rumson, enjoying their new community. The three oldest children were all in school. Ellen joined the Girl Scouts; Kitty learned how to sail. The girls listened to Pat Boone records. Charlie took swimming lessons and, already an athlete, began bringing home medals from swimming races. Mason took Charlie rowing in a small rented skiff in the swift current of the Shrewsbury River and afterward bought him a small skiff of his own with a three-horsepower Evinrude outboard motor. The Salk polio vaccine came out, and lines of families stretched around the block to receive it. Everyone still got chicken pox and measles, but scarlet fever and polio were gone. It was the 1950s. Life was good, or so it seemed. What could go wrong?

CHAPTER 9

Rutgers v. the Red Scare, 1954

*I am not afraid of communism, which has only taken deep root in countries
which are basically rotten. I cannot help but feel that it [communism] might
be an important factor in the ultimate liberation of the peoples of Central
Europe. Something else would be more ideal, but somehow a government
must be provided for these people now.*   —MWG, 1945

Immediately after the war, radio industry executives miscalculated, dismissing television as a toy. At the end of 1947, there were only 172,000 television sets in operation in the United States and only twenty television stations. Within a year, televisions would be selling at the rate of 250,000 per month.[1] Ellen and Kitty remember that all the families had a television except for ours. Finally Mason bought a television, not for Howdy Doody or Milton Berle or the 1952 Democratic Convention, but in order to watch the McCarthy hearings.

This period is referred to as the McCarthy era. Wisconsin senator Joseph McCarthy and the black-and-white videos of his slanderous anticommunist witch-hunt trials evoke an amazement that such a travesty could have happened here in the democratic United States, where one is hypothetically innocent until proven guilty. Yet, McCarthy was only a small part of the American anticommunist hysteria. He is a most vocal and most easily recalled icon, the tip of an iceberg that is itself the half-hidden anticommunist fervor that continues to dominate American politics after almost a full century.

Fear of communism had arisen in the United States after World War I and the Russian Revolution. The most convincing lies always contain some grain of truth, and the half-truth behind the anticommunist witch hunts was that a few Americans indeed had been turning over government secrets, as well as nuclear data, to the Russians. In 1948 the Soviet Union exploded its first atomic bomb, much to the surprise of Americans who believed that their monopoly on the ultimate weapon would guarantee their peaceful hegemony over a new world order. It soon became clear that atomic secrets had been stolen and that there was evidence of Soviet agents busily infiltrating American government, industry, unions, and universities.

In retrospect, Mason's first brush with socialism had begun while he was in Aberdeen and later Cambridge, when he witnessed the massive poverty, hunger, and disease in postwar Britain. At the time, hunger marches were converging on Parliament demanding relief. Mason expressed sympathy for the socialist causes that were challenging Britain's class-dominated imperial and colonialist establishment. He lambasted the inept British government and allowed that if able, he would have voted for socialist candidates.[2]

In his letters home, Mason never mentioned the small cadres of communist student groups that had sprung up in British universities, but he did note that only the communists were providing any consistent resistance to the fascists during the Spanish Civil War.

While he was in Italy during the war Mason recognized, as did many others, that the United States and the Soviet Union would emerge as the two strongest global powers in the postwar era. Some American voices, believing that war with Soviet communism was inevitable, advocated continuing the war, driving east through Europe and defeating the Soviets. Several in Mason's squadron had expressed the belief that a war with the Soviets was coming, so they should probably stay in Europe and get it over with. These thoughts were not accompanied by any discussion of goals, strategy, logistics, or the simplest of all conclusions, namely that Americans were sick of war and wanted it over.

In a letter home from Italy in 1945, Mason described a discussion with his squadron chaplain.[3] This letter was unusual due to its length and its detail. The chaplain had wanted to understand why the Allies were supporting the Yugoslavian communist partisan Josef Broz, more commonly known as Tito. Mason pointed out that those countries that had been decimated by war were populated by millions of refugees, all suffering poverty, disease, starvation, and lack of clean water. He proposed that these countries needed a strong government "immediately" in order to provide the necessities, such as food, shelter, and coal. In Yugoslavia, Tito's forces were the most organized of all anti-Nazi groups and therefore the most effective not only in defeating the enemy but also in providing for the Yugoslavian people. However, this effectiveness came with a price; that is, it was accompanied by unprecedented internecine savagery. In 1945 all of Europe was a boiling cauldron of such violence and reprisals for collaboration, all of which were perpetrated by not only European communists but also the anticommunist Free French and the Dutch resistance, to name just a few.

Mason's point was that in Yugoslavia as well as other states, the communists may have been in a position to provide the greatest good to the greatest number in the shortest period. The rebuilding of a capitalist economy under democratic government in societies that had never functioned under democracy, such as Yugoslavia, would take time.

———

Mason tried to explain to the chaplain how the impoverished people of Europe needed basic sustenance immediately. More than communism, Mason feared most a return to the situation after World War I, that "some thoroughly rotten regime . . . with its own internal problems would allow that country to fall prey to the next Hitler who comes along." Noting that the communist partisans of Yugoslavia, with which in his position as intelligence officer he had firsthand knowledge, were the most organized and the most effective, he felt that in some countries the communists could more quickly get the people back on their feet, fed, sheltered, and clothed.

Mason told the chaplain that he was "not afraid of communism" and anticipated that once peace with some degree of economic stability had returned to the regions, the people would push back against a strong central communist government and would select a more capitalist economy and democratically elected government and institutions. Regardless of whether he was right or wrong, naive or realistic, Mason saw communism as a temporary expedient solution and had faith that the human spirit would eventually cast it off and rise above it. He believed that after a while, people under a communist system would overthrow a system that repressed speech, thought, education, and free press. Mason did not live to see the fall of the Berlin Wall and the democratization of Eastern Europe, which is in danger now, but he did predict it in 1945.

After the war, worldwide communist insurgency was ascendant. In the postwar United States, now that the Soviets also had an atom bomb, now that China had been "lost," an intense dragnet resulted in order to discover the real threat, but this became a nationwide anticommunist hysteria. Baseless accusations were cast without merit, often due to personality clashes, envy, or jealousy. This panic destroyed many lives and careers while adding no benefit to national security.

Although McCarthy's televised Senate hearings provide a most dramatic record, the hearings of the House Un-American Activities Committee (HUAC) were equally insidious. HUAC had been formed in the 1930s to identify Nazis and other subversives but rose to full prominence during the Truman administration after the war.

Rutgers was not immune to the anticommunist hysteria. The climate for academic freedom at Rutgers University at this time was extremely chilly. Mason was now provost, the second-in-command of an administration that chose to draw a clear line in the sand against the threat of communism, whether real or imagined.

Rutgers professor M. I. Finley, a Newark campus historian of ancient Greece, was identified as a communist by a prior colleague, Karl Wittfogel, who had testified before the Senate Internal Security Subcommittee. Finley testified that he had run a communist study group at Columbia before the war. He stated that he was not a communist, but when queried if he had ever been a communist, he declined to answer, invoking the Fifth Amendment. Upon his return to Newark, the Rutgers Board of Trustees declared that this was grounds for immediate dismissal, stating that Finley had violated Section 3.92 of the University Statute, a fixed policy that provided that "it shall be cause for immediate dismissal of any member of faculty or staff" who invoked the Fifth Amendment before an investigatory body in refusing to answer questions relating to his or her communist affiliation, whether real or supposed.[4]

Thus, Rutgers became the first American college or university to dismiss a faculty member for relying on his constitutional privilege against self-incrimination.

Sources differ in how many Rutgers faculty were caught in the web. In 1952 several other Rutgers professors were called to testify before HUAC. Mason's close friend Dick Schlatter, with whom he taught "The Traditions of Western Religious Thought," had been accused of being a communist by a former Harvard colleague, Robert G. Davis. Schlatter testified on February 18, 1953. Under oath, he stated the following: "From 1935 until 1937 I was a member of a communist student organization at Oxford. From 1937 until 1939 I was a member of a small communist group composed exclusively of members of the Harvard faculty. We wanted to oppose fascism, which we felt was not inconsistent with being a loyal American. I left the group as soon as I learned that they did not believe in democracy."[5]

Before his testimony Schlatter contacted all the people from his group at Harvard, all of whom agreed that he was at liberty to divulge their names. When HUAC learned that Schlatter had done so, they dropped their investigation and cleared him. Dick Schlatter was Mason's best friend and closest colleague at Rutgers. Mason was unnerved at how the trauma of the experience had affected Dick emotionally.

On March 18, 1953, law professor Michael Glasser was subpoenaed. Glasser had been accused of being a communist in the late 1930s when he worked for the U.S. Department of Justice (DOJ). Apparently, he had given some unclassified DOJ information to a journalist who was later determined to be a Soviet agent. In an internal DOJ hearing, Glasser had answered that he was not a communist and was cleared. When called to testify at HUAC, he had been again accused by a former associate of being a communist when he worked for the DOJ. When asked if he was or had ever been a member of the Communist Party, Glasser refused to answer, evoking the Fifth Amendment and stating, "There was a prior adjudication, under oath, that I was not a member of the communist party."[6]

When Glasser returned to Rutgers, President Lewis Jones immediately suspended him, citing again Section 3.92 of the University Statute.

Historian and brilliant scholar Dick Schlatter, a midwestern butcher's son, was a Harvard graduate and a Rhodes Scholar who came to Rutgers in 1946. Mason's right-hand man and best friend, Dick accepted the role of provost when Mason was inaugurated. During Mason's absence, Dick dealt with the initial pushback from the April 1965 teach-in. Also, when told he needed to choose a color for repainting the interior of the Kirkpatrick Chapel, then a dull and faded institutional yellow, he and his wife Suzanne chose a bright Rutgers scarlet, which it has remained since that time. Dick was like a second father to me. (Photo credit: Rutgers University Library Special Collections and University Archives)

When asked if he was a communist, why did Glasser not just come out and deny it? The word was out; namely, "Keep your mouth shut." Witnesses knew that the prosecutors were setting traps. If any person testified under oath that he or she was not a communist and if HUAC could find another witness to state that the person either was or had been a communist, whether true or not, then the accused would risk a conviction for perjury and possible incarceration for having committed no crime.

A Rutgers faculty committee reviewed the records of Glasser's case, but he was not permitted to meet with the committee. The faculty review com-

mittee concluded that Glasser could elect to "resign without prejudice" or
he may be dismissed.

Professor Glasser chose to resign.

On April 23, President Jones also suspended economics professor Myron
Hoch for refusing to state to HUAC whether he had been a communist. As
a result of these cases, the American Association of University Professors
(AAUP) placed Rutgers on its list of censured administrations, citing their
1940 Statement on Principles of Academic Freedom and tenure and its provision on extramural speech: "University teachers are citizens, members of
a learned profession and officers of an educational institution. When they
speak or write as citizens, they should be free from institutional censorship
or discipline."[7] An AAUP special committee found that Rutgers's policy of
automatic dismissal "violated the right of a faculty member to a meaningful hearing in which his fitness to remain in his position would be the issue,
and attempted to turn the exercise of constitutional privilege into an academic offense."[8]

Mason had kept uncharacteristically silent in any official communications pertaining to Glasser's case. As provost, Mason treaded softly. On the
one hand, he was the voice of the university and its authority and could not
speak out against President Jones's decisions. On the other hand, Mason
learned from Dick Schlatter what the hearings were like and knew that this
whole process was a political show and a witch hunt.

Once Mason became president of Rutgers in 1959, he initiated a retroac-
tive review of the case that exonerated Glasser several years later. Although
no record exists of his conversations with Dick Schlatter, we know how
Mason felt about communism itself and about the "emotionalism, fear and
stupidity" of the anticommunist investigations.

––––––

We will see how this issue comes up again in 1965, when Mason will step up
to defend the right of a citizen to speak his own mind. Only then will Mason,
as president of the university and free from any restrictions, fight back and
speak out on his own.

CHAPTER 10

Philosophy of Education v. the "Big Lie"

The real test of an education is whether or not the students have acquired the habit of individual pursuit of truth, a habit which will not leave them when they leave college.
                                                                —*MWG, June 13, 1958*

The Rutgers University Special Collections and University Archives contain many carbon copies of Mason's letters in response to parents inquiring why their child was not admitted to Rutgers, to football fans who wanted him to fire the coach, and to citizens angry over their own assessment of Mason's alleged incompetent mismanagement of the latest campus crisis.

One January, Mason received a handwritten letter from a New Jersey citizen, Miss Adriana DiGiacomantonio, a fifth grader at Washington Elementary School in Raritan, New Jersey. Ten years old, Miss DiGiacomantonio aspired to a career as a teacher and, as a part of a school project, wrote to the president of Rutgers seeking his advice on the best preparation for that profession.

In his answer to Miss DiGiacomantonio, Mason advised her the following:

The profession of teaching in all its ramifications is the one to which we must look for eventual solution to our problems in civil rights, the elimination of poverty and the creation of the kind of society in which we all hope to live happily. The best possible preparation that a young person can have is conscientiously to make sure to do the best possible job . . . in learning the skills of reading and writing that will be so essential to you and never being satisfied with less than your best effort every day.[1]

In another letter, a response to a similar query from the fourth grade at Green Knoll Elementary School in Bridgewater-Raritan Township, Mason emphasized "the same lessons that we learn day-by-day; namely, the importance of individual effort toward excellence in whatever our field of interest lies."[2] One can imagine that Mason had learned this early in his life, and we must wonder who had passed this lesson on to him.

As we have seen, a very few individuals had unknowingly guided and influenced Mason in the arc of his life. These included his mother's first cousin Deming, the cattle rancher who taught the bookish adolescent to grow up, become an independent man, and take responsibility for his own life. There was Reverend Willis Howard Butler of Hartford's Asylum Hill Congregational Church, who personified both theology and philosophy. Butler had taught Mason the difference between faith in action and rote religious dogma, stating in one of his sermons that "the Kingdom of God comes only by doing his will by those who are clear-eyed enough to see it."[3] At Cambridge, it was not Mason's classics professors who most influenced him. Rather, it was the famous Cambridge rowing coach Steve Fairbairn, under whose tutelage Mason had decided that his calling was teaching. Noting that Fairbairn had chosen rowing as a means of expressing his own philosophy, Mason added that he had learned more of permanent value from Steve than from all of the rest of his teachers put together.

Finally, to what degree Rutgers philosophy professor Houston Peterson was a mentor rather than a colleague and great friend is lost to history. But on Mason's roster of what the world now calls mentors, there is one who most influenced Mason's philosophy of education and who stands out among the rest, whom Mason once called the most inspiring man he was ever associated with, namely, Harvard's philosophy professor Alfred North Whitehead.

Whitehead was born on the Ides of February 1861 amid the Roman ruins at Ramsgate in Kent. His father was a schoolmaster and a clergyman. At the age of fourteen Whitehead was sent to the Sherborne School, where he studied the required classics, including the New Testament in Greek, and where he excelled in mathematics. Going up to Trinity College, Cambridge, in 1880, he specialized in pure and applied mathematics. Ten years later he married

Evelyn Wade, who had grown up in military and diplomatic circles but whose spirit impressed him most, exhibiting in her life how "beauty is the aim of existence, and that kindness, love and artistic satisfaction are among its modes of attainment."[4]

Having published the *Treatise on Universal Algebra*, Whitehead then wrote, with his former pupil, Lord Bertrand Russell, the great work *Principia Mathematica*. In 1910 Whitehead left Cambridge for the University of London, where he began to write and lecture on the philosophy of science. In his 1925 Lowell lectures in Boston, he examined such topics as relativity, quantum theory, and the interface of religion, science, and philosophy. In 1924 at the age of sixty-three, Whitehead accepted an invitation to join Harvard's philosophy department, from which he retired in 1937, only a few years after Mason had himself arrived from Cambridge.[5]

Whitehead's "speculative philosophy" finds little space in twenty-first-century surveys on the history of Western philosophy, partly perhaps "because of the apparent difficulty of his technical language"[6] and also because the study of philosophy has taken a different route since that time. Whitehead's proposed synthesis of mathematics, science, and religious experience no longer stimulates much discussion in the higher elevations of the ivory tower.

Prior to the war, Mason's publications on Whitehead referred mostly to the latter's position relative to metaphysics and the more empirical "logical positivists." But after the war when Mason came home seeking a new role for himself as something more than an "eccentric philosophy professor,"[7] he rediscovered the relevance of a little-known jewel in Whitehead's work, a series of essays the nucleus of which was first published in 1917 under the title "The Organization of Thought, Educational and Scientific." Written from 1912 to 1928, these essays were collated and first published in 1929 in a collection titled *The Aims of Education*. In numerous public addresses, Mason continuously referred to a few key phrases from these essays. The full driving force behind Mason's own philosophy of education is best encapsulated by Whitehead's own words: "Culture is activity of thought, and receptiveness to beauty and humane feeling. Scraps of knowledge have nothing to do with it. A merely well-informed man is the most useless bore on God's earth. What we should aim at producing is graduates who possess both culture and expert knowledge in some special direction. Their expert knowledge will give them the ground to start from, and their culture will head them as deep as philosophy and as high as art."[8]

Whitehead had come to his analysis of education late in his career. While in London, he became acutely aware that only a small percentage of British citizens even knew how to read or write effectively. Britain's antiquated educational system, which allowed only for the education of the very elite, did not serve the needs of a political system that was on the threshold of embracing universal suffrage and in which a larger segment of the populace needed education in order to participate. In London, Whitehead saw that "the problem of higher education in a modern industrial civilization" included a "seething mass of artisans seeking intellectual enlightenment" and "young people of every social grade craving for adequate knowledge."[9]

At Rutgers Mason discovered the same issue, at first among the rising tide of veterans eagerly seeking education under the auspices of the GI Bill of Rights and later as the university began a large building program to accommodate the anticipated influx of baby boomers.

Mason had written in his letters to Julia during the war that only education could prevent the world from falling again into the grips of dictators such as Mussolini, Hitler, and Stalin and that the future of our own fragile democracy was dependent on the ability of citizens to reason and not succumb to bombastic hate rhetoric and shallow promises, whose best and most recent historical example had been Nazi propagandist Joseph Goebbels's "Big Lie," of which the guiding principle was to "keep it simple, . . . keep saying it," and enough people will eventually believe it. There exist many contemporary examples as well.

As the postwar New Jersey legislature had not fully grasped the enormity of financing a state university, numerous bond issues were presented to New Jersey voters seeking to ameliorate the severity of the educational crisis that would loom as the children of the World War II generation entered primary school. Most of these early bond issues, requesting support for education at all levels, failed.

Beginning in 1948, and for the next eleven years until his selection as the sixteenth president of Rutgers, Mason gave scores of addresses, speeches, and interviews as he tried to generate public support in New Jersey not only for the state university but for also public education at all levels, primary and secondary, vocational and adult extension. He first addressed small gatherings, such as PTAs and local B'nai B'rith chapters. Soon he was invited to address university commencements, urban planning commissions, and meetings of professional societies, such as the annual meeting of the Essex County Medical Society. To the New Jersey Welfare Conference in November 1950, he claimed that he was competent to speak on only two issues: "either on a philosophical matter or on the theory and practice of higher education."

At each of these meetings, Mason spoke both passionately and persuasively about education, its importance, its value, its necessity, and its cost. Little by little the voters came around, passing bond issues and electing representatives to the state legislature who recognized the necessity of funding for education at all levels.

Mason became New Jersey's strongest advocate for support of public education. To what extent his role assisted these electoral victories is unmeasurable, but his effort was enormous. He reported to a colleague, "I am out many evenings." Mason himself also noted that his experience on the quiz show *Two for the Money* made him a recognizable and credible face when he was campaigning for the bond issues. He later stated to his daughter Kitty, "I'd been in their living rooms once a week for five years. They knew me."[10]

In Mason's many addresses during this period, Whitehead's influence on him is evident. Mason found the voice for which he had been searching since his service in Italy in 1945.

Whitehead emphasized the individual student, noting that ultimately all education is self-education and personal. He advocated that a student should aim for "expert knowledge in some direction," be it physics, Latin, or the hydraulics of plumbing. However, the student's education must also be

Mason participated in numerous fundraisers. On this occasion in October 1951, he and several New Brunswick community leaders were voluntarily jailed. Donations for the United Way were solicited to bail them out. At 2 A.M., Mason was released on his own recognizance when Julia went into labor. For posterity, I get to state that my father was in jail the night that I was born. (Photo credit: Rutgers University Library Special Collections and University Archives)

accompanied by "activity of thought" and not just knowledge itself. White-head wrote that education is not just the accumulation of knowledge; rather, it is the "acquisition of the art of the utilization of knowledge." He spoke against the accumulation of "inert ideas," that is, ideas that "are merely received into the mind without being utilized, tested or thrown into fresh combinations." Whitehead cautioned also against the "passive reception of disconnected ideas," that is, subjects that are excessively disparate and presented with no relation to each other.[11]

In an attempt to create a well-balanced education, early twentieth-century educators had developed the concept of the core curriculum, a well-intentioned premise that a student should have some general knowledge outside the main area of her or his expertise. The proposed core curriculum included one hundred "Great Books," which purportedly included all of "the 104 great ideas" that an educated person needed to know. Of this endeavor, Mason had his own opinion: "We have been told that about all a man needs to be cultured and moral is contained in roughly one hundred Great Books. . . . Unfortunately, there doesn't seem to be any reason to believe that this is true."[12]

This theoretical concept of core curriculum was codified into educational canon with the 1945 Harvard publication of the *General Education in a Free Society,* also known as the Harvard Redbook. It reconfirmed the importance of a multidisciplinary approach in general education. Accepted by many educators in theory, this concept entered practice mainly as a multiple choice menu, requiring that an engineer must take so many courses in humanities and that liberal arts students must take a science, either physical science or biology. The intended value of this approach was soon lost in the tall weeds of its dogmatic implementation.*

For many students and teachers alike, the core curriculum became just another boring and burdensome graduation requirement, what Whitehead

---

* At UC Berkeley where I was an undergraduate, science majors could get an easy A by enrolling in "Film Appreciation" and watching old movies once a week. Other students could satisfy their science requirement with a "gut" course, Geology 10, also known as "Rocks for Jocks."

called "cross -sterilization, . . . the fatal disconnection of subjects which kills the vitality of our modern curriculum."[13]

Mason brought Whitehead's philosophy down to earth, noting that as a result of Rutgers's rapid growth, "faculty and students tended to become more self-contained, and to know less about what was being done in other departments."[14] In order to counter this "cross-sterilization" due to the dogmatic approach to core curricula, Mason and others developed a series of interdepartmental courses, the first of which was "The Civilization of the European Renaissance," and featured lecturers from history (Dick Schlatter), art history (Helmut von Erffa), English (Rudolph Kirk), Italian and French literature (Terry Turner), and, of course, philosophy (Mason Gross). The unique feature of this course was that all professors attended each class. Thus, if the philosophy professor "touched on subject of art," he did so "with the knowledge that there was a trained art historian in the room," leading to "fascinating debates" and some "fairly exciting disputes on the floor of the lecture room itself."[15] Initially, students were "hesitant to ask questions with so many professors in the room,"[16] but their reluctance dissipated in time. David Mars (Rutgers class of 1949) recalls this class, "taught by five professors," as extremely popular "primarily because of the opportunity to interact with a large and stellar" group of faculty. He calls the class "unquestionably one of my outstanding experiences . . . at Rutgers."[17]

Norman McNatt (Rutgers class of 1964) recalls that this "team teaching" became prevalent at Rutgers. Mason cotaught a class with an English professor titled "The Philosophy of Rhetoric." In a class titled "Traditions of Western Religious Thought," which Mason taught together with Dick Schlatter, they came to class together, and rather than lecture separately, they debated with each other in front of the students in order to demonstrate that ideas are not static but instead need to be discussed and argued.

For Mason, one aim of education was to develop a sense of truth that will not be deceived by half-truth. "A half-truth is a statement which purports to be true and offers some evidence of the truth, but which is such that the whole truth would either prove it to be false or would radically change its meaning. It appeals to people who have been taught to demand evidence but are not critical about the quality of the evidence provided. . . . [T]herein lies our peculiar vulnerability. . . . [T]he successful demagogue will be the one who can turn this condition to his advantage."[18]

Paraphrasing Whitehead's "Aims of Education," Mason proposed that there exist two goals of education, which he labeled objective and subjective. It was a university's clear duty to provide objective education, which referred to any body of knowledge in a given field, whether it be engineering, medicine, physics, or Spanish literature, which allows one to function proficiently in that field. Objective education can be measured by examinations of a student's ability to demonstrate the acquisition of the required body of information.

On the other hand, subjective education is what Whitehead referred to as "activity of thought and receptivity to beauty and humane feeling." It cannot be quantified or forced onto a spread sheet. Subjective education includes "the development of such character as would ensure that its value judgments and choices would be soundly based and intelligently shaped. . . . We are not concerned merely with the qualities which give one success in college, but the qualities which society needs in order to function properly."[19]

In short, subjective and objective educations must be conjoined. Purely objective education, without the joy of discovery, an aesthetic sense of humane feeling, or the sense of how all experience is linked, leads to Whitehead's description of a "well informed man as . . . a useless bore."[20]

As a guest lecturer in a senior class in business policy, Mason summarized the study of philosophy as the quest for a rational explanation of why you are doing what you are doing. Derived from the search to discover what is life and its circumstances, Mason defined philosophy as "an attempt to re-examine the principles upon which you have based your entire life. Philosophy in all its history has never gone beyond Socrates' classic phrase, the motto of all philosophers, that 'the unexamined life is not worth living.'"[21]

Mason further distinguished critical philosophy from speculative philosophy. He noted that Socrates was the prototypical critical philosopher, a gadfly, challenging assumptions and making people think about them.

"Every individual has basic assumptions, expressed or not expressed, which he makes about himself, his activities, and his relationship to people and to his society, all those beliefs upon which a person acts without really knowing that he is doing so. Critical philosophy is a way of bringing these beliefs into the cold light of day."[22]

Mason then described speculative philosophy not as pure Socratic criticism but instead as the attempt to replace inadequate or outmoded ideas with more adequate systems. The natural sciences offer many good examples of a scheme of general ideas with a logical relationship between them, such as in physics, chemistry, and biochemistry. Mason often quoted Whitehead's own definition of speculative philosophy as "the endeavor to frame a logical, consistent scheme of general ideas in . . . which every element of human experience can be interpreted."[23] A proponent of a unifying or coherent scheme, Whitehead opposed any unnecessary conceptual bifurcation, such as that of René Descartes's separation of mind and body, or the study of medical sciences without the social sciences.

For Whitehead, philosophy was a "speculative and not merely a critical enterprise. It must not be afraid to employ the results of science and it must not ignore the claims of religious experience."[24] Whitehead's proposed unification of philosophy into a single scheme of ideas rarely caught any traction in academic circles. Whitehead himself never expected to achieve a single "explanation of everything" but saw the value of moving in that direction, ever simplifying and ever clarifying.

Reflecting Whitehead, Mason also chose to distinguish the study of philosophy by another axis, that of objective judgment of facts versus subjective judgment of values. His point of a judgment of fact is that a fact is verifiable, testable against experience, as in "it is a cloudy day." Conversely, a judgment of value states preferences, such as "I like a cloudy day." This is personal and can result in passionate discussion, but there are no facts to dispute. Mason distinguished these two branches, objective versus subjective, as follows: "From the judgment of facts derive all our sciences. From judgment of values, all our systems of ethics, of politics, and the whole realm of aesthetics as well: judgments of beauty or goodness."[25]

Mason pointed out that our "educational institutions have been fabulously successful in answering the question of "how" to do something, but "equally important in education is the question 'why.'"[26] For example, a chemist might use an objective judgment of facts to learn how to design a new herbicide but might use a subjective judgement of values to determine why we might want one.

Plato attempted to "prove that the statement 'this is good' is not a statement of value but a statement of fact . . . by assuming that there existed in some non-temporal realm an external form of the 'good.'"[27] Other philosophers, such as Kant, insisted that this could not be done, noting that there are absolute values that exist regardless of facts. Kant's famous categorical imperative illustrates that we must adhere to "the ultimate dignity of every human being"[28] even if this imperative is not based on verifiable fact.

Mason repeatedly spoke about how subjective educational experience, however unmeasurable, is as vital to education as is the objective. Objective education proceeds by dogged and dutiful study of the subject matter, be it calculus, chemistry, or the irregular Spanish verbs. But subjective understanding advances by leaps and bounds, by flashes of insight. The teacher cannot predict when it will come or in what form it will arise. In Mason's experience, it may have occurred when he read Hamlet aloud in the desert and discovered that "some words are too beautiful to be read while sitting down."[29]

Mason's main point was that subjective education is "intensely personal, unpredictable and involves self-education."[30] Not just in music, visual arts, philosophy, and history but even in physics and calculus, it is the joy of self-discovery, the flash of understanding, that cannot be measured but is essential to one's education. D. W. Rogers (Rutgers class of 1954) recalls that "the most important lesson that I ever learned at Rutgers was how to think."[31]

––––––

State legislators know how to fund objective education. They can measure it, such as by comparing the number of degrees granted in a given year to the annual budget. If more degrees are offered at less cost to the state, that is measurable success. But the legislators cannot put a monetary value on the experience of two Rutgers students who rowed to victory, winning a gold medal in the 1952 Olympics, or on the sense of humanity that a Rutgers medical student brought home having sung a requiem with the Kirkpatrick Chapel Choir in a pouring rain outside the gates of the ruins of Auschwitz. Legislators cannot always understand how the humanities and social sciences are as important a part of university education as are chemistry, physics, and engineering. They cannot measure how a student's understanding of Thucydides's account of the civil war in Corcyra could promote a better understanding of struggles in Birmingham, Alabama. They cannot see, nor can they measure, how a student's understanding of the power of propaganda sees its reflection in the current polarity of American politics or how "neglect of fact leads to ignorance, superstition, bigotry and prejudice, as well as failure to establish any control over the hard facts which do surround us."

———

By the time of his inauguration in May 1959, Mason was clearly at the top of his game as an orator and an administrator but, most important of all, also as a professor of philosophy, a former cattle-roping cowhand who had shouted Shakespeare to the desert sky and rowed to exhaustion, a free spirit who now stood as the president of the university that he had joined as a junior faculty member thirteen years before, who saw it his "duty to bring the topic of education before as many people as possible."[32]

CHAPTER 11

The Inauguration, 1959

The fundamental aim of education as we know it is, simply, freedom . . . , that freedom of spirit which . . . comes about when ignorance, superstition, hatred and fear yield to clear and adequate ideas.   —MWG, May 6, 1959

The canopy of elms that had not yet succumbed to Dutch elm disease shaded the academic procession, which meandered from Old Queens down the hill, across Hamilton Street, and through the Nielson campus* to the bronze statue of William of Orange, also known as William the Silent.

It was auspicious that Mason's inaugural procession was led by representatives from some of the oldest universities of Europe and North America, including the University of Cambridge (1209), the University of Aberdeen (1495), and Harvard University (1638), all three of which Mason had attended. Leiden University (1575) was included in the ceremony as a reminder that colonial New Jersey had been settled originally largely by the Dutch and that Rutgers, originally Queens College, had been founded in 1766 by ministers of the Dutch Reformed Church in order to train young men for the clergy.[1] The presence of Leiden University was even more auspicious to the inauguration of this philosophy professor as university president in that the founding of Leiden University in 1575, by William the Silent, had co-occurred with the adoption of the Dutch constitution guaranteeing religious freedom, freedom of speech, and freedom of intellectual inquiry (also known as academic freedom) and introduced the hitherto unknown spirit of religious and racial tolerance. Decades later to provide the intellectual environment for such philosophers as René Descartes and Baruch Spinoza, the founding of

---

* Now known as Voorhees Mall.

Mason was inaugurated in May 1959, when universities were seen as the salvation of the American way of life. On that spring day, the turbulence of the following decade was unimaginable. That summer the first two American soldiers died in Vietnam, a country that most Americans had never heard of and could not have located on a map. (Photo credit: Rutgers Archives)

Leiden University precipitated "the moment when modern higher education was born."[2]

Despite the shade from the thick canopy overhead, the Rutgers faculty and the representatives from most of the universities in the United States were warm under their academic regalia, mostly black robes but occasionally bright colors reflecting the institutions where they had received their doctorates. Mason's gown was a brilliant Harvard crimson and stood out in the crowd. On the raised platform were other guests, who included Governor Robert Meyner, New Jersey Supreme Court chief justice Joseph Weintraub, and special guests including Ms. Betty Durham, a 1917 graduate of the first class of the New Jersey College for Women, now Douglass College and a part of Rutgers University.[3] Conspicuously absent was former president Lewis Jones, who had suddenly announced his resignation the previous autumn. During his administration Rutgers had gone through tremendous change, including near bankruptcy, low enrollment, faculty departures, unsuccessful bond issues, and a new administrative oversight by the state. Jones had never enjoyed a collegial relationship with the new Board of Governors and was impatient with the frustrations inherent in fractious New Jersey politics. He had departed suddenly not due to illness but instead for reasons that remain, as Mason later stated when queried on the matter, "not for public record."[4]

Having taken the oath of office, Mason stood to read his inaugural address, which he had handwritten in pencil on a yellow legal pad.[5] In his deep baritone voice with a hint of British accent retained from his years overseas, he spoke of the shrinking world.

After paying homage to the four oldest universities whose representatives had led the inaugural procession, Mason talked about tradition, describing how universities, out of necessity rather than design, had become essentially conservative, that is, conserving and preserving the "culture of our common past and transmitting it to the young." He reflected on the ubiquitous "core curricula" that errantly proposed to include everything a citizen needs to know. Mason suggested that this was a disservice, offering to "prepare our youth for tomorrow by giving them the tools that were satisfactory only until yesterday." He believed that this was a university's erroneous expectation that the world and "society would remain as stable as the curriculum itself."[6]

Mason proposed an alternative. Although he did recognize the value of a resurgence in Latin and Greek, which he had studied as an undergraduate at Cambridge, as a way to combat the "perilous lack of enthusiasm for our own heritage," he cited the recent advances in nuclear science and microbiology as examples of the acceleration in the rate of change of knowledge.

Mason proposed looking to the emerging postcolonial peoples to study the vitality of these cultures suddenly set free from colonial domination and then stated, "The stresses and strains that are being placed upon our society cannot be understood in terms of our civilization alone. The sudden surge to freedom in the former colonial societies have demonstrated that the world of ideas has exploded, . . . ideas which have set the world on fire."[7]

Mason stated, "Freedom is the essential condition for any great intellectual vitality." Universities that have "wrapped western civilization into an easily marketable package are . . . partly responsible for this loss of a sense of excitement about ideas and for their consequent loss of urgent vitality."[8] He pointed out that 35 percent of the world's populace spoke one of six languages: Russian, Hindustani, Arabic, Chinese, Portuguese, and Japanese. Of these six, in 1959 Rutgers taught only Russian.

Under the watchful eyes of the tall bronze statue of William the Silent, Mason closed his inaugural address: "I can think of no words in the English language more beautiful than the words 'free spirit.' It must always be the ultimate aim of the university to provide the atmosphere and the intellectual conditions by which alone the free spirit can survive."[9]

Mason had a vision. He envisioned that Rutgers would enter the ranks of the truly great state universities of his day, citing both the University of Michigan, as the "fourth arm of the state government,"[10] and the University of California, Berkeley, "one of the greatest universities in the world," whose "contributions to the safety and well-being of this country have been tremendous."[11]*

Mason stood firmly for free speech, academic freedom, civil rights, and civil liberties and against poverty and racism. He had been born into privilege, a child of the American aristocracy virtually untouched by the Great Depression that had decimated so many American families. Mason's wife Julia had worked two jobs concurrently for four years before Mason had even been employed. World War II was his great leveler. Thrown as he was into the anonymity of the U.S. Army, he saw men in his squadron, younger than himself and with little education and no savings, give everything that they

---

* I had no idea that he felt this way. Much later when I was accepted to Berkeley, he never said a word to me about my choice. I assumed that he disapproved.

had. The experience pulled Mason away from the ivory tower and threw him, like Socrates, into the agora, the marketplace, in order to, again like Socrates, bring philosophy down from the clouds.

In 1959 as Mason was taking this newest biggest step in his career, there were other challenges looming besides increasing enrollment, a massive building plan, and bond issues in support of education. Already he had recognized that minority students and minority faculty were underrepresented at Rutgers. These challenges were like the fluttering of the butterfly's wings that can someday build into a hurricane.

In another beginning and soon another challenge that would reach back to Rutgers, halfway around the world in 1959 the first two Americans soldiers* died in Vietnam,[12] a country that most Americans had never heard of and could not have located on a map.

---

*Master Sergeant Chester Ovnand and Major Dale Buisand, two of the three hundred members of the U.S. Military Assistance Advisory Group.

CHAPTER 12

Into the Fishbowl, 1959

The strain of public life is positively terrifying.
—MWG, 1932

Our family moved into the Rutgers President's House in Piscataway in late August 1959. It was a fishbowl. Built in 1929, the original owner, Robert Nicholas, had donated it to Rutgers in 1939 when he and his wife, a daughter of Robert Wood Johnson, the founder of Johnson and Johnson, retired to Arizona. The house, which still stands but is no longer used for the president's residence, sits on a hill at the corner of River Road and Metlar's Lane, now the four-lane Route 18 that runs less than one hundred yards from the house. Overlooking Piscataway's Johnson Park and the Raritan River, the residence stands on a forty-three-acre property, maintained by the university, and is adjacent to the athletic fields and only a ten-minute walk from the football stadium. We had only one neighbor, Marshall Wilver, the superintendent of buildings and grounds at University Heights, and his wife and son, Gene (Skip), who was my brother Charlie's age. The University Heights campus, across open fields about a mile from the President's House, consisted of a cluster of new buildings for physics, engineering, and chemistry and the Microbiology Building, erected following Selman Waksman's Nobel Prize–winning development of the antibiotic streptomycin.

Aside from these few structures, the University Heights campus was a mostly barren and windswept undeveloped rural countryside in the then unincorporated Piscataway Township. Much of this campus was used for practice fields for football and lacrosse, a nine-hole public golf course managed by the university, and a field house and seventeen-thousand-seat football stadium, built in 1937, that was at the time considered more than adequate size for intercollegiate football. The left-field fence of the baseball field abutted the President's House property, and any over-the-fence home runs ended up in our backyard.

Each autumn, the sounds of a football game, the cheers of the crowd, and the marching band's bass drum echoed across the fields to the house. In late March, Julia, an ardent Dodgers fan and a longtime admirer of Branch Rickey,[1] always knew that spring had arrived when, looking at the bright yellow forsythia through the newly opened windows, she could hear distant shouts of "hey, no batter, no batter" and the staccato crack of a hardwood bat.

My two older sisters, Ellen and Kitty, were no longer living at home. Kitty was a junior at Milton Academy outside of Boston, and Ellen, having just graduated also from Milton, was on her way to England for a postgraduate year at Shelborne School under the auspices of the English Speaking Union. My older brother Charlie and I lived at home. Instead of the Piscataway public school system, Mason enrolled us both at Rutgers Preparatory School, which in 1957 had been separated from formal association with Rutgers itself.

The President's House had five bedrooms upstairs and a separate apartment over the attached garage for a university cook to live. The upstairs was considered the family's private residence and was not furnished by the university.

But the house was not just a residence; it was also used for many university functions, such as faculty receptions, meetings, and dinners hosted for guests, including recipients of honorary degrees. The lower floor of the residence was furnished by the university, and a day staff member was assigned to keep it clean, which freed Julia from having to maintain such a large property. The university also assigned a groundskeeper, Mr. Fred Dilalo, a U.S. Army veteran of the Battles of Salerno and Anzio, to supervise the maintenance of the large gardens.* Groundskeepers also maintained the stadium

---

* Mr. Dilalo ("Freddie") also taught me how to drive and accompanied me to my driving test.

In 1959, on our last vacation all together, Mason took our family to the Elkhorn Ranch south of Bozeman, Montana, where forty years earlier he had first ridden the high country to the headwaters of the Gallatin River and into the Valley of the Yellowstone. In 1928, he had written his parents that he loved the West and wanted to remain there for his entire life. (Photo credit: Courtesy of Montana Picture Gallery, Virginia City, MT)

and athletic fields and provided mowing and snow removal under Mr. Wilver's supervision.

Humans seek routine. Mason was no different.

———

Mason awoke daily to the quiet buzz of his G.E. electric alarm clock, set for
7:00 A.M. By 7:25, I heard his footsteps outside my room. He knocked on my
door before entering and, on the colder mornings, crossed my room to close
the window for me, then departed, followed by one if not both of his large,
loud, and poorly disciplined dogs. If I was not downstairs for breakfast within
ten minutes, Mason knew that I had fallen back asleep. His deep baritone
resonated from the bottom of the stairs, tersely barking his displeasure,
which sounded like anger but was difficult to distinguish from his characteristic impatience.

Sitting at a small table that looked out through a bay window, Mason quietly enjoyed a breakfast prepared by the university's cook. His breakfast
rarely changed, namely eggs, bacon, Arnold whole wheat toast, Dundee
Orange Marmalade, and wicked-strong iced Maxwell House coffee with
cream and sugar. He shared little or no conversation as he read in their
entirety two morning newspapers, the *New York Times* and the *New York
Herald Tribune*. Bristling whenever anyone tried to read parts of an article
aloud to him, he interrupted, saying, "I've already read the newspaper, thank
you." He read each article on the front page, and instead of turning to where
each article later was continued, he read the papers front to back, picking
up each continued article in turn as he got to it. Although not one to listen
to sports or watch them on television, he was an "ardent Yankee fan."[2] He
read the sports pages and knew the standings of the professional teams.
He could easily converse intelligently on recent games despite the fact that he
hadn't seen them. He did follow college football very closely, especially
the Ivy League and the Mid-Atlantic conference, of which Rutgers was
a member.

To work every day Mason wore a charcoal gray worsted Brooks Brothers
suit over a white cotton button-down oxford shirt and a scarlet-and-black

striped official Rutgers freshman tie. The width of the tie and the size of the stripes changed every year, but they were always red-and-black striped. Every year he bought several at the Rutgers Bookstore and wore them constantly, even in unofficial situations. Occasionally he wore a light suit, but he never wore jeans, T-shirts, sweatshirts, or any article of clothing displaying either a manufacturer's logo or a slogan. A blue button-down oxford cloth shirt was suitable for only the most casual of situations. He never loosened his tie, rolled up his sleeves, or kicked off his shoes, even while napping in his armchair after Sunday lunch while listening to his favorite singers, Joan Sutherland and Marilyn Horne. Once at a picnic high in the mountains of Montana along the banks of the headwaters Gallatin River, he wore a white cotton button-down oxford shirt open at the neck, without a necktie, to signal to everyone that he was, yes, finally, on vacation.

In his suit's breast pocket Mason kept a soft pack of Old Golds, unfiltered, with a pack of matches slid inside its clear cellophane cover. He never used a lighter and always made certain that the number of cigarettes remaining equaled the number of matches in the pack. In another coat pocket he kept his spectacles and a small pocket calendar with a pencil to make note of his schedule. He also kept a small yellow tin of Bisodol, a chewable antacid that he used constantly throughout the day for the chronic heartburn that had plagued him since college. He repacked the tin every night before bed from a cotton-stoppered brown glass stock bottle atop his tall dresser.

Up close, Mason smelled like tobacco, old scotch, and antacid. By age fifty he had developed a slight resting tremor, most pronounced in the morning, that may have been due to his body's craving for nicotine or alcohol, both of which he consumed daily in generous quantities, habits that were de rigueur among successful professional men of the postwar era. He once admitted that he would like to stop smoking but was hopelessly hooked.[3]

Carrying no briefcase but tucking under one arm a zippered leather folder adorned with his initials, Mason left for work just after 8:00 A.M., driving in his big V-8 gray Oldsmobile four-door sedan with a ring of nicotine stain in the overhead liner. He made certain that he arrived at 8:15 every day, ahead of everyone else, in order to have a quiet moment before the day began. He

Mason's day was busy with constant meetings, yet his students were never turned away. He never lost touch with what a university is all about—namely, the education of the young. Mason saw himself as a part-time executive but a full-time teacher. (Photo credit: Rutgers University Library Special Collections and University Archives)

stopped at the first floor to check in with Bob Ochs, chief of campus police, to see what disasters had occurred during the night.

Visitors to Mason's second-story office in Old Queens reported shelves of hardbound classics, all of which Mason had read, as well as rowing prints, many by Currier and Ives, and a constantly visible cloud of stale cigarette smoke. The window sills, a side table, and every other flat surface held stacks of books, but his desk was generally uncluttered. His day was busy, with constant meetings, yet his students were not turned away. Visiting officials would wait while the students were ushered immediately into his office, because Mason saw himself as a part-time executive but a full-time teacher.[4] Even as president, every year he taught at least one undergraduate class and one graduate seminar in philosophy. Unlike many college presidents, he never lost touch with what a university is all about: not research, not grants, not capital improvement but rather "the education of the young, the handing on of the best of the past, the exploration of the present and the future with the fine tools of intellectual method and discipline."[5]

Mason believed, like Alfred North Whitehead, that all education is personal. Education is not simply the transfer of facts, which could easily be performed in a correspondence course or, as they are now, online. The role of the educator is to stimulate students to want to teach themselves.

Students remember less about what Mason was like in class but more about how the class made them feel. He never took off his suit jacket; he did not hide behind a lectern. Jim Shokoff (Rutgers class of 1960) remembers that Mason was always "on his feet, thoughtfully moving to different parts of the room to assure that every student felt involvement and participation in the class."[6] Mason had a mesmerizing enthusiasm, as if the subject was trying to burst out of him. He sometimes sat on the edge of a wooden desk leaning forward, one leg crossed over the other, as he asked questions. Sitting forward, he seemed to be looking at you all the time, trying to convince you.

Dick Schlatter wrote that Mason "was a popular teacher in the best sense. . . . He was a master of the dialectic and students were devoted to his clash of ideas and to the principle that the unexamined life is not worth living. . . . Like all great teachers, he liked students."[7]

Mason sometimes used his own notes, handwritten in pencil on yellow legal pads,[8] but many students recall that he spoke extemporaneously, using no notes at all. He had a way of clarifying very difficult works by Plato, Saint Augustine, Baruch Spinoza, Immanuel Kant, and, of course, Whitehead.

Many of Mason's former students cannot remember any details of why he was such a good teacher; they just recalled that his classes were well enrolled, well attended throughout the semester, and well worth the effort. Mason's classes were not easy. One former student said, "He challenged you." Another former student quipped that he had to bring a dictionary to class just so he could keep up. Mason didn't make philosophy simple, but he opened the door to understanding. It was presumed that you had to come to class prepared or you'd be left in the dust. But the preparation would be worth the trouble. One student noted that he could never take notes, because he was too busy thinking about what Mason was saying. Students cannot recall if he smoked during class, but he definitely lit one up immediately afterward, even in classrooms where smoking had been prohibited.

Norman McNatt (Rutgers class of 1964) recalls the atmosphere on campus, calling it "an intellectual ferment"; those were "the best years of Rutgers."[9] According to Mark Singley, Mason "radiated enthusiasm and hope."[10]

Mason had a reputation for looking after the students. All colleges receiving federal grants under the 1862 Morrill Land Grant Agricultural and Mechanical College Act were mandated to provide education in military tactics. Rutgers had always satisfied this mandate by requiring freshmen to participate for one year in the Reserve Officers' Training Corps. There was a weekly requirement of all cadets to march in uniform. In 1956, freshman Jerry Jacobs was not allowed to march because he did not have a uniform. He did not have a uniform because he had refused to sign a loyalty oath, and therefore the uniform was not issued to him. But he felt that the loyalty oath was ethically unsound and perhaps illegal, so he refused to sign. He was due to be expelled if he did not march, and he could not march without a uniform and could not get a uniform unless he signed the loyalty oath.

Jerry was sent to Mason's office. According to Jerry, Mason leaned back in his chair and put his feet up on the desk. The two agreed that Jerry could

Students recall Mason's mesmerizing enthusiasm. Mason knew that all education is "self-education" and that the role of an educator is to stimulate students to want to teach themselves. (Photo credit: Rutgers University Library Special Collections and University Archives)

march in civilian attire if he did so "with a respectful attitude" and expressed no "pretense of carrying a weapon." This incident, well publicized by word of mouth, increased Mason's stature among the students. Jerry was not unpatriotic and in fact after graduation was drafted into the U.S. Army, received a high-level security clearance, and served honorably in Korea.[11]

According to Norman McNatt (Rutgers class of 1964), anyone who wanted a conversation with Mason Gross could count on finding him in the late afternoon at the faculty club, where he would stop on his way home for a martini or two with his colleagues.[12]

Then, unless Mason had an evening meeting, he departed for home between 5:00 and 5:30 P.M., driving across the old Landing Lane Bridge. He announced his arrival home with a "Hi-de-ho" and expected to be answered. He refreshed himself with an iced tea on warm days and hot tea in the cooler months. Removing his suit jacket, folding and draping it carefully over the back of an armchair, he sat down on his favorite couch with a blended scotch and water on the rocks and three afternoon newspapers, the *Newark Evening News*, New Brunswick's *Daily Home News*, and the Rutgers *Daily Targum*.

Even in midsummer, Mason never rolled up the sleeves of his cotton oxford. The cuffs stayed buttoned. He never loosened his necktie. The tie was either on tight or off, and he never took it off during evenings at home until he went upstairs to bed. None of his family members ever recall him wearing just a T-shirt.

In decent weather, Mason enjoyed walking to the university fields to watch the teams practice. An unlocked gate in the anchor fence gave him access across the baseball outfield. Head football coach John Bateman recalled how the players appreciated Mason's interest. Mason stopped to talk to the coaches, Bateman, Frank Burns, and Matt Bolger; in springtime Bolger was also the head baseball coach.

Although Mason enjoyed watching athletic events, he never attended any of those in which his children were playing. He did not play tennis, squash, or even golf and participated in no regular exercise. I never saw him run. He never threw a football, a baseball, or a tennis ball for the dogs or even a snowball. He had developed an intermittent right shoulder bursitis, very likely secondary to his arthritic illness back in high school, that kept him from playing many sports. When the bursitis flared up, he could not move his right arm. While driving, instead of shifting his transmission with his right hand, he reached through the steering wheel and shifted with his left while still smoking.

No radio played in the President's House except during the day when Julia listened to National League Baseball. No television blared; it was hidden in the basement. Having read five newspapers that day, Mason saw no need to watch the television news. In fact, he rarely watched any television. On Sunday evenings, he enjoyed Walter Cronkite's weekly documentary titled *The Twentieth Century*. Although Mason was an avid fan of college football, the only sports he ever watched on television were the New Year's college championships—the Sugar Bowl, the Cotton Bowl, and the Rose Bowl—but never in their entirety.

We knew that we were not to bring our report cards, complete with accompanying excuses, family squabbles, or other adolescent dysphorias,* to him at the door. Julia protected him from that, knowing that he needed some down time before addressing the problems of this smaller world than the one that he had just left. Family drama could wait its turn.

Supper was at 7:00 P.M. sharp. Mason enjoyed meat: roasts, chicken, pork chops, or lamb and fish every Friday. He was always pleased with leftovers, such as shepherd's pie, beet stew, hash, creamed chicken on rice, and even creamed chipped beef on toast, which in the army often had been called by another more colorful and colloquial expression.† He enjoyed organ meats, such as liver, kidneys, cold beef tongue, and sweetbreads, all of which my older brother Charlie and I found especially gross.

Speaking of that, the adjective "gross" was not used in Mason's house. The word was not forbidden, but when uttered, it always drew a look from over the top of his tortoiseshell bifocals. In truth, the word was not then as common a component of the American lexicon as it is today. As children, we resisted the taunts of our classmates when the word appeared on our school vocabulary lists and we discovered that "gross" means more than simply "twelve dozen."

Mason smoked constantly, two packs per day of unfiltered Old Golds, a carton of which had been given out weekly by the sponsors during his

* Dysphoria: A profound state of emotional unease or dissatisfaction, sometimes accompanied by depression, anxiety, agitation, or histrionics; in other words, typical normal adolescent behavior.
† S.O.S., or "shit on a shingle."

television appearances on *Two for the Money.* A column of smoke always rose from the ashtray by his seat. Most evenings he was attentive and conversant, but if left alone, he lost himself in whatever he was reading, and the room remained quiet.

After supper, Mason was approachable to deal with whatever family drama could not wait. He had a look. It was the very same look that a cobra uses to hypnotize and then paralyze its victims. If a question was especially puerile, Mason would look over the top of his bifocals and just stare motionless. He often used this glare in lieu of speaking whenever a comment or question had not met the minimum criteria to qualify for a verbal response. On those few occasions when a verbal response was indicated, it was usually brief. He then returned to his newspaper, and that would be the end of what had qualified as a "discussion."

Julia often joined Mason after supper, sitting across the room in an armchair of her own. They conversed or read quietly, both smoking and sipping scotch, until retiring shortly after 10:00 P.M., Mason first, then Julia an hour or so later. They slept in adjoining twin beds.

It's not clear how much alcohol Mason drank, although he did drink every day but never before noon. Some days during the week he drank a dry martini or more at lunch at the faculty club, perhaps one or two more in the afternoon before driving home, and only 21 Club blended scotch in the evening. He never drank beer and had a single glass of wine at holiday dinners. He had two to three scotches at night but sipped them slowly throughout the evening. Mason never seemed intoxicated, and nobody has ever reported seeing him so. Except for his tolerance, his alcohol use meets none of the other criteria for a formal diagnosis of alcohol dependence. Multiple sources have corroborated the legend that Mason Gross could hold his liquor. Professional men of his era were noted for a very high tolerance for alcohol, which seemed normal at the time but in retrospect has been shown to be much more harmful than had been suspected. There were nights when Mason was especially impatient and short-tempered, which may have been precipitated by innumerable stresses at work that he had been unable to unload until he got home. A few drinks would not have dampened his irritation. To what extent the distance that I felt between us was due to his alcohol consumption I'll never know, but even moderate alcohol consumption is well documented as disrupting family dynamics and communication.

Mason enthusiastically attended all the Rutgers home football games, which involved a reception and lunch before the game at the President's House for selected alumni and VIPs from the opposing team, followed by a walk through the practice fields to the stadium. Visitor parking stretched out on the lawn behind the house. One Monday morning after a very close home game, Mason was very hoarse during his 8:00 A.M. class. He then said, "If anyone here was at the game and isn't hoarse, he should be ashamed of himself." Mason and Julia attended most of the away games as well, driving Saturday morning at least as far as West Point, Lehigh in Pennsylvania, or the University of Delaware. Their attendance was expected at the season opener, the annual Rutgers-Princeton football game, commemorating the oldest college football rivalry in the country. Dating from 1869, the game was always played at Princeton because Palmer Stadium had twice the capacity of that at Rutgers. Very casual tailgate parties were the order of the day, with deviled eggs, chicken salad sandwich triangles, and ice tea or scotch and water on the rocks in a plastic cup. Mason always wore a suit, a button-down white oxford, and his scarlet-and-black striped Rutgers tie.

On Sundays, Mason slept in until 7:30 A.M. After breakfast, he read the Sunday *New York Times* until exactly 10:30, when he got into the Oldsmobile to drive to the nondenominational Sunday services at Kirkpatrick Chapel. I accompanied him, but Julia often stayed home. As we know, she had made her peace with organized religion when she was a teenager.

A large Sunday lunch was served precisely at 1:30 P.M., always roast chicken, rice, and one overboiled vegetable followed by ice cream and chocolate sauce. Often, the chapel's guest speaker and the university chaplain, Bradford S. Abernethy, would come for lunch, often with several of Mason and Julia's friends, the Schlatters, Metzgers, or Camerons.

Once the guests had left, Mason adjourned to listen to his favorite music, mostly opera, to which he would regularly fall asleep in his chair. It was the only time I ever saw his feet up on the coffee table, with his wingtip shoes, the sleeves of his long-sleeve shirt rolled down and buttoned, and his red-and-white striped Rutgers necktie, never loosened.

Mason's life was very much in the public eye. There is no single list of the many boards and committees he served on, and I know that I have failed to document them all. He served on the boards of trustees or directors of Vassar College, St. Peter's College, the U.S. Merchant Marine Academy at Kings Point (New York), and the New Jersey Symphony Orchestra and chaired the Taft School Board of Trustees. Mason was a trustee also of the Institute for International Education, the Educational Testing Service, the English Speaking Union, the Rutgers Preparatory School, the Rutgers University Press, the Kingsport Press, and the Howard Savings Institute. He chaired or was president of the New Jersey Labor Mediation Board, the Center for Analysis of Public Issues, Middlesex General Hospital, the National Book Committee, the New Jersey State United Negro College Fund, and the American Council on Education. At last count he had honorary degrees from eleven American universities, not including one from Rutgers in 1971, but I am certain that I have missed a few.

In the evenings, Julia often accompanied Mason on speaking engagements or dinners when spouses were typically included, often in New York City. Together they traveled to alumni meetings across the country.

But unlike Mason, Julia was not extroverted and was not comfortable with life in the fishbowl where your home was not private. The President's House was not a place where you could make your own breakfast in your pajamas. Julia chose to be at the house during the day as little as possible. Having studied library science at Rutgers, she worked part-time at the Highland Park public library. Julia was not as stiffly attired as Mason and preferred to spend her day in a wraparound blue denim skirt tied at the waist, a loose cotton blouse, and espadrilles, with her extremely long hair always tied back in a bun.

Since Mason and Julia owned their residence at the Jersey Shore, they elected to keep it as their permanent home, knowing that their stay in the President's House was temporary. They maintained their house in Rumson, voted there, and spent their vacation time there, Thanksgiving, Christmas, and all summer. It was great to get out of the fishbowl every now and then. Many of their closest friends, Robinsons and Freemans, whose children were the same age as us, lived in that neighborhood.

Mason loved Christmas. Every December during finals week, he went to the Rutgers College Student Center, sat in a large chair, and read aloud to gathered students and staff Clement Clarke Moore's "A Visit from St. Nicholas." Mason thrived on the classical Christmas music, such as the "Festival of Lessons and Carols" broadcast live on Christmas Eve from Kings' College Cambridge. Every December during final exam week, we attended a similar event in the Kirkpatrick Chapel, a concert of sacred and secular Christmas music sung by the Rutgers Glee Club, led by F. Austin "Soup" Walter, and the Kirkpatrick Chapel Choir, under the direction of David Drinkwater, university organist and choir director.

Mason also enjoyed the secular seasonal music. Rutgers graduate Phillip "Sandy" Greene, a Rumson neighbor, remembers a "truly memorable, annual event." Every year on December 23 in Rumson, Mason and Julia hosted a large party, with catered finger foods, an open bar (as was the custom at the time), and two hours of loud singing as Mason played his grandmother's Steinway, working through the FAO Schwartz Christmas Carol book at least three times. It was the only occasion when I ever saw this once virtuoso pianist play the piano. The whole family had spent the entire day decorating the house with fresh-cut boughs of spruce, pine, and balsam. Mason stoked huge fires in the house's two fireplaces. I never saw him happier.

Mason never asked Julia to buy the Christmas gifts for us. He did that on his own, often books or music, naturally. One year he gave me a collection of Leonard Bernstein's Young Peoples' Concerts, hoping to stimulate an interest in classical music.* Knowing my interest in boats, the following year Mason gave me Howard Chappelle's *History of the American Fishing Schooners* and then Admiral Samuel Eliot Morrison's two-volume history *The European Discovery of America*. Mason always wrapped the gifts himself,

---

* Charlie liked Stan Getz. Kitty and Ellen played Elvis Presley, whose music Mason once described as "certainly passionate." Mason once asked Ellen to buy him a Dave Brubeck record.

alone, quietly late at night, very carefully and precisely, tying them with ribbon and never using adhesive tape. The best part of Christmas for him was
having his whole family home, often dragging their college friends along,
resulting in hours of music and conversation. Like Socrates himself, Mason
was always more alive when he was surrounded by active young minds who
would fence with him.

Mason was clearly the opposite of what we now call a "helicopter parent"
or a "snowplow parent." His own father had attempted to push him to Yale,
intervening excessively, but in the end helped with the details of getting him
into college and pursuing his career. Mason recoiled from that, and although,
as his children, we may have sensed his distance from us, we have to thank
him for the independence that resulted so that we would learn to get through
our issues and our troubles on our own.

––––––

The late biographer William Manchester once wrote that "most public men
have one personality for the world and another in private."[13] When my oldest sister Ellen was seventeen, she approached Mason seeking advice as to
what colleges she should apply. (Extremely smart and focused like Mason,
Ellen was cum laude, aced the SATs, and could have gotten in anywhere.)

Mason answered, "Well, Harvard is the best."

Ellen, always as quick-minded as Mason, retorted, "But Harvard doesn't
admit women." But the moment had passed; the conversation was over.[14]

Another seventeen-year-old, our neighbor and my former elementary
school classmate Marion Freeman, called one day asking if she could come
over to seek Mason's advice about colleges. He ushered her into his study
and closed the French doors. They talked for over an hour. The following
year, she entered the first women's class at Princeton.

I heard Mason speak once at Kirkpatrick Chapel, but at age ten I didn't
understand a word of his sermon. I have learned that he was the best teacher
his students had ever known, but I never sat in on one of his classes. I never
saw that side of him. I knew that he was a great pianist but only heard him
play carols for his friends once a year. When I asked to borrow his book on

Charlemagne for a school report, he said, "Yes, but you won't understand it." (He was probably correct.) He was always generous to me whenever I asked for something, but I never found the keys to unlock this charismatic and witty professor at home. After I had experienced a few well-deserved confrontations with his impatience and short temper, I chose to keep my distance. Mason apparently never lost his cool at work, but his best friend Bill Robinson recalled to me occasions when he was "edgy as a wounded bear" and "verbally abusive to Julia."[15]

Mason favored some routine in his life. His life at home was generally predictable. But starting in the autumn of 1959, his life as president of Rutgers quickly became anything but routine.

CHAPTER 13

The Cultural Wasteland, 1959

The culture of a community is the outward manifestation of the interests, desires, hopes, aspirations, delights and emotions of its inhabitants. . . . As a community acquires its own diverse ways of satisfying the demands of its citizens for a better life, its culture is therefore peculiar to itself.

—MWG, April 1963

The community leaders who had gathered in 1959 for the twelfth annual review of the 1947 New Jersey Constitutional Convention may not have known that the newly inaugurated president of their state university was "prone to hyperbole" and had once been cautioned by his high school headmaster to "moderate the strength of his opinions."[1] They would not have read Mr. Horace Taft's 1928 assessment that Mason liked to present an argument "intended to incite conflict" and would sit back and "watch the fur fly." They would not have heard that as a Rutgers philosophy professor, Mason was the university's gadfly who, like Socrates, delighted in stirring up controversy in the agora, the marketplace. As such, they may have been taken aback when Mason, a Harvard-educated Connecticut Yankee, stood before them in September 1959 and scolded them that New Jersey was "culturally almost bankrupt."[2]

The local press got wind of this very quickly, as one might expect. The *New York Times* called it a "bombshell."[3] Mason received some highly opinionated pushback. Some responders applauded what everyone already knew; others were deeply insulted.

With the 1959 election day approaching, a major bond issue to support public education was on the ballot. Mason was only pointing out that two-thirds of New Jersey's residents who were seeking a college education were leaving the state, a much higher percentage than any other state. In other words, New Jersey was perilously dependent on other states for the education of its citizens, an unsustainable situation now that all state universities were about to be besieged by the influx of their own children of the baby boom generation.

Mason stated that "on the subject of higher education in the state, the constitution had nothing to say." He then added that New Jersey's educational dependence on other states paralleled a cultural dependence as well. In his attempt to connect education to culture, his point was that there was no demand for culture within New Jersey, and if there was no demand for culture, then the demands for higher education would be weak as well. "For one community to defend itself by arguing that its members can find cultural opportunities in another community is for that community a way to brand itself as impoverished and sterile."[4]

At the time, New Jersey had "no legitimate theatre," no opera, and no ballet and "minimal galleries capable of attracting first class exhibits of painting or sculpture."[5] New Jersey was dependent on New York and Philadelphia, which for some people meant only a short drive across the river. But who cares if people go to New York or Philadelphia to hear the symphony? What difference does that make?

As I've mentioned, Mason often quoted Alfred North Whitehead, who had written that "culture is activity of thought, and receptiveness to beauty and humane feeling." But the concept of "culture" required careful definition, as the term resonates with overtones of snobbery, elitism and false gentility. Connotations of the word "culture" clashed in opposition to another powerful ideal of American society, namely equality. Rutgers provost Richard Schlatter wrote that "proponents of culture have been haunted by the fact that culture, even when defined as 'activity of thought' and 'receptiveness to beauty' has been perceived as the exclusive possession of aristocracy."[6]

Cultural anthropologists list 164 definitions of the word "culture."[7] Culture is not found in a ticket to the opera. Culture is the "resonance of a community,"[8] synonymous with consciousness, or the lens through which one society sees itself in the world. Culture may be "epiphenomenal, a reflection of underlying social relations."[9] A society can choose, as a part of its culture, to have a public library or not, an excellent school system or not or to turn a blind eye to racism or not or ignore poverty or not. Critical to an understanding of both Whitehead's and Mason's thesis is that culture is not just an evening at the Metropolitan Opera or standing in line to see the *Mona Lisa*. Those are examples of "culture of the past." Culture is not something that I can pay someone to do to me.

No, culture is not "the exclusive possession of aristocracy." Culture says "something fresh and new about the world in which we ourselves live" and includes equal parts of Eugene Ormandy and Quincy Jones, Mikhail Baryshnikov and Gene Kelly, soprano Joan Sutherland and Ella Fitzgerald, or Luciano Pavarotti and Paul Robeson (Rutgers class of 1919, Phi Beta Kappa and valedictorian), whom Mason once described as "Rutgers' greatest graduate."[10] Culture includes what a society chooses to see in its own mirror, be it Selma, Watts, the Kardashians, school shootings, the Super Bowl, the dramatic rescues during Hurricane Katrina, or a chief executive who brags on camera about grabbing women "by the pussy."

Mason believed that education and culture were linked, again not merely in an appreciation of Shakespeare or Beethoven or Picasso. Invited to address a meeting of the Jersey City Planning Commission, Mason spoke of the cultural resonance of a community and how it could be built into a city. But how does one plan for "activity of thought" or "receptiveness to humane feeling?" Mason suggested that a city's "schools must exhibit as high a standard of educational performance as can be secured, . . . where the pupils are stimulated by exciting teaching and not worn down by uninspired routine." He advocated for a strong public library, not just as a repository for dusty books but also as a center for "the intellectual vigor of a community" and an important barometer of "a city's commitment to culture and activity of thought."[11]

But how was education linked to culture? Mason believed that a college education engendered in its graduates certain habits over a four-year period, habits that become "an integral part of one's personality."[12] One habit was that of critical analysis, whether learned in chemistry, differential calculus, or English literature, the habit of logical analysis (rather than knee jerk reactivity), critical evaluation (of facts rather than "fake news"), creative imagination, sensitive appreciation, and independent judgment. In short, culture and education would join together in a search for the meanings and significance in our human experience.

In Rutgers graduates, Mason saw a "grass roots movement of critical intelligence, moral and aesthetic sensitivity and social responsibility, building up the quality of our society . . . in the greatest movement toward cultural advancement that the world has ever known."[13]

Mason described American universities as "the greatest opportunity which history has offered for transforming our society from one in which fear, ignorance and naked power are dominant forces, to one where intelligence, human sympathy and love of freedom will shape our destiny."[14]

That is what Mason meant by "culture." He recognized that a community's commitment to its own culture would complement its commitment to education at all levels. He insisted that a community could not have one without the other.

CHAPTER 14

Nothing at Rutgers Was
Ever Easy

*In 1900, only five percent of the boys and girls between the ages of 18 and 22
were in college. Today, nearly forty percent of New Jersey high school graduates go on to college. When you multiply these percentages by the increasing
population, you understand why the colleges are facing such pressures.*
—*MWG, October 31, 1960*

After his inauguration there was little time for Mason to relax into his new
job, even though he had been the acting president since President Lewis
Jones's hasty departure the previous autumn. A statewide education bond
issue was on the November 1959 ballot. Jersey voters had shot down the previous two.

New Jersey voters and their legislators had always been reluctant to open
their wallets in support of higher education, especially since for any college-
bound student New Jersey was surrounded by high-quality out-of-state
institutions, both private and public, willing and eager to welcome New Jersey residents who could afford the high tuition. Into the 1960s New Jersey
ranked forty-eighth, near the very lowest of states, in financial support of
higher education.

The magnitude of Rutgers's capital expansion during Mason's presidency
becomes even more astounding if we consider where Rutgers had been previously and how closely it had come to bankruptcy and complete failure.

Rutgers had been financed on a shoestring ever since its inception in 1766
as Queens College. With the 1862 Morrill Act, the first federal aid to education,[1] Rutgers became one of only a few private colleges nationwide to be des-

ignated as a Land Grant college, as most of the grants went to state universities, many of which were started with these grants in mind. As noted previously, many of the Land Grant state universities founded at this time were in states that were just entering the union, such as Kansas and Iowa, so that state support for higher education was required and specified in their new state constitutions.

Rutgers was not so fortunate. By 1925, Rutgers was growing but was still a private institution, with three separate campuses and several colleges. Still, the state legislature balked at supporting higher education, and the Rutgers Board of Trustees, a private governing body made up predominantly of Rutgers alumni, was reluctant to cede autonomy to the state. In 1932, Rutgers president Robert Clothier challenged the Board of Trustees to decide whether "Rutgers was to be a state university under state control or a private university under private control."[2]

An opportunity to clarify Rutgers's status arose in 1943 when New Jersey governor Walter Edge initiated a massive reorganization of the state government in anticipation of a new constitutional convention scheduled for 1947. Some parties to the discussion, such as the representatives from Hudson and Essex Counties, located closest to New York City, opposed the selection of Rutgers as a state university for New Jersey. Other parties lobbied for a state university administered by the state Board of Education. Rutgers's loyal alumni were able to pass legislation that would designate Rutgers as the state university of New Jersey but with a relationship coordinated with, not subservient to, the New Jersey Board of Education. Annual budget proposals and requests for capital expansion would go straight to the governor's office to be included in his budget submission to the legislature. On March 26, 1945, Governor Edge signed the legislation, and Rutgers became the state university of New Jersey, absorbing also the University of Newark, including its law school and pharmacy school, which were housed in a few rundown houses and an old brewery. The campus at Camden would be absorbed in 1950. President Clothier had successfully obtained legal recognition for Rutgers as the state university and had retained both its fiscal separation from the Board of Education and its autonomy under its own Board of Trustees. Unfortunately, he had anticipated increased state appropriations for operating costs and for capital expansion, which would not be forthcoming. Despite the legislative victory creating the state university, the public continued to view Rutgers as a private college and did not support it financially as did those voters in states with a well-defined relationship to their state university.

In 1946 as Mason considered a move from Columbia, he proudly wrote to this father that "Rutgers is now a state university." But Mason did not write that the physical plant was antiquated and that the state was supporting only one-third of the operating budget and was providing no funds for capital expansion. The total university enrollment in 1945 had been seven thousand students; by 1948 it jumped to sixteen thousand. Rutgers charged the highest tuition of any state university in the nation and paid the lowest faculty salaries, such that two-thirds of the faculty sought either loans or outside employment.*

The New Jersey legislature was unwilling to back any loans to the university but did support a 1948 statewide bond issue, which failed by a huge margin. Historian Richard McCormick calls the defeat of this bond issue "a multiple catastrophe for the university" during a time of decreasing enrollment, as the floodtide of World War II veterans on the GI Bill was rapidly ebbing. The defeat "dashed the hopes for any capital improvement" but also resulted in a query by the new governor, Alfred E. Driscoll, to clarify why a state university, dependent upon state funding, was administered totally by a private alumni Board of Trustees.[3]

The defeat of a second bond issue in 1954, which had been aimed partially at starting a medical school, tacitly presumed to be at Rutgers, forced further clarification of Rutgers's status in the state. Democratic governor Robert Meyner, although personally highly supportive of Rutgers, recognized that "unless the state were given a larger voice in the control of the University, there was little prospect for an increase in capital expenditure."[4] Meyner insisted "that the ambiguous status of the institution must be resolved."[5]

---

* Mason started his first television job in 1949, and in 1951 he became chairman of the New Jersey Mediation Board. Both part-time positions paid well.

Rutgers continued to evolve. As of August 10, 1956, new legislation mandated that Rutgers was now to be directly managed not by the private Board of Trustees but instead by a public Board of Governors, six of whose eleven members would be appointed by the governor and five by the Board of Trustees from its membership. The name of the organization was also changed, giving birth to the corporate entity known since that day as "Rutgers, the State University."

Financially, Rutgers was not out of the woods. Now subject more than ever to the whims and biases of politics, the Republican legislature slashed the amount of funding the new Board of Governors had requested through the governor's office. The state Board of Education, which held no proprietary relationship to Rutgers under the new arrangement, still recommended decreased funding, creating a contentious relationship that would smolder for decades. With budgetary emergencies, requiring heavily raised tuition and dormitory rates, Rutgers's financial situation in 1957 was critical.

Then, a miracle happened.

Sputnik!*

On October 4, 1957, the Soviet Union placed the world's first satellite into Earth's orbit.[6] One is tempted to ponder what all the fuss was about. It wasn't about the 180-pound satellite no bigger than a beach ball and emitting a radio signal, a weak "beep-beep-beep" that even amateur radio operators around the world could pick up. Within three weeks the batteries had died, and Sputnik went silent. So what? No, the fuss was not about the beach ball but instead about the intercontinental ballistic missile that had lifted it up there. Americans were accustomed to technological superiority, in cars, airplanes, washing machines, toilet paper, and toothpaste. But the Russians proved that they had a better missile than we did, one that now could lob a nuclear weapon anywhere in the world, while our missiles were regularly blowing up on the launch pad. Our missile scientists and engineers were all foreign-born, mostly German, having surrendered to the Americans and emigrated from Europe at the end of the war.

---

* "Sputnik," Russian for "fellow traveler."

Within months on the heels of a massive public hysteria that we were behind the Russians, federal money started to flow. The National Defense Education Act of 1958 and later the Higher Education Facilities Act opened the floodgates for scholarships, student loans, and capital construction. Federal spending for education and university-based research went up tenfold between 1957 and 1964.[7] Politicians discovered that education, from the primary level through the graduate level, including vocational and technical education, had become a sacred cow to the public. The legislatures opened the taxpayers' wallets.

When Mason was inaugurated, this largess was just beginning. The next seven years would be the high-water mark for federal funding for general higher education on its own merit, separate from later goal-directed funding for defense research. The well dried up in early 1967 when a new Republican Congress, angry over the juggernaut that had ruled Congress since the 1964 Democratic landslide victories, shut down President Lyndon B. Johnson's "Great Society" so that he could not even pass a rodent-control bill.[8]

But Mason was unable to build his dream. He wanted to build at Rutgers a center for the performing and visual arts, with an auditorium that would accommodate world-class orchestras. That would have to wait.

CHAPTER 15

Crisis, 1961

Having been told that you are expecting twins, imagine being told now that you are having triplets. —MWG, 1961

The year 1961 began with the hope and enthusiasm of President John F. Kennedy's "New Frontier." Although Kennedy had won his election over Richard Nixon by the slimmest of margins, within two months over 65 percent of voters claimed that they had voted for Kennedy.[1] The Bay of Pigs fiasco put an end to Kennedy's honeymoon, followed by his embarrassing performance in a debate with Nikita Khrushchev at the summit conference in Vienna in May. Some historians have claimed that the 1961 Berlin Crisis, which that summer followed the building of the Berlin Wall, brought the world closer to the brink of nuclear war than did the following year's October confrontation over missiles in Cuba.[2] In 1961, the Soviets put a man into orbit and exploded a fifty-megaton hydrogen bomb, the largest nuclear weapon ever exploded. They also claimed to have built a one-hundred-megaton bomb, six thousand times more powerful than the atom bomb that had incinerated Hiroshima. The front page of the morning *New York Times* showed a map of the expanding concentric circles of complete destruction by each weapon, assuming the Empire State Building was ground zero. That day I stood at my school bus stop, looking in the direction of New York, wondering if I would actually see the fireball over the city or if it would immediately vaporize me.

At Rutgers, in March 1961 Mason announced that a crisis had developed. Increases in the undergraduate body were accelerating more quickly than had been anticipated, now due to double from 1959 to 1964. That March, Rutgers stopped accepting applications for the following school year due to a shortage of facilities. Projections of high school graduates, made a decade earlier, had underestimated and totally missed the mark.

The tidal wave of the baby boom generation had been anticipated in the first few years after World War II. During the war, the American birth rate had been three million babies per year. Although some postwar increase was anticipated, social scientists misread the tea leaves and were surprised to discover an annual birth rate in 1946 of four million and almost five million in 1947. By 1959, there were thirty million more Americans than had been anticipated, most of them under eighteen years old. As Mason himself had pointed out in 1948, the harbinger of the coming crisis in education was not then in the universities but rather in the overcrowded hospital nurseries and kindergartens throughout the state.

In 1948, the California state legislature had commissioned the "Survey of the Needs of Higher Education," which aside from enrollment trends also offered a master plan for the development of higher education in the state. Known also as the Strayer Report, it was widely accepted nationwide as a cogent needs assessment for American higher education.

Additionally, in 1959 New York governor Nelson Rockefeller commissioned a study of "the increasing demand for higher education in New York State." Known as the Heald Report, it predicted "an unprecedented rise in university enrollments, a rise so dramatic that it will significantly alter the shape of higher education." The Heald Report summarized the situation for many states, including New Jersey, and estimated that the college population would double by 1970 due to four factors:

1. An increased number of people of college age;
2. Within that number, an increased proportion of high school graduates;
3. Within that number, an increased percentage seeking college education; and
4. A decreasing number of students leaving the state to attend college.

But both the Strayer Report and the Heald Report were incorrect. The college-age population was not going to double; it would triple, with a probable peak predicted for 1974.

Traditionally, over 80 percent of New Jersey's students had sought college education outside of the state, a higher percentage than any other state. However, out-of-state public universities were now all under the same pressure to accept their own residents and so had less room for New Jersey students. University of California, Berkeley chancellor Roger Heyns would state later that New Jersey had to make room for its own students, as "California had no more room."[3] Yet in 1961, New Jersey legislators and New Jersey taxpayers remained unwilling to support increased funding. However, the state legislature did pass two bills, Assembly Bill A619 to establish two-year community colleges to take the pressure off of Rutgers and Assembly Bill A535, which allowed Rutgers to increase enrollment immediately by 520 students and appropriated $1 million for new dormitory construction.

In 1961, Governor Meyner was ineligible for re-election. Based on new studies, Mason had estimated a tripling of enrollment by 1970. The Republican Party gubernatorial platform included increased support for Rutgers, but the party's gubernatorial candidate, former U.S. secretary of labor James Mitchell, had campaigned against the 1959 education bond issue, stating that Rutgers would become a threat to New Jersey's private colleges, presumably Princeton, for example. Mitchell supported the concept of a new medical school for New Jersey as long as it was free-standing and not associated with the state university. Democratic candidate Richard Hughes was the first candidate to openly consider new taxes if needed. Hughes also wanted a new study, as the Strayer Report was considered an "inside job"; that is, like the proverbial fox sent to guard the henhouse, legislators doubted the report's credibility, as it had been drafted by academics who stood most to benefit from its recommendations.

Mason repeatedly looked to two other state universities, the University of Michigan and the University of California, and its crown jewel, Berkeley, as the ideal. He called the University of Michigan a "fourth arm of the state government,"[4] noting that Michigan's support for higher education was written into the state constitution.

Meanwhile, in 1961 Rutgers was expanding in not only total student population but also the scope of expanding numbers of individual programs.

For example, in 1961 Yale University's Center for Alcohol Studies, founded in 1921, was looking for a new home. The center was established to study the social, biological, psychological, and sociological aspects of alcohol, and Rutgers could not pass up this opportunity. The development of such a center requires more work than is well known. Would the current faculty agree to transfer, and what salary would they receive? What were the housing costs compared to Connecticut? Where would the center, with its required lecture halls, offices, and laboratory facilities, be located on an already crowded campus until its own facility could be built? Every detail from faculty appointments, tenure, research grants, and even budgets for custodial and secretarial help crossed Mason's desk, if not for approval then at least for concurrence. Mason and the Rutgers administration lobbied heavily and received a grant from the National Institute of Mental Health. The center's building, Smithers Hall, would be dedicated in 1964.[5]

In 1961, the W. K. Kellogg Foundation provided Rutgers with a $1 million grant toward the cost of planning and establishing a medical school. In 1963 the Institute for Labor and Management Relations, founded over ten years earlier, would move into its own building, funded almost entirely by union contributions.

Also in 1961, Rutgers dedicated the new Eagleton Institute "to improve the study and practice in the science of government." Already designated for Woodlawn on the Douglass campus, similar detail work was required. Other programs were established, including the new College of Engineering; the Graduate Schools of Library Science, Social Work, and Education; at Newark the Colleges of Pharmacy and Nursing; and the new Law School at Camden. Each program required committees, telephone calls, correspondence, and most of all funding from federal and state governments, bond issues, and grants. Rutgers meanwhile relied on the handouts from a reluctant legislature and support for bond issues from a general public that remained uncertain as to the place of Rutgers in the state government.

The U.S. Army's Camp Kilmer had been named for the New Brunswick poet Joyce Kilmer, who had died in World War I. Bordering Piscataway and Edison Townships, the camp was slowly deactivated after World War II.

During the 1956 Hungarian Revolution, large numbers of Hungarian refugees spent their first weeks or months in the United States in the leaky tumbledown barracks of Camp Kilmer. The army finally decided to dispose of the 1,600-acre property. Rutgers University, as a branch of the state government, was awarded 540 acres in 1964.

Mason had planned not one but three new colleges, each with 3,500 students, in federated liberal arts colleges on a single campus, modeled after the new University of California at Santa Cruz.[6]

UC Santa Cruz had been designed throughout the 1950s and had opened its doors in 1964. Due to low availability of housing within the community, the designers had planned on a residential college system whereby students within each of ten modular colleges would live at the college as well. The intent was also to provide cross-disciplinary courses and progressive and innovative teaching methods, including a "pass versus no record" grading system.

Unlike the 1963 state bond issue that failed, the 1964 New Jersey state bond issue passed, providing $40 million for new construction including the first of three colleges of the new Livingston College on the Kilmer property, which planned to open for its first classes in 1968.[7]

Summaries of activity at Rutgers during this period emphasize the amounts of money being spent, the increasing numbers of students, and the size of the budgets, which now after fifty years of hindsight and inflation seem pitifully trivial. The numbers alone do not reflect the amount of detail work that each project entailed. By the time of Mason's retirement in 1971, fully three-quarters of the physical plant of Rutgers University at all of its campuses had been built during his presidency, at a total cost in 1971 dollars of $112 million.*

It is easy to quote numbers, detailing how much more construction was taking place, how many dormitories and classrooms were added, how much increased capacity was obtained, and how many millions of dollars were spent, but that misses the point. Numbers would represent a mere objective

* This sum approximates over $1 billion in 2020 dollars.

and quantitative assessment of what was changing at Rutgers, more like a report card or a grant proposal. A subjective, or qualitative, assessment is more appropriate, because it will show not just numbers of students, graduates, or buildings but also how the next years of Mason's administration would change the footprint and the face of Rutgers as well as its soul, to take its place as a major American state university with all that implies: new departments such as Anthropology; an enlarged graduate school, with research in both sciences and humanities; community involvement; nurturing of the arts; a world-class faculty; noteworthy athletic accomplishments; increased facility for education, undergraduate, graduate, and postdoctoral; and national recognition for Mason and the Board of Governors for their highly contested 1965 support of academic freedom.

CHAPTER 16

Faith and Reason

*It is safe to say that anyone who is moved at all and in any way by religion,
and specifically the Christian religion, will sooner or later have to face the
bipolarity of faith and reason and, consciously or unconsciously, come to grips
with it.* —MWG, 1959

In November 1959, Rutgers University chaplain Bradford S. Abernethy
invited Mason to deliver a sermon at the Sunday nondenominational services in the university's Kirkpatrick Chapel. In this setting, Mason introduced his views on the bipolarity of faith and reason.

The history of Western philosophy and the development of Christian religious thought have struggled with this topic of faith versus reason even to
the present day, as faith in the literal interpretations of the various translations of the Bible stand in stark opposition to the discoveries of Copernicus,
Isaac Newton, Charles Darwin, Gregor Mendel, Albert Einstein, and even
James Watson and Francis Crick, discoveries that have formed the founda-
tions of modern science, medicine, anthropology, psychology, and political
philosophy.

In his sermon, reflecting on his own experience with faith and reason,
Mason stated that "probably the first time when most of us have had to face
it is during our undergraduate years in college."[1] He added that undergraduates, newly immersed in studies of anthropology, archaeology, history, biology, and philosophy, might query whether or not the simple instruction of
their Sunday school lessons adequately addressed their many questions. He
stated, "They need not lose their faith nor become religious skeptics as a
result of these discoveries, but they must come to recognize that there is a
problem here which must be wrestled with."[2]

Mason had attended Hartford's Asylum Hill Congregational Church every Sunday during his childhood and adolescence. His early religious training under Reverend Willis Howard Butler had stirred Mason to a life of action rather than pure religious contemplation to occur once a week on Sunday mornings.

Mason also went to church regularly at Jesus College and later while in graduate school at Harvard. When visiting Palestine in 1945, he recoiled from the hypocrisy of the commercialization of early Christian sites, but still he stated in a letter to Julia that "he preferred to be a believer."[3]

As a parent, Mason sent all four of us children to Sunday school but never spoke to us about it. Once at Rutgers, he rarely attended church himself until he was inaugurated as president. He then attended weekly Sunday services at Kirkpatrick Chapel, requiring me to go with him once I had been confirmed at Christ Church in downtown New Brunswick and therefore was presumably old enough to sit still for over an hour. But when the university was not in session and there were no services on campus, Mason did not attend church elsewhere.

Mason's undergraduate studies at Aberdeen and Cambridge had taken him deeper and deeper into Greek philosophy and into the writings of the early Christian theologians who relied so heavily on Greek culture and whose "thinking and preaching constantly revolved around the two poles of Faith and Reason."[4] His own ability to read these early texts in their original language, noting how the translations had changed over the centuries, had clearly amplified his awareness of this conflict and drew him to a personal understanding of the confluence of the Greeks' reason and the Christian faith.

For the Western mind, the controversy of faith and reason began in ancient Ionia, where early Greek philosophers began to question whether the world was totally under the whim of the gods or was subject to some natural laws. Socrates was sentenced to death for corrupting the minds of Athenian youth in part by denying the gods. Yet even Socrates insisted that there was "an element of the divine in human experience."[5]

Saint Paul used the Greek Pan-Mediterranean infrastructure to spread the word of Jesus, tying the similarities of the Greek philosophers' rational deduction of a singular divine wisdom, the Greek Logos, to that of the "Word" of the Gospel according to John.* Philo of Alexandria "appears to have been the first to have attempted to integrate Christian revelation and philosophy, faith and reason."[6] Later, the Neo-Platonists were instrumental in further joining Greek philosophy with Christian theology, culminating in the writings of Saint Augustine, who stated, "I have faith in order to understand."[7] Mason paraphrased this to "have faith, in order that reason may lead you to wisdom."[8]

Saint Thomas Aquinas and William of Ockham offered a short-lived reconciliation to the bipolarity. The irreconcilable wedge between faith and reason truly began with Copernicus, whose calculations indicated that Earth was not the center of the universe. The Copernican Revolution and the subsequent Age of Science further divided the faithful from the scientists. Darwin's theory, followed by Mendel's discovery of the genetic code, seemed to make the schism permanent.

Mason's interdepartmental course, titled "The Traditions of Western Religious Thought," which he cotaught with his colleague and best friend, Provost Dick Schlatter, fenced frequently with the roles of theology and philosophy. With his characteristic hyperbole, Mason stated that "theology and religious philosophy" had "made no progress since the eighteenth century."[9] He stated that theologians, who had once served to explain to people the divergence of religion and science, had failed to address that ever-widening split and thereby weakened their own authority. They thus widened the gap between those who believed in a literal, infallible, and somehow divinely inspired English translation of the Bible, no matter whose translation, and those who chose to assimilate into their faith some of the new discoveries of science, such as the genetic code and fossil records. Mason believed that it is the purpose of theology to provide the spiritual leadership to consolidate the apparent divergent paths of faith and reason, allowing people to trust the

* "In the beginning was the Word." John 1:1. In the original Greek, the "Word" is "Logos," thus tying Greek philosophy to Christian faith. This is well summarized in Tarnas, *The Passion of the Western Mind*, 101–103.

advances in science without having to violate the essential tenets of their religious faith.

Mason's moral compass was a combination of faith and reason. From the side of the philosopher, Mason adhered to Immanuel Kant's categorical imperative, a moral command with no conditions and no strings attached. This imperative commanded "the absolute and ultimate and irreducible dignity of man, every man, regardless of his color or his religion or his nationality or his achievements or his talents or any other peculiar and separate qualities he may possess."[10]

Mason was also a strong proponent that the teachings of Socrates are as valid today as they ever were. "We need not be disciples of Socrates to accept the validity of his principle that 'The unexamined life is not worth living.' Every one of us pushes out of sight elements in our experience which are unpleasant reminders of a more sordid kind of life. . . . Today the searchlight of contemporary events is forcing us to do a little of the self-examining which Socrates recommended. If this can free us to act as we know in our heart of hearts we must, then Socrates will not have died in vain."[11]

Mason believed both in Kant's moral imperative and, like Socrates, that there is an objective standard of right and wrong. Mason's belief was based on both his philosophy and his religion. Like Socrates, Mason rejected the moral relativism of the Greek Sophists, which allowed for a situational morality that could fluctuate with the times. But Mason's compass was not set exclusively by philosophers alone. There were moral absolutes that burned inside him, and the teachings of Christ were a moral absolute. "Another principle suggests a way out of the moral frustration and paralysis which characterizes so much of our national behavior today. Its source is Leviticus, is made central by Jesus in the Gospel according to Luke, and is illustrated by the parable of the Good Samaritan: 'Thou shalt love thy neighbor as thyself.' It is a program for immediate action."[12]

Mason taught how Plato's Allegory of the Cave describes "a sudden flash of understanding" and the metaphor of "truth by illumination," equally similar not only to Newton's sudden insight "under the apple tree" but also to Saul's on the road to Damascus. Christians will state that faith and illumination can come only from the grace of God through Christ, which even though unverifiable is "supported by the understanding that it conveys."[13]

In his 1959 sermon in Kirkpatrick Chapel, Mason's best fix for the bipolarity was from Saint Augustine, who concluded that truth "comprises both faith and reason. Without faith, reason works in the dark, . . . but faith cannot be achieved by reason alone."

Whether one calls it faith or hypothesis, Mason concluded that Sunday morning that "the power and goodness of a loving God has enabled us to deduce that life is meaningful and purposeful; that personal and social morality are not merely the conventions of the moment; [and] that human beings can to a greater and greater extent hope to grasp by reason, and understand, the significance of both the moral and the physical order of the universe."[14]

Was Mason's faith simply a product of his New England Protestant upbringing, or was there more to it for him than sitting in a wooden pew for one hour per week? We know that he had once moved toward a career in the ministry, only to be exasperated by its rigid dogma. We know that he advocated a thoughtful self-examination of one's own beliefs and motivations, to "attempt to re-examine the principles upon which you have based your entire life."[15]

Alfred North Whitehead's influence on Mason is most keenly evident in this controversy. Mason had struggled with this polarity as an undergraduate when he first translated the religious texts for himself. As a graduate student, he later found resolution in Whitehead's cosmology, which proposed to relieve the controversy between religion and science, and noted that philosophy "must not be afraid to employ the results of science and it must not ignore the claims of religious experience."[16]

We can see from Mason's own words that he believed in the divine. We can never know his view of the nature of that divine or to what degree his belief was best described as the philosophical divine wisdom, the Logos of the Greeks, or his faith in "the power and goodness of a loving God," but it is clear that in his search to resolve the bipolarity of faith and reason, Mason found his own peace in combining the elements of both.

CHAPTER 17

Score Once More, 1965

A college which has a sports program for any other reason than an educational reason is soon going to lose control of the program. If the college goes in for sports as a part of a program of public entertainment and public relations, then the public, and not the university, will dictate what kind of entertainment it wants.   —MWG, December 8, 1960

In the autumn of 1964, my older brother Charlie was at a freshman orientation at the University of Wisconsin. Standing at the exit was a tall athlete holding an oar, known among rowers as a "sweep." The athlete was stopping all the tall freshmen and asking if anyone wanted to go out for freshman crew. Charlie was 6'3", just like Mason, and broad-shouldered like our mom's brother Walter, who had rowed at Harvard. Charlie was also a trim athlete, having lettered in varsity football and lacrosse, but except for rowing his small skiff on the Shrewsbury River, he had never rowed before. He joined the crew on a whim, exactly the same as Mason had thirty years before. Just like Cambridge, American colleges did not recruit high school rowers for crew. First of all, there weren't many high schools that even offered it. But more importantly, in that era intercollegiate athletics were viewed as an adjunct to scholarship. As Rutgers All-American tailback Billy Austin (Rutgers class of 1959) once agreed, "At Rutgers, football is a part of college; college is not a part of football."[1] The Wisconsin crew had no gate receipts like Big Ten football; a spectator could watch the races for free from the campus.

For the freshman crew, everyone was a walk-on. New to the sport, all were learning at the same time. At Rutgers in 1964, athletics still fit that model. It was the model with which Mason was most accustomed, in 1930 having been a walk-on for the crew at Cambridge. The coaches had all been volunteers, former oarsmen themselves. Having not been an athlete in high school, Mason had found that regular strenuous athletics improved his strength, his mental outlook, and his studies. His time on the Jesus crew was instrumental to his education and to his future career.

Mason had enjoyed attending football games in high school, although he did not wish to play. Once while recuperating from his arthritis at the Devereux Rehabilitation Hospital in Marblehead, Massachusetts, he even talked his physician into letting him out of the hospital so he could attend the Harvard-Yale game with his father and his brother Spencer. As a graduate student at Harvard and later as a junior faculty member at Columbia, Mason enjoyed attending the football games. At Rutgers, he did the same. The games were always played on Saturday afternoons. As president, he could walk to the home games and, during his entire presidency, rarely missed an away game.

Mason strongly supported the initial decision of the National College Football Foundation to locate the National College Football Hall of Fame at Rutgers, since the very first intercollegiate football game had been played in New Brunswick between Princeton and Rutgers, commencing the longest-standing college football rivalry between the two schools.

But Mason's favorite sport, obviously, was crew, difficult for spectators who only get to see about fifteen seconds of a seven-minute race. At Rutgers, Mason quickly endeared himself to the rowing coaches and was soon invited regularly to assist with timekeeping. This got him a front-row seat in the official launch so he could watch the whole race.

A Rutgers legend exists that Mason, ever articulate, rarely swore. Apparently, in 1952 the class of 1914 was searching for a gift to Rutgers and was considering an ornamental mace* for the College Avenue gymnasium. This was a time when Rutgers finances were at their worst. Faculty were threatened with layoffs, and many had to seek extra part-time employment, such as Mason's work on the quiz show *Two for the Money*. An apocryphal story maintains that when asked for his recommendation for the class of 1914

---

*Mace: A medieval heavy bludgeon or war club, sometimes used as a symbol for athletic prowess.

Mason's enthusiastic support of the Rutgers crew, which included obtaining funding to send rowers to the Olympic Trials, new rowing shells, and alumni support for a new boathouse, won him an open-ended invitation to serve as a timekeeper for the races, giving him a front-row seat to his favorite sport. How many university presidents get to do that? (Photo credit: Rutgers University Library Special Collections and University Archives)

donation, Mason allegedly replied, "We don't need an ax; we need a fucking boathouse."[2] The class of 1914 donated a beautiful boathouse.

Also in 1952, the crew coach came to Mason with a problem, knowing that Mason would understand. Two rowers, Tom Price and Chuck Logg, had qualified for the new Pan American Games, but there was no money to send them. Fortunately, Mason had an answer.

In early 1950 Mason had sent a memo to the Rutgers comptroller, Mr. A. S. Johnson. Mason had received a $100 honorarium from the New Jersey Parent Teachers Conference. He had decided that the money was not really his, since he had been invited to speak because of his position at

Rutgers. He also felt that it was impolitic to refuse to accept the honorarium. Mason asked Mr. Johnson if the honorarium could be placed in a cash account where it could be used to benefit the students for those situations that fell outside the budget, noting that especially in the lean years of the early 1950s, "there is no possibility for setting aside in the regular university budget extra funds for such purposes."[3] Johnson agreed that there were many similar accounts for alumni monetary donations for specific purposes, such as study grants and music scholarships. Johnson set up the account, calling it the Mason Gross Special Students' Aid Fund (27-9111-935), in order "to provide those special attributes of a superior college education which cannot be covered or anticipated in the annual budget."[4] In the early 1950s while campaigning throughout New Jersey for increased funding for public education, Mason spoke as many as one hundred times per year. Honoraria included $100 from Brooklyn College, $50 from the New Jersey Dental Society, and $15 from the Carteret High School Student Organization for speaking at its commencement. Mason also donated half of his per diem from the Labor Mediation Board whenever a labor dispute in any way involved Rutgers, as he felt that he was double-dipping. In 1953, Mason donated $1,000 of his own money into this fund.

As a result, in 1952 Mason was able to fund the crew coach's request to support the travel for rowers Tom Price and Chuck Logg to the Pan-American games. They won in their event, "pair without coxswain," and then went on to win the Olympic Gold medal for the United States in Helsinki in 1952. Without the financial assistance, they could not even have made it to the Olympic trials that year.

Over the following two decades, funds from this account were used for many purposes, including sending the freshman crew to Florida; buying a new shell when the university budget could not support the purchase; assisting with a Glee Club European tour, which was typically financed though specific alumni donations; and rebuilding the Kirkpatrick Chapel Aeolian-Skinner pipe organ.

For many university presidents, athletics is the elephant in the room. Regardless of which division the college plays in, a winning football season always calms the alumni and helps to open their wallets. In 1961, Rutgers experienced its first undefeated football season.* In March 1966, the Rutgers basketball team advanced to the Final Four of the NCAA Championships. In both years, the alumni were ecstatic.

For Mason's entire twenty-five-year career as Rutgers was growing and changing, the role of college athletics was changing even more radically at Rutgers as well as nationwide. Policies that had been suitable for a small private college in 1945 were woefully vague and inadequate for a state university in 1970. Athletic policy would be used to guide choices of facilities, capital expenditures, the hiring of coaches, scholarships, and the overall role of college athletics, if any, in a student's education.

Mason recognized that his anachronistic view of the role of athletics in college education would not last and that "the ideal of participatory athletics" had "come from another world."[5] Deep inside, he knew that he was going to lose this one, but that did not keep him from drawing a line in the sand and holding out throughout his own administration.

There was "a mounting pressure to move Rutgers in the direction of big-time athletics. . . . [M]uch of the pressure was coming not from alumni but instead from New Jersey politicians and businessmen."[6] In the early 1960s college football was king, with televised bowl games and playoffs. The Monday morning *New York Times* listed all the college sports scores from the weekend. Professional football games were poorly attended and rarely televised.

David "Sonny" Werblin (Rutgers class of 1931) changed all that. As a previous producer for Music Corporation of America and president of its television division, Werblin knew how to work the power of television. He bought the New York Titans football team and changed its name to the Jets. He drafted quarterback Joe Namath from the University of Alabama for an unprecedented high salary and made Broadway Joe into the first professional

---

* Before the last game of the season, against Columbia, Rutgers was 8 and 0. The old stadium was packed, standing room only. At the end of the third quarter, Columbia was ahead 19–0. It was dreadful. Then, Rutgers scored *five* times in the fourth quarter and won. What a game!

football superstar, paving the way for dozens of others. Werblin's AFL Jets defeated the powerful NFL Baltimore Colts in the third Super Bowl. Werblin later built and managed the New Jersey Meadowlands Sports Complex, securing his legacy as being instrumental in the development of professional football into the economic and entertainment powerhouse that it is today.

As an alumnus, Werblin was a strong supporter of Rutgers. From the early 1960s, he began providing gentle pressure on Mason that Rutgers football should expand in scope. Elected to the Rutgers Board of Trustees in 1966, Werblin lobbied for a New York Jets game to be played at Rutgers's old stadium, even to the point of offering to pay for lights to be installed so the game could be played at night.

Sources differ as to the extent of Werblin's goals. Werblin understood television, and he understood sports. He stated that Rutgers could never succeed in a league such as the Big Ten because of the likely failure of attendance and subsequent minimal gate receipts,[7] since football fans in the New York metropolitan area already had so many choices due to the proximity of professional teams in nearby Baltimore, Philadelphia, and New York City.

When Mason retired in 1971, Governor William Cahill selected Werblin for the Rutgers Board of Governors. Mason's successor, Edward Bloustein, was more easily convinced. At that time, "it unexpectedly turned out that the small group of loyal alumni boosters whose demand for big-time athletics had been so stoutly resisted under Mason Gross would find themselves, under Edward Bloustein, receiving powerful support from a Trenton political culture whose model of public universities was sport centered schools like Nebraska and Oklahoma and Ohio State."[8] Bloustein agreed to push for big-time football and so dropped Rutgers's long-standing rivalry against Princeton.

Controversy has existed throughout the years about the role of athletics, especially football and basketball, in university education. Mason's key point was not to argue against one kind of program or another but instead to emphasize that all participants must understand the nature of that program, its governing policies, and its limitations and thus to generate a similar set of expectations among all parties.

Mason knew that once college athletics relies on gate receipts, the customers of the athletic program are no longer the students trying to get an education but instead are the spectators, who then demand something for their money beyond a football game against Princeton. Once the spectators dictate the program, he added, the university has lost control of it.

Mason asked, "If professors are evaluated on the basis of scholarship, how should coaches be evaluated?" If athletics was truly a part of a student's educational process, then were coaches to be faculty as well? Were they to be evaluated on the number of their players who graduated with honors? Classically, coaches were evaluated by the extent of their victories. Therefore, the coaches' success and their professional advancement depended on attracting the players who could provide those victories. This could get expensive. Werblin assured Mason that "if the university financed the transition to a higher level of competition, the program would ultimately pay for itself."[9] Promises that increased gate receipts and television contracts would improve a university's financial condition and pay for athletic scholarships never panned out. Decades later, the final result is that the high cost of the football and basketball programs has forced the elimination of many varsity sports, including Mason's favorite, the crew, and, ironically, even Werblin's own favorite from his days at Rutgers, namely intercollegiate varsity swimming.

Mason argued that if athletics was to be considered a part of an educational process, then it needed to be a part of the university budget and not subject to the fluctuation of gate receipts and concessions contracts.

Lost in the controversy was that Mason was only trying to maintain Rutgers as a university where the student's education and ultimate success as an educated individual took precedence over any athletic program. As New Jersey governor Thomas Kean later stated, Rutgers needs to "care more about having the best English department in the country than about having the best football team."[10]

Mason supported athletics, just as he supported music, as long as that goal of value to the individual student was not lost. He even traveled once to an

NCAA meeting in Denver to provide his personal support for a prospective student football player on a Barr athletic scholarship. The NCAA had ruled that the student's poor high school class rank, from a small and competitive private school, predicted that he would not do well academically. The NCAA had planned to penalize Rutgers for admitting an athlete who was not likely to perform above the NCAA's arbitrary minimum GPA,[11] called the 3.0 Rule.* Mason viewed this action as another of many artificial barriers that existed only to limit equal opportunity and access to education for minority students from disadvantaged backgrounds. In Denver, he explained to Walter Beyers, the NCAA president, that the student was *going* to play at Rutgers regardless of the rule, and the NCAA could revoke Rutgers's right to participate if it chose. The NCAA yielded to Mason's argument and allowed the student to play.

In June 1965, Mason flew our entire family from Newark to Syracuse to watch Charlie and the Wisconsin freshman crew rowing in the IRA (Intercollegiate Rowing Association) National Championship Regatta, a race considered to be the U.S. collegiate championship of rowing. Mason had attended this annual event regularly for many years and used the occasion to revisit with his first cousin Bill Welch, who was teaching political science at Hamilton College. But this year, Charlie was participating in the race. I was thirteen, and this was my first airplane flight ever. Mason sat me by the window, explaining what was going to occur and what the sounds from the aircraft engine and hydraulics all meant so I would not be alarmed. He warned me that the Boeing 727 "WhisperJet" would climb very steeply, and right after liftoff, in compliance with noise abatement regulations, the pilots would pull the power so far back that it might sound like the engines had quit. Mason assured me that they would not. He was warm, pleasant, and conversant, and in my experience he seemed so out of character at that moment. He was with his family and was en route to see his son rowing in

---

* The 3.0 rule combined SAT score and class rank to determine a student's eligibility under NCAA auspices.

his own favorite sporting event. I think at that moment Mason was as happy as I'd ever seen him.

Meanwhile, there was trouble brewing in New Brunswick over comments that had been made during an April teach-in on the U.S. conduct of the war in Vietnam, comments that would draw Mason more into the public eye and would have long-lasting effects on his administration.

CHAPTER 18

The Inflection Point, 1965

Does a man have a right to speak out freely and to state his convictions in a controversial area, . . . or does he accept a limitation on his civil rights solely by virtue of becoming a member of a tax-supported institution? If we ever lose sight of that point, we are in serious trouble. —MWG, August 8, 1965

In October 1965, I was thirteen years old, standing behind another customer at the Vargas Hobby Shop on Easton Avenue, waiting my turn to pay for a spool of electrical wire. The customer, a slender man in his mid- to late fifties, raised his voice in anger to the store owner.

"If I were the governor of New Jersey," said the customer, pounding his fist on the counter, "I'd take Mason Gross out, stand him up against a wall, and shoot him."

It was only a few weeks before the election in the most venomous gubernatorial campaign in the history of New Jersey, a state that specializes in venomous politics. The main issue was not the state budget deficit but instead whether or not the incumbent governor should fire the university president who had upheld a professor's civil liberty to speak his mind.

This issue began the previous April over a teach-in pertaining to the Vietnam War. The story has a lot of interwoven moving parts besides the Vietnam War, including academic freedom, constitutional rights of free speech, anticommunist fervor, and a nascent conservative backlash against civil rights legislation, President Lyndon Johnson's Great Society, the March on Selma, and the 1965 Watts riots. But let us start with the event itself.

Ironically, perhaps the single most seminal public event in Mason's presidency occurred while he and Julia were out of the country on a three-month

Carnegie Travel Grant in Africa, the Middle East, and the Soviet bloc. Provost Dick Schlatter was acting president during Mason's absence.

On the evening of April 23, 1965, a new type of event called a teach-in occurred in Scott Hall on the College Avenue campus. The organizers of the event had planned an all-night session in order to generate an open discussion on the Vietnam War, in which the involvement of American troops was still in its infancy. Faculty members known to have strong opinions on the war, those both in favor of and those opposed to increased American involvement, had been invited to express their opinions. It was clear that this was a public event, an extracurricular activity and not a formal class.

The event was well attended, with 1,300 students and faculty seated about on the floor of a lecture room with seats for 500. Serious arguments, with some raised voices, were expressing the opposing concerns. In the early hours of the following morning, an unimposing history professor in his second year on the Rutgers faculty stood up to speak.

Professor Eugene Genovese had been born in Brooklyn in 1930 to a working-class Italian immigrant family. His father was a dockworker. Genovese had expressed communist sympathy as early as age fifteen. He graduated from Brooklyn College in 1953 and earned a PhD in history from Columbia in 1959. He was a specialist in the history of the American South and slavery in America, and his excellent scholarship was never in question. His promotion to associate professor and his tenure had already been approved by the time of the teach-in.

As he spoke, Genovese first precisely expressed his frame of reference for the teach-in, reminding the audience that this was not a classroom but instead was an open forum where each speaker was invited to express his or her personal concerns of "vital questions not normally proper in class." Genovese specified that speakers each had the responsibility to outline their own prejudices at the outset and that "no matter how deep the ideological and political divisions among us, it is vital to our country's survival that we find a common basis on which to defend the peace."

Then came two sentences that would launch Rutgers into the epicenter of the 1965 gubernatorial election and, more importantly, would resonate throughout the remainder of Mason's presidency. Genovese spoke the following exact words, which later were widely misquoted: "Those of you who know me know that I am a Marxist and a socialist. Therefore, unlike most of my distinguished colleagues here this morning I do not fear or regret the impending Viet Cong victory in Vietnam; I welcome it."

Vietnam in 1965 was not the same Vietnam it would become by 1968. The conflict was still considered by some a civil war. To others it was the front line of communist global aggression. Prior to the spring of 1965, the only American ground forces in Vietnam had been advisors and trainers originally assigned to the Military Advisory Assistance Group, which had been in-country for the previous ten years. But only one month prior to the teach-in, President Johnson had committed the very first American combat troops, a battalion of marines whose specific assignment was the protection of those U.S. air bases in Vietnam, which had come under increasing threat of attack by Viet Cong forces. By the spring of 1965, there were 16,000 U.S. military personnel in Vietnam. Since July 1959, 315 American soldiers and airmen had died there.

For Americans, the Vietnam War was not yet the quagmire that soon began to enflame and divide the United States. But for many Vietnamese, 1965 was just another year in a decades-long battle for their independence from foreign control.

———

In the nineteenth century resource-rich Indochina, a territory that included what would later become Vietnam, Cambodia, and Laos, was under colonial control of the French, who introduced Catholicism, often by force, and required the use of French for all official communication. The brutality of each of the European colonial powers is well documented, and the French were not shy in forcing themselves on the Vietnamese, whom they considered racially inferior.

At the beginning of World War II, the Nazi invasion of France led to the formation of the French Vichy collaborationist government, which allowed the French the illusion of nominal control over their own affairs. In 1941 the

Japanese, in response to an American embargo of strategic raw materials, especially Vietnamese rubber and Indonesian oil, occupied French Indochina with the tacit agreement of the powerless Vichy government.

The racist brutality of the Japanese occupation is well documented and exceeded even that of the French. As the world war turned against the Japanese, American operatives under the auspices of the Office of Strategic Services (OSS), predecessor of the Central Intelligence Agency, had parachuted into Indochina in order to bolster anti-Japanese resistance. The most powerful, most organized, and most effective anti-Japanese organization was also communist, led by an expatriate named Ho Chi Minh who had lived in Paris and Moscow before returning to Indochina in the 1930s. Any nationalists hoping effectively to fight the Japanese joined Ho's organization, the Viet Minh. Thus, the Viet Minh became both a nationalist and a communist entity, a combination that was unique to Southeast Asia.

Ho had read the Atlantic Charter, the 1941 agreement between British prime minister Winston Churchill and U.S. president Franklin Roosevelt that had promised support for the independence of the former European colonies. Ho also received assurance from the OSS representatives that Roosevelt advocated independence for colonial peoples.

But by September 1945 when the Japanese surrendered, Roosevelt was dead, as was his postwar vision. His promises were long forgotten. On September 2, V-J Day, Ho published Vietnam's declaration of independence. It began with the words, quoted from an eighteenth-century American document, "All men are created equal,"[1] and reflected the degree to which Ho had accepted OSS assurance that the United States would support independence for Indochina.

But the world had changed. The Americans wanted to protect war-torn Europe from the threat of communist insurrection. In order to do so, the Americans needed the support of the French. And the French wanted their colonies back.

So, consistent with the political quid pro quo that lubricates all international diplomacy, the Americans turned a blind eye when the French Army, grossly undermanned, released Japanese soldiers from Allied prisoner-of-war camps, armed them with their own confiscated weapons, and sent them to fight the Viet Minh.

The world has come to recognize the cost, in both lives and matériel, of resistance against movements of national liberation. But in the late 1940s that lesson had not been learned, and the American conservatives were crying madly over who lost China to the communists. By 1954, the French resistance against the Viet Minh was going poorly. The French repeatedly requested American support. U.S. president Harry Truman had begun support of the French in Indochina, and President Dwight Eisenhower continued it, responding only with military supplies, ultimately providing 80 percent of the support for the war.[2] Eisenhower resisted requests from his own military advisors to consider supporting the French with American combat troops or even with the use of atomic weapons. After the disastrous French defeat at the mountain redoubt of Dien Bien Phu, the French capitulated and departed Vietnam in accordance with the Geneva Accords of 1954.

The U.S. representatives did not sign the Geneva agreement but did agree to adhere to its covenants, which included a military withdrawal such that Vietnam would be temporarily divided into a northern territory, governed by the communists, and a southern territory under a noncommunist administration. The agreement stated that Vietnam would reunite subsequent to elections in 1956.

Ho and the Viet Minh agreed to the Geneva Accords solely because of elections. They knew they could eventually win militarily or also politically, so why not stop the bloodshed? It appeared to be the path of least resistance to an ultimate victory that they felt was assured.

The domino theory was prevalent in American foreign policy circles at the time. With his own upcoming re-election campaign, President Eisenhower could not appear to be soft on communism or to condone the loss of another country to communism, having himself come to power accusing the Democrats of losing China. Consequently, when President Ngo Dinh Diem, having seized power in South Vietnam, cancelled the 1956 elections, the Eisenhower administration did not protest.

The civil war in Vietnam heated up again, as Ho and his allies in South Vietnam, the Viet Cong, proceeded to increase their influence both militarily and politically, albeit often with increasingly violent reprisals against Diem's supporters. One must remember that throughout history one rarely finds such brutality as in civil wars, as the sequelae from our own American Civil War continue to resonate. It becomes pointless to ask whose brutality came first or whose was the most inhumane. Internecine warfare is always the most vicious and the most violent.

Diem declared South Vietnam an independent country and successfully lobbied the U.S. government for assistance, such that by the time of the John F. Kennedy administration, still smarting from its own early foreign policy snafus, especially in Cuba, and sensitive to accusations of itself being soft on communism, American advisors of the Military Advisory Assistance Group were actively engaged in combat operations. Civil unrest in South Vietnam intensified, including self-immolation by Buddhist monks, as Diem's regime brutally suppressed any resistance. The South Vietnamese Viet Cong, which involved both military and political branches, were clearly gaining in power. Diem's brutal regime was itself violently overthrown in November 1963, only weeks before Kennedy's own assassination. A succession of military coups in South Vietnam left the world to wonder who the hell was really in charge.

American military support for South Vietnam increased under the new Johnson administration. On August 10, 1964, subsequent to a fabricated event suggesting that North Vietnamese torpedo boats had attacked the U.S. destroyer *Maddox*, the U.S. Senate, in a vote of 98–2,* and a unanimous (!) vote in the House of Representatives, passed the Gulf of Tonkin Resolution, authorizing the president to use all necessary force to protect American assets in Vietnam. With this action, the U.S. Congress abrogated to the executive branch its own constitutional authority to declare war.

---

*It was opposed by only two senators, both Democrats, Wayne Morse (Oregon) and Ernest Gruening (Alaska).

In his 1964 reelection campaign, Johnson vowed not to send American soldiers to die in Asia, knowing that he was already in a quagmire that would be difficult to resolve. But in early 1965, the American airbase at Pleiku, from which, under the authority of the Tonkin Gulf Resolution, the U.S. Air Force was launching bombing raids against North Vietnam, came under mortar attack by Viet Cong forces, resulting in significant casualties. In March 1965 Johnson ordered the 9th Marine Expeditionary Brigade into Vietnam to protect the American bases. In a dramatic amphibious assault for which they had become justifiably famous in many previous conflicts, the marines stormed ashore at Danang, unopposed. According to Lieutenant Phil Caputo, a platoon leader in the same brigade, "they charged up the beach and were met, not by machine guns and shells, but by the mayor of Danang and a crowd of schoolgirls . . . who placed flowered garlands around the Marines' necks."[3]

It is critical to note that the American public's view of the conflict was very different in 1965 than it would become in 1968 or 1971. In 1965, there was considerably more support for Johnson's actions, as the American public and the press to some degree still believed him.

With this background began the Rutgers teach-in debate in April 1965.

———

Genovese's comments were not the highpoint of the teach-in, which was dominated by a vociferous argument between two other faculty members. The following day, Provost Dick Schlatter, as acting president in Mason's absence, commented that the event was well attended, calling it a "dignified discussion at a high level, and a legitimate part of the education in free debate which all universities wish to offer their students."

The *Daily Targum*, the Rutgers student newspaper, devoted an entire issue to the teach-in but misquoted Genovese's remarks, stating instead "I am a Marxist and a Socialist and I welcome a Communist victory in Vietnam."[4] Other press coverage of the teach-in was sporadic and resulted in some negative editorials in regional newspapers.

The controversy first garnered more widespread attention in the end of May at the annual convention of the New Jersey Federation of Young Republicans, who passed a resolution questioning Genovese's fitness to teach at a public university. In June, Governor Richard Hughes, disagreeing with the content of Genovese's remarks, nonetheless responded to mounting criticism of his failure to take action by defending Genovese's right to speak his mind. By midsummer letters and editorials increased in frequency, hostile not only to Genovese and accusing him of treason but also to Mason's refusal to fire him. Hughes was steadfast in his refusal to fire either of them.

In June, state Senate majority leader Wayne Dumont won the Republican gubernatorial primary, narrow defeating conservative state senator Charles Sandman.

Having heard that Dumont was going to make Genovese a campaign issue, Mason invited Dumont to a July 29 meeting with himself, Rutgers University secretary Karl Metzger, and Board of Governors members Archie Alexander and chairman Charles Brower (Rutgers class of 1925).

On the day prior to this meeting, President Johnson had announced a "dramatic turning point in the Vietnamese conflict."[5] Relying on the authority defaulted to him by the congressional passage of the Tonkin Gulf Resolution and only one year after his campaign promise not to send "American boys" to die in Vietnam, Johnson declared that the United States was "at war in Vietnam."[6]

On the following day in his meeting with Rutgers administration, candidate Dumont expressed his strong opposition to their unwillingness to take action against Genovese but stated that in his campaign he would "not bring it up myself; I'll just answer any questions about it." That same day, however, he reversed this position and announced his intention to make this the pivotal issue in his campaign, promising if elected to fire both Genovese and Mason Gross. Dumont's remarks received widespread press coverage, reigniting the controversy.[7] Fueled by Dumont's insistence that Genovese be fired and by Mason's refusal to do so, public outcry erupted further after Johnson's July 28 declaration.

The issue garnered national attention. Both Vice President Hubert Humphrey and freshman New York senator Robert F. Kennedy campaigned in support of Hughes. Several prominent Republicans, including former president Eisenhower and New Jersey senator Clifford Case, campaigned for Dumont but remained silent on the Genovese issue.[8] Private citizen and former vice president Richard Nixon came to New Jersey to campaign for Dumont. Nixon launched into his famous red-baiting rhetoric, stating that Genovese had given "aid and comfort to the enemy" and that Genovese's actions were reflective of those occasions "when the individual's rights and the nation's security come into conflict."[9] Nixon asked if "the principle of freedom of speech requires that the state subsidize those who would destroy the system of government which protects freedom of speech."

As we know, Rutgers and the anticommunist hysteria had a history. Under Mason's administration, the climate for academic freedom at Rutgers University in 1965 had risen from the chilly 1950s, when Rutgers had become the first college or university to dismiss faculty members for relying on the Fifth Amendment's privilege against self incrimination in appearances before a congressional committee's investigation into alleged communist infiltration of academia. The American Association of University Professors (AAUP) had then censured Rutgers for summarily dismissing the professors without following Rutgers's own policy guaranteeing due process for those accused. Mason had reopened those cases when he was in charge.

Mason refused to fire Genovese, stating that he had no justification to do so. In a letter to candidate Dumont, Mason emphasized that "the American concept of free expression covers any citizen provided he violates no laws and provided there is no clear and present danger involved."[10]

By the time of the November election and my witnessing of the threat against my own father, the U.S. involvement in Vietnam had heavily intensified. Meanwhile Genovese, intoxicated by this fifteen minutes of fame, wouldn't shut up. His next statements, such as those recounting his history as a member of the Communist Party as a youth, continued to inflame the public and worsen the situation for Mason, the Rutgers Board of Governors, and Governor Hughes.

The actions of Rutgers students also helped to unsettle the situation. The student Committee for Free Speech and the Rutgers chapter of the Students for a Democratic Society proposed another Vietnam teach-in for the middle of October. Unlike the April teach-in, this meeting clearly had a partisan antiwar agenda with no pretense of allowing open discussion. Citing this agenda, Mason disapproved the request for the meeting to be held on campus, but one must surmise that he had one eye on the political ramifications.

On Tuesday, November 2, Hughes handily won re-election, with the Democrats also winning both houses of the state legislature for the first time since 1913. The Genovese affair, which had dominated pre-election news and commentary, dropped off the front page.

Yet, Mason's refusal to fire Genovese resonated in academic circles. In 1966, the AAUP awarded to Mason and to the Rutgers Board of Governors its prestigious Meiklejohn Award for Rutgers's defense of academic freedom in the Genovese affair. Interesting enough, when queried later on this matter, Mason insisted that what was at stake during the Genovese affair was not academic freedom but rather civil liberty. "Academic freedom, strictly speaking, means that a scholar who has been appointed to your faculty by reason of his competence in a particular field shall be allowed to speak within that field of competence."

Mason proposed that academic freedom is "the preservation of an atmosphere in which ideas, no matter how novel or revolutionary, can be dispassionately examined by intellectual and rational methods, free from emotionalism, fear and stupidity."[11] But, Mason insisted, the Genovese affair was not about academic freedom but instead was about civil rights, about the right to speak one's mind, when queried, on a specific issue not related to one's scholarship or area of expertise.

———

Mathematicians refer to an inflection point as that point on a curve where trends slowly reverse course and move in an opposite direction. In 1965, there occurred an inflection point in the American involvement of the Vietnam War. By the end of the year, the number of American troops in Vietnam rose to over 150,000. President Johnson had declared in July that we were "at war," substituting the Gulf of Tonkin Resolution for a de facto declaration of war from Congress.

I never told my dad about the conversation that I'd heard in the hardware store, but I did query him about the effect of the Genovese affair on the governor's race. He dismissed my concern and stated that the real issue in the race was not Genovese but rather the state deficit. In 1965, New Jersey was one of only three states with neither income tax nor sales tax, and the budget deficit was looming. Governor Hughes campaigned for re-election acknowledging that he would seek the first income tax in the state's history, a platform always unpopular with an electorate.

But, 1965 was the last good year to be a Democrat. Still riding high on the momentum of the Democrats' 1964 landslide victories at the federal level, Hughes readily defeated his Republican opponent, despite Genovese and despite Hughes's call for increased taxes. Even with Democratic majorities in both chambers of the New Jersey legislature, Hughes's proposal for a state income tax was later defeated by one vote.

This year there was also an inflection point in American race relations. Vietnam has been described as the first television war. This year would also bring televised coverage of Selma and the Watts riots. It would usher in the 1965 Civil Rights Act, mandating access to voting without discrimination. This year would prove to be a high-water mark, an inflection point, for the Democratic Party and its last ever elective cakewalk. President Johnson, by forcing the 1964 Civil Rights Act and the 1965 Voting Rights Act through a reluctant Congress, had broken the back of the invincible southern Democratic caucus, a good deed that would not go unpunished.

This year there was also another inflection point in American politics, a sharp swing to the right. By 1966, a nascent conservative backlash against the perceived threat of communism as well as against civil rights legislation, urban riots, inflation, high interest rates, and the War on Poverty returned control of the U.S. House of Representatives to the Republican Party, effectively shutting down all of Johnson's pending legislation and signaling the political renaissance of Richard Nixon.[12] This backlash also scapegoated

American universities as hotbeds of communism, anarchy, and liberalism, an accusation that American higher education remains to this day impotent to refute.

This year also served as an inflection point in Mason's presidency. The archives of Rutgers University contain many folders of the mail on this issue that Mason received from both New Jersey politicians and the public. The hate mail outnumbered the approvals by about ten to one. There are some letters mostly from alumni and many from university presidents across the nation who had been watching this situation very closely, expressing that despite their disagreement with Genovese's comments, they fully endorsed Mason's stand for academic freedom and civil rights. On the other hand, the majority of the letters reflect the writers' vehemence over Genovese's advocacy of a communist victory that would come at the cost of American lives. Many demanded that Mason fire Genovese; some recommended that Mason himself be dismissed. Over ten years after Joe McCarthy vanished in disgrace his legacy was still active, reflecting that the majority of the American public only believes in freedom of speech when that speech agrees with their own point of view. This myopia is not restricted to conservatives; it is equally present among liberals as well. Even now in the twenty-first century, our founders' core belief that freedom of speech is essential to our democracy is no longer widely supported.

The Genovese affair was a critical moment in Mason's presidency. University historian Richard McCormick noted that in 1964, the most politically active student group at Rutgers had been the Students for Goldwater. One year later, the Genovese affair "marked the boundary, the introduction of a new era,"[13] which represented the first instance of the public's new perception of the university as a breeding ground for "rebellion, radicalism and changes in the whole youth culture."[14]

Mason dismissed any significance of the Genovese affair. He saw it only as a headache. "These things turn up frequently," he said, "and they're always headaches."[15] Only with the lens of history can we look back and see that for academic freedom and civil liberties, this was a victory. But for Rutgers and for Mason we will see that it was a Pyrrhic victory, a watershed. It was the inflection point when slowly, very slowly, everything started to unwind.

CHAPTER 19

The Silent Steinway, 1965

I must have heard the Schubert C Major Symphony many times before the critical performance when all of a sudden a phrase brought a gulp to my throat and, uncontrollably, tears to my eyes. . . . That day lifted my joy in music to an entirely new plane. —MWG, June 1961

Exactly one week after Governor Richard Hughes's reelection, after the Genovese affair passed into history, on a chilly but clear November Tuesday afternoon in 1965, Vladimir Horowitz, one of the greatest pianists of all time, sat alone on Carnegie Hall's large stage, playing his first public recital in over a decade. There were only fifty people in the audience, a small and select group including Mason, Julia, and several members of the Rutgers Music Department. It was a moment to be cherished, to sit in that exquisite hall with its impeccable acoustics and to witness one of the greatest classical pianists of all time coax himself back into the public eye. Why were Mason and Julia there?

———

In Mason's living room there stood the 1895 Steinway "A" model grand piano that had belonged to his grandmother and on which he had first learned to play as a boy in Hartford. This same piano in 1938 had gone up three flights of stairs to his apartment at Columbia. By the time I was seven, my sisters were off in boarding school, and nobody at home played the piano. It gathered dust quietly in a corner of the living room.

As noted earlier, Mason had once been a virtuoso pianist in England, playing for hours every day. He had considered becoming a professional musician. He could play any music, classical or popular. We know that one of his colleagues at Cambridge, Samuel McCollough, called him the best pianist in England and that Mason gave solo recitals and even performed on RMS *Mauretania* when crossing the Atlantic.

When Mason's grandmother passed away she bequeathed the piano to him, as nobody else in his family had the slightest inclination either to play or even listen to music. Mason was living in New York City before the war and moved the piano into his apartment in Morningside Heights. He continued to play daily. Even in Italy during the war, he found occasion to play a piano when on leave.

Once on the Rutgers faculty and living in Highland Park, across the river from the campus, Mason was still playing frequently. My sister Kitty recalls that he would come home from work and play the piano. Young Ellen had requested to take piano lessons, probably having heard the music that Mason played in the evening.* In 1947, Mason purchased an Ansley record player and remarked to his parents how the LP records could contain an entire symphony on one disc. He began to play the piano less often and instead would come home and listen to the recordings after supper. Julia later told me of Mason's remark that the recordings were better than he himself could play. Having been such a gifted pianist at one time, it would be frustrating to watch one's skill deteriorate and not have the time to maintain it. It was easier just to let it go.

Ellen and Kitty also remember Mason playing songs at Houston Peterson's house on Cape Cod during summer vacations, but those trips had stopped by 1950. By the time the family had moved to Rumson in 1954, he had stopped playing almost entirely. When the family moved from Highland Park to Rumson, his daily commute had changed from five minutes to fifty minutes each way. Many evenings he was out at meetings. He may also have been too tired to play. Perhaps he was just hungry and wanted to relax. Perhaps he did not want to wake the youngest children, or perhaps the details of family life precluded any serious attempt to play regularly. Somehow dur-

---

*Ellen began her lessons at age six from Ms. Olga Von Till, a Hungarian pianist who had studied under Bela Bartok and lived two blocks from the Gross family at 400 Second Avenue with her husband, Samuel Carmell, a virtuoso violinist who was conductor and music director of the Plainfield Symphony Orchestra.

ing this period, the desire to play disappeared. Kitty recalls once when she was practicing a sonata that Mason, sitting in the same room and having heard her play it over and over, suggested brusquely that she could now move on to something else.

With rare exception the piano sat quiet, no longer a "friend and confidant"[1] but just a large piece of dusty and sun-faded cherry-wood furniture with yellowed ivory keys and a squeaky damper pedal. The dogs cowered under it during thunderstorms.

———

Immediately adjacent to the main Rutgers administration building, Old Queens, stands the Kirkpatrick Chapel, built in 1873 in memory of Sophia Kirkpatrick.[2] The widow of a Rutgers trustee, she had left her entire estate to the college. Originally intended for religious training, the chapel briefly housed the college library but eventually became the site for weekly mandatory religious services, a common practice in private colleges of that era. Built in German gothic style in 1873, the chapel still features four opalescent stained-glass windows by Louis Tiffany. In 1917, music professor Howard McKinney (Rutgers class of 1913) oversaw the installation of a pipe organ built by Ernest M. Skinner, the premier organ builder in the United States, whose pipe organs are located also at Harvard University and at New York City's Saint Thomas Episcopal Church and Cathedral of St. John the Divine.

In 1955, Rutgers was looking for a new chapel organist. A superbly qualified applicant, David Drinkwater, had been born in Kokomo, Indiana, in 1928. Graduating from the University of Indiana with a BA in music, he served two years in the U.S. Air Force as an intelligence officer, assigned to Puerto Rico to run an air force country club. Leaving military service in 1954, David then attended the School of Sacred Music in New York City, which was at the time associated with the Union Theological Seminary and Riverside Church but has since relocated to Yale. His music professor at Indiana had told him to get to the seminary a week early in order to be first in line for any job postings. David found immediate employment as the assistant organist at Temple Emmanuel and at St. Paul's Chapel. He also saw a notice for a part-time university organist at Rutgers University, an hour away by train in New Brunswick, New Jersey.[3]

David interviewed with F. Austin "Soup" Walter (Rutgers class of 1932) and Howard McKinney (Rutgers class of 1913). McKinney took David over to Old Queens to meet the university provost. David recalls that after a few pleasantries, Mason immediately began to query him on the condition of the Kirkpatrick Skinner pipe organ, which had become significantly worn out. David was floored that the provost knew so much about music and specifically pipe organs. Mason knew that it was a Skinner and knew the names of all the stops, ranks, and registers. He even recommended adding a register for French horn. Mason found discretionary funds for a $35,000 rebuild of the organ, which took three years to accomplish.

When later interviewing for a full-time position at Rutgers, David was also offered a position in a well-endowed church in Kilgore, Texas, an oil town of ten thousand people one hour from Shreveport and two hours from Dallas. Kilgore offered an annual salary of $14,000. Rutgers started at $3,800 per year but quickly upped the ante to $4,800. David preferred the opportunity of music at a university and so turned down the Texas job.

When David came to Rutgers, now a state university, Sunday services were still available but no longer required for students. In 1958 David took over the direction of the Kirkpatrick Chapel Choir, mixed voices of men from Rutgers and women from the music program at Douglass College. They performed weekly for Sunday services, singing challenging motets from classical composers such as Brahms, Stravinsky, Verdi, and Ives. During fall finals week, with the Rutgers all-male glee club under the direction of Soup Walter, the choir hosted an annual free Christmas concert, "Christmas in Carol and Song," a program similar to the famous "Lessons and Carols" performed every Christmas Eve by the Kings' College Chapel at Cambridge University.

David's mother once came for a visit from Indiana. David offered to introduce her to Mason Gross. She agreed, not sure of the importance of meeting the university provost. She performed a double take when David introduced them.

"You!" she exclaimed when Mason met them at the top of the stairs. She recognized him as the former onstage moderator of her favorite quiz show, *Two for the Money.*

David and his own organ students from Douglass College gave weekly organ recitals every Tuesday at 12:15 P.M. David recalls fondly that Mason would frequently try to pin him down way ahead of time, asking what pieces he proposed to play in recitals that were weeks in the future. David had never planned that far in advance. Mason's pocket calendars, which outline his entire professional life from 1951 to 1971, include an entry for every Tuesday during the school year, "12:15 KC organ recital," where he sat alone in the darkened back row, one leg crossed over the other, his chin resting in his fingertips, in his "aural oasis," his only peaceful moment in a busy day at Rutgers.

Kirkpatrick Chapel was eventually caught in the cross fire of church versus state. As Rutgers struggled to grow into its new role as a state university, one of the questions ultimately asked was what is the role of Christian-based Sunday services in a public university. Such a question never came up at Princeton or Columbia, private universities that were not responsible to state authority or voters. Meanwhile, during the 1950s and 1960s, as Rutgers eased into its new role, weekly Sunday services at Kirkpatrick Chapel continued, led by Chaplain Brad Abernethy, with music provided by David Drinkwater and the Kirkpatrick Chapel Choir, and operated quietly under the radar.

———

Music professor Howard McKinney (Rutgers class of 1913) was well known in music circles in both New York and Philadelphia. His 1934 book *Discovering Music: A Course in Music Appreciation* was used for high school music education throughout the nation.

McKinney first made the connection for Eugene Ormandy and his Philadelphia Orchestra to come to Rutgers. Later, the Los Angeles, Baltimore, Cleveland, and London Symphony Orchestras played there as well. These orchestras were often on tour, with weekend concerts scheduled in New York

City. McKinney arranged for them to play at Rutgers in the College Avenue gymnasium on Thursday evenings. Ormandy was especially impressed with the Rutgers University Choir and used them frequently.

In November 1963, the Rutgers University Choir had been rehearsing the Brahms Requiem under Ormandy's direction. For the evening of Monday, November 25, immediately prior to Thanksgiving, Ormandy had scheduled a performance of the Brahms Requiem in the Rutgers College Avenue gymnasium, since Rutgers had no auditorium. However, on the preceding Friday, November 22, President John F. Kennedy was assassinated in Dallas, Texas. That same evening, Ormandy called Mason asking if the University Chorus was available Saturday morning for a concert. The chorus traveled into New York City and, with Ormandy and the Philadelphia Symphony Orchestra, on Saturday morning performed a live radio broadcast of the Brahms Requiem, which was rebroadcast on Sunday.*

Many colleges cancelled classes and all other events for Monday, November 25, the day of Kennedy's funeral. Some closed for the week, sending their students home. Home for part of the day, Mason was tense, edgy, and angry; he watched the funeral quietly. He was visibly shaken.

My sister Kitty recalls being home from college that Monday. After watching Kennedy's funeral on television, she and Mason went to the Rutgers College Avenue gymnasium where Ormandy was holding the originally scheduled Brahms concert. She remembers mostly that at the end of the concert, there was no applause. Everyone just got up and left quietly.[4]

Having performed at Rutgers consecutively for fourteen years, Ormandy finally admitted to Mason his frustration at playing in the gymnasium. The acoustics were clearly inadequate, and there was no facility for his musicians

*David Drinkwater and baritone David Thaxton recall going into New York City to Carnegie Hall. Others recall that they went to Philadelphia. It was a turbulent weekend, and accounts will vary. The important point to remember is that Ormandy called for the choir, and Mason sent them.

At a December 1961 dinner noting the selection of Rutgers as the future home of the National College Football Hall of Fame, Mason shared the head table with President John F. Kennedy and General Douglas MacArthur. Kennedy's famous comment on this occasion was that Americans had become a nation of spectators, and their favorite sport was sitting and watching other people exercise. (Photo credit: Rutgers University Library Special Collections and University Archives)

to dress or to tune their instruments except in the men's locker room.* The musicians had to leave their instrument cases on the pool deck, noting that the two-hundred-year-old violins did not tolerate the humid and steamy chlorinated atmosphere.

Finally, in 1965 Ormandy wrote Mason to express his regret that he could no longer perform with the Philadelphia Symphony Orchestra in the Rutgers

---

* There was no women's locker room in the men's gym.

gym. Mason's search for funds for an arts center with a suitable auditorium continued without success.

———

On a chilly but clear November afternoon in 1965, Vladimir Horowitz sat alone on Carnegie Hall's large stage playing his first public recital in over a decade. Born in Kiev in 1903, Horowitz, a skillful pianist since childhood, had immigrated to the United States in 1925. Always willing to record his music, he was anxious that his live performances were not good enough. Mason had heard him play before the war, once in England and again in New York. Horowitz had stopped performing for several long periods during his life. This most recent hiatus had begun twelve years previously in 1953.

Julius Bloom, the Rutgers director of concerts and lectures, was one of Horowitz's closest friends.

Julius Bloom (Rutgers class of 1933, Phi Beta Kappa, philosophy), born in Brooklyn in 1912, had been the director of the Brooklyn Academy of Music and in 1960 became the executive director of New York's Carnegie Hall. He helped save the venerable concert hall from its destruction by the same forces that were modernizing New York and razing such structures as the original Metropolitan Opera House, the original Madison Square Garden, and Pennsylvania Station, which by now were all rust, rubble, dust, and fading memory.

It is not clear how Mason and Bloom first met, but the Rutgers College alumni group in New York was very strong, including Bloom, David A. "Sonny" Werblin (Rutgers class of 1931), and Rutgers trustee I. Robert Kreindler (Rutgers class of 1925), president of the 21 Club ("Jack and Charlie's") that had been founded during the 1920s by his brother Jack and cousin Charlie. Mason hired Bloom in 1959 to a new position as director of concerts and lectures to organize the many different concert venues at Rutgers, to the consternation of many Rutgers music department faculty who felt that Bloom's presence was an unnecessary imposition on their turf.

In 1965, Bloom had slowly encouraged his friend Horowitz to come out of his self-imposed exile. Bloom wrote to Mason that "there is a strong possibility of Horowitz giving a concert" at Rutgers. Horowitz agreed to perform his first concert in twelve years in the College Avenue gymnasium at Rutgers. Horowitz insisted, however, that prior to the first concert in New Brunswick he be allowed to perform in front of a small and select group. This first recital was scheduled for late afternoon Tuesday, November 9, on the main stage at Carnegie Hall, where he had last performed many years previously.

At Carnegie Hall, the house lights dimmed as Horowitz began his first concert in front of a live audience in twelve years.

––––––

That Tuesday was clear and cold, colder than anticipated for so early in November. As people throughout the Northeast United States and Canada came home from work that day, they turned on their electric heaters and their electric stoves to start making supper, pushing power demands to peak capacity. In Ontario near Niagara Falls, a protective relay slowly heated under the load. Finally, it tripped off-line as it had been programmed to do. The electric load cascaded to the east, slowly tripping more relays as it went. More and more parts of the power grid went off-line.

In Carnegie Hall the lights, already dimmed for the recital, went out suddenly. By the glow of the exit lights, Horowitz, playing by memory, never skipped a beat, never missed a note, as if he hadn't even noticed. He certainly didn't need to read any music.

A stage hand emerged from backstage with an emergency lantern and set it on the floor by the piano. David Drinkwater remembers that Horowitz's shadow cast by the lantern reflected upward so that there was a shadow image of the maestro, forty feet tall, playing against the tall white curtain upstage behind him. Horowitz continued to play. Everyone assumed that a fuse had blown somewhere in the old building.

Nobody knew until they went outside that the power failure had extended beyond the concert hall itself. The total failure affected New York state,

Ontario, and much of New England. Julia recalled no light on the street except for headlights. Naturally, the New York City traffic at rush hour was a snarled mess, more than usual. The buildings were dark. David Drinkwater remembers that some people, still at work, had lit candles in the windows of the midtown office buildings. New Jersey State trooper Sergeant Kurt Ralph had been assigned as Mason's driver for official business. Not knowing the cause of the blackout, he had been waiting on the street for Mason and Julia to emerge. Sergeant Ralph hustled them into the university car and skillfully expedited their short drive to the Lincoln Tunnel. Emerging from the tunnel's west end, New Jersey was awash in light; the power blackout had not affected any but a small northern part of the state. Coming out of the Lincoln Tunnel, they saw a once-in-a-lifetime scene: the entire Manhattan skyline silhouetted in total darkness.[5]

———

David Drinkwater recalls a small recital that had been arranged for new music department faculty at the President's House. David arrived early and let himself in. In the distance, he heard a piano. He assumed that the pianist was one of the new faculty. He followed the sound and came upon Mason, sitting alone at the university's piano playing a Mozart sonata flawlessly and from memory. As soon as Mason noticed David's presence, he stopped playing and stood to greet him. David later told me that he had no idea that Mason played so well.

Except for the annual Christmas party and one occasion in the summer of 1968 when he banged out some duets with a childhood friend from Hartford, Patsy Huntington, Mason never played his old Steinway again.

As a man of routine, Mason consistently spent Sunday afternoons, eyes closed with his feet up on the coffee table, listening to music, which stirred a passion that burned inside him but that he showed to nobody. Julia saw it, but she never spoke of it. His music reached down inside him and resonated in his every victory and every defeat, with its soft fingertips touching his every heartache that he kept hidden inside, such as the loss of his closest friends in the war, his mother's recent passing, and the memory of his son Charlie's burned arm.

———

Throughout his career, Mason had publicly advocated for increased support for the arts in the university. "The physical environment provided by a university for its various disciplines is a valid means of judging a university's respect for the full spectrum of man's knowledge. Let's provide the leadership necessary to establish respect for the arts in New Jersey."[6]

Mason had first proposed the concept of a school for music and the arts in 1953 when he asked the faculty if "there is sufficient interest in a proposed Rutgers Theatre of the Arts to begin full scale fund raising."[7] He later reintroduced the topic, adding that most universities had heretofore studied solely music theory and history but not performance itself, which was taught mostly in specialized schools and conservatories.[8] At Rutgers music history and theory were taught on the College Avenue campus, but courses in performance were only available at Douglass College. Mason advocated that universities must develop their own centers for training of professionals in the arts. He envisioned one school that would incorporate all aspects of the performing and visual arts.

Early in his administration, Mason cited to the Plainfield, New Jersey, Chamber of Commerce that nowhere in central New Jersey was there an "auditorium satisfactory for performing orchestras." The only possible indoor venue for music at Rutgers was the College Avenue gymnasium, with the acoustics that one would expect from the inside of a rectangular basketball court that also smelled of sneakers, old sweat, and wafts of chlorine rising from the nearby indoor swimming pool. As president, Mason had tried since 1959 to raise money for an arts center, to include an art museum, a full-sized theater, and a concert hall. However, the National Defense Education Act and subsequent legislation, born out of the Sputnik scare and the nuclear arms race, clearly favored capital construction in the sciences, to the detriment of any emphasis on the arts or humanities.

Upon his 1959 arrival at Rutgers, Julius Bloom immediately recognized that the biggest problem in scheduling events was the "absence of a suitable auditorium." At a 1962 meeting of the Rutgers Board of Trustees, Mason again urged them to support private sources of "funding for a concert hall, auditorium and art gallery in time for the Rutgers 1966 Bicentennial celebration."

Bloom wrote to Mason that "more and more, the main concert auditoriums of our country are being built at state universities." Emphasizing to the Board of Trustees in 1962 the role that universities play in the cultural life of the country, Bloom noted newly built auditoriums for opera, dance, and theater at a dozen other state universities, including Michigan (4,500 seats), Indiana (3,800 seats), Connecticut (3,600 seats), and Ohio State (3,100 seats). He added that these auditoriums were being used not just for music but also for film, lectures, jazz festivals, and special events, such as debates and chess tournaments.

Mason felt strongly that the arts needed to be a vital part of any university community. In 1962, he gave an address to the Fine Arts Council at Michigan State University titled the "University and the Arts." In this address, he outlined a university's four responsibilities to the arts.[9]

Noting that only the largest cities in the nation (New York, Chicago, Philadelphia) could raise the funds to develop world-class museums, orchestras, theater, and ballet, Mason added that a university, by supporting the arts, would bring world-class exposure to smaller cities, not just the university community but also the surrounding community. The first responsibility of the university was therefore to bring into their community high-quality artistic performances, such as those by Ormandy and Horowitz at Rutgers. The second role for a university was to train and develop young artists, not leaving this role to conservatories, and in doing so would bring the art and music students into closer proximity and more frequent exposure to the university's scholars in literature, art history, and musicology. Third, students of other professions would be able to exercise their amateur talents by performing on an elective basis, such as those in the Rutgers Glee Club had experienced with such great artists as Erich Leinsdorf and Leonard Bernstein. Finally, most importantly, the university could reach a larger segment of the general public than ever before by becoming a center of excellence in the arts, open to the public for all to experience.

There was considerable opposition. Mason received a letter from an irate New Jersey citizen who articulately stated that she was a supporter of every bond issue but with a caveat: "to those who are interested in opera, ballet, symphonic music and chamber music, let them spend their own money in interests of this kind and not expect the New Jersey taxpayers to pay these bills for them."[10]

Mason repeatedly told his audiences that proponents of higher education had done a poor job of convincing voters what was needed:

> We must be more explicit in what we are trying to do. We cannot assume the acquiescence of the general public in our "wise and benevolent leadership." We are going to cost the public a lot of money . . . and they have every right to know more clearly what we propose to do with that money. It is much easier to raise money for something that has a direct and immediate impact . . . , but it becomes more difficult to explain what seem to them to be the frills, such as the humanities, the arts and the social sciences.[11]

In 1966, a report from the Commission to Study the Arts in New Jersey stated that the state "should establish a college of fine and performing arts as a part of the university system." In March 1967, Rutgers provost Dick Schlatter formed a committee to create a faculty for a school of fine arts, music, and drama, stating that the "present anonymity of the scattered college programs in the arts places the university in a disadvantageous position when seeking support for the arts."[12]

By the late 1960s there was less money for capital expansion, and there were more hungry mouths to feed. As Rutgers was able to purchase a nuclear accelerator, there was clearly plenty of money for engineers and physicists but very little for music. The medical school, which was transitioning from a two-year to a four-year program in order to offer a medical degree rather than a masters in medical science, would require more classroom and laboratory space as well as clinical facilities. Livingston College was funded by the 1968 New Jersey bond issue to build its second full campus. Rutgers-Newark was clamoring to divert $7 million of the Livingston funds for increased facilities to support its own expansion as well as the promised programs for disadvantaged students.

The college of fine and performing arts, with its own auditorium, would have to wait.

Mason's old Steinway continued to gather dust in the corner.

CHAPTER 20

The Jewel in the Crown

*At the risk of seeming to show favoritism, I must single out one small group
here for special mention. . . . These are the first group of medical students to
receive a degree from Rutgers University in its two hundred and two years,
and [it] is an occasion for special rejoicing.*   —MWG, May 29, 1968

In June 1968, Rutgers Medical School graduated its first class. Historian
Paul G. E. Clemens calls the development of the medical school one of the
two greatest endeavors of Mason's presidency.* It had been an uphill battle,
and at Rutgers, if you recall, nothing is ever easy.

The original idea for a medical school at Rutgers had arisen in the early
1950s. At the time, Rutgers was a new state university and sought the best
directions into which to expand. Mason had no special interest in medicine
but realized that our country's greatest state universities also contained a
medical school. There was no medical school in New Jersey at the time, so
any New Jersey student desiring to study medicine had to leave the state. Subsequently, very few returned to New Jersey to practice. New Jersey already
experienced a shortfall of physicians that, with a rapidly enlarging postwar
population, was destined to worsen.

The Republican governor Alfred E. Driscoll, President Robert Clothier,
and the Rutgers Board of Trustees all agreed to support the development of
a medical school. But in 1954, a state bond issue and referendum for that specific purpose failed to interest the New Jersey electorate. The proposal to
build a medical school was shelved, perhaps forever.

---

* The other is the creation of Livingston College.

In September 1959, only months after his inauguration, Mason, citing the defeat of the medical school referendum "a few years ago," formed a committee to investigate building a medical school at Rutgers. He noted, "It is very interesting to see the topic of the medical school coming up again in the state."[1] The physician shortage in New Jersey was worsening, as it was elsewhere in the country. In 1960, the Bane Report of the U.S. surgeon general's office reported that twenty new medical schools would be needed, two of which needed to be in New Jersey.[2] The report also noted that the public medical schools restricted admissions to in-state residents, which limited opportunities for New Jersey residents who had to leave the state in order to study medicine. In November 1960 the W. K. Kellogg Foundation, citing the need for 3,600 more medical school graduates by the year 1975, issued $1 million grants each to the University of Connecticut and the University of New Mexico to start to build a medical school.

In March 1961, Mason's committee submitted a grant request for $1.072 million to Kellogg for the establishment of a two-year program in basic medical sciences, culminating in a master's degree of medical sciences. That grant was approved in June 1961.

In October 1962, Rutgers announced the appointment of Dr. DeWitt Stetten as dean of the Rutgers Medical School, due to matriculate its first class in 1965.

DeWitt Stetten Jr. was born in 1909 and completed his medical degree and PhD in biochemistry at Columbia. He trained further at Bellevue Hospital in New York and served on the faculty at Columbia and Harvard before moving to the National Institutes of Health in 1954.

———

Training to be a physician takes a minimum of seven years after the completion of one's undergraduate degree. For the first four years, one is enrolled in a medical school. The first two years of medical school are an intensive yet mind-numbing marathon, often compared to drinking water from a fire hose. The training is primarily didactic, with some laboratory work and extensive study of anatomy, pathology, and related disciplines but minimal patient contact. Students, mostly sedentary, must master a vast quantity of material in preparation for the second two years, which are almost exclusively clinical, hospital-based, with required rotations through the clinical specialties.

After four years and after passing Parts One and Two of the National Medical Board Examination, a student graduates and earns the medical degree, with the privilege to add "MD" to one's name. However, at this point an MD cannot get a license to practice. After one year of postgraduate training, called an internship, one can complete Part Three of the National Medical Board Examinations and actually obtain a license to practice in any state. However, further postgraduate training, from two to four more years, is required to enter even the most basic of specialties, such as internal medicine, family practice, pediatrics, and general surgery.

As Rutgers had no teaching hospital available, Rutgers Medical School initially would offer a two-year curriculum culminating in a master's degree of medical science, at which time the medical students would transfer to a four-year medical school to complete the clinical portion of their education. A two-year medical school did not have to provide hospital or clinical experiences for its students and so could operate at much lower expense, hoping that four-year schools could be found to absorb its graduates. The Bane Report had recommended an increase in the number of two-year programs, noting that the Universities of North Carolina, Missouri, and West Virginia all had two-year programs. Well-established medical schools in other states maintained affiliations with a number of training hospitals and had agreed to absorb the Rutgers medical students into their student body for their final two years of clinical hands-on training.

———

The chronology of successful fund-raising and legislative victories cloaks the vicious political turf battles that ensued. Major political opposition, mostly from Essex, Hudson, and other northern counties, centered around the fact that by this time New Jersey already had a medical school. In 1954 Monsignor John McNulty, the president of Seton Hall University, had announced the completion of negotiations with the Jersey City Medical Center to obtain some vacant facilities at the hospital for the creation of a private medical school, sponsored by the archdiocese. In 1956 the New Jersey College of Medicine and Dentistry inaugurated its first class of four-year students, due to graduate in 1960. However, by 1961 this medical college was already struggling, and the archdiocese sought to divest itself of this unpredictably large financial burden.

Republican state Senate majority leader Wayne Dumont and state senator Charles Sandman both opposed the creation of a medical school at Rutgers in New Brunswick. They proposed instead that Rutgers University simply take over the struggling New Jersey College of Medicine and Dentistry and build Rutgers Medical School in Jersey City. Dean Stetten and the Rutgers Board of Governors opposed this for several reasons, mostly that the facilities were unsuitable, were not conveniently located, and would not provide an education that was colocated in a university setting, the importance of which both Mason and Stetten continually had to reinforce.

Their insistence that Rutgers Medical School be located on a Rutgers campus is reminiscent of Alfred North Whitehead's philosophy and his caution against "cross sterilization." As we have seen, Mason was a firm advocate that in addition to developing expertise, a university experience should lead a student to a more enhanced appreciation of the humanities and the arts, not merely as a subject for study but also in the management of the arc of one's own life.

In 1964, the New Jersey State Assembly approved Governor Richard Hughes's request for $6 million, supplemented with federal matching funds, and additionally voted separately to take over the New Jersey College of Medicine and Dentistry but not as a part of the Rutgers Medical School system.

A $40 million education bond issue passed in November 1964 and included $19 million for capital construction. The federal government provided $8 million. Rutgers also obtained funding from corporate contributions, including $750,000 from Merck Pharmaceuticals, headquartered in nearby Rahway, and from New Brunswick's own Johnson and Johnson (J&J) and Colgate-Palmolive.

Contracts for construction were not awarded until 1966. Simultaneously, Mason was in constant negotiation for Rutgers to obtain Camp Kilmer, a closed U.S. Army base in Piscataway. The army intended to dispose of the property by turning it over to the General Services Administration. Rutgers wanted it for expansion. The transfer should be simple; it wasn't. Rutgers's primary purpose for this land was for the other huge simultaneous construction endeavor, the creation of Livingston College, another Rutgers campus intended to absorb the increasing enrollments that were continually projected. Meanwhile, sixteen students had been admitted to Rutgers Medical School in the fall of 1966. There was no medical education building on the Busch campus* yet, so they started their medical education in the leaking, dilapidated railroad storage sheds at Camp Kilmer. The biochemistry laboratory was housed in an old wooden temporary army barracks with a tar paper roof. It was struck by lightning and burned in August 1967.

Stetten had insisted as a part of his agreement to come to Rutgers that there be adequate salary to attract highly qualified faculty and suitable funding for a first-class medical library, having noted that "the library is the heart of any academic endeavor."[3] The library construction grant was awarded in April 1967.

However, the initial problem had not been solved. These New Jersey students were moving out of state to complete not only their remaining education prior to attaining their medical degree but also the subsequent internship and residency programs, where their four years of medical education would mature into practical and professional competence. Therefore, in 1965 the Rutgers Board of Governors voted to move forward, expanding Rutgers Medical School to offer a four-year medical degree. Governor Hughes requested from the legislature a total of $40 million in support.

In order fully to develop a four-year medical curriculum leading to a medical degree, Rutgers required clinical training facilities. Planners initially had proposed to purchase Raritan Valley Hospital in Somerset, which would

* Until 1971, the Busch campus was known as University Heights and hosted many of the Rutgers natural science departments, such as engineering, physics, chemistry, and microbiology.

become the training site for the remaining two years of medical education, intending that the medical school would be able to offer a four-year medical degree by 1972. The Board of Governors had approved the plan, which was still in early planning stages by the spring of 1970.

The development of a teaching hospital would wait. But gradually the medical education complex, with a medical library and the School of Pharmacy, rose out of the windswept red shale of the University Heights campus. The complex was appropriately situated next to the Microbiology Building, in homage to Selman Waksmann's Nobel Prize–winning discovery of streptomycin at Rutgers in 1943.

CHAPTER 21

The Year Everything Went Wrong, 1968

If you always remember that the individual in front of you, with his loves and his hates, his desires and his aversions, his hopes and his fears, is like you, a segment of mankind, you will recognize that he shares with you the irreducible dignity of a human being. Then you will not be in any danger of losing any of your own dignity or humanity in your dealings with him.

—*MWG, June 3, 1963*

The year 1968 still resonates as one of the most chaotic and unsettling in American history. The late historian and biographer William Manchester describes 1968 as "the year everything went wrong."[1] The year is fresh in collective memory. It is a significant waypoint in that all the unsettling international and national events trickled down into everyone's daily life and into everyone's heart.

The year had started badly. In Vietnam, in the tiny North Highlands village of Khe Sanh, the U.S. Army commenced the single most intense artillery barrage in the entire history of human conflict.[2] The army had chosen this site, in the far northwest corner of South Vietnam just south of the demilitarized zone, in order to stop the enemy's flow of arms and personnel down the Ho Chi Minh Trail. The North Vietnamese Army responded with concentrated mortar and artillery attacks besieging the American base, followed by focused infantry assault. The U.S. media noted the similarities of this siege to the ultimate defeat of the encircled French garrison at Dien Bien Phu in 1954. At President Lyndon Johnson's insistence that Khe Sanh would be held at all costs, U.S. commander General William Westmoreland then rushed reinforcements from all over South Vietnam to relieve the surrounded marines at Khe Sanh.

With American forces diverted north to Khe Sanh, the end of January saw the surprise attacks of the Tet Offensive throughout the cities of South Vietnam. In Saigon, Viet Cong forces fought their way into the American embassy, which was soon retaken by the Americans. The ultimate battle occurred in the ancient capital of Hue, where enemy forces had seized the fortified citadel. There is no denying the dogged resistance, courage, and selfless heroism of the American troops in Hue, as elsewhere throughout South Vietnam, but for the American public watching on their television sets, the winter of our discontent due to Tet was jaw-dropping. Although heralded by some revisionist historians as a tactical American military triumph, it was a Pyrrhic victory at best because strategically it was an American disaster. The Tet Offensive further alienated much of the American public past the point of no return. Even now, more than fifty years later, some still blame the "liberal media" for betraying the U.S. military effort, but the political catastrophe was there for all with open eyes to see. Presidential candidate Richard Nixon saw it. Walter Cronkite saw it in Vietnam, in person. The voters in the March New Hampshire Democratic primary saw it and voted heavily for the antiwar candidate, Minnesota senator Eugene McCarthy. Robert F. "Bobby" Kennedy saw it, throwing his hat into the ring in March. President Lyndon Johnson saw it and threw in the towel instead.

I was sixteen. My first cousin Dev was a U.S. Army enlisted man in Vietnam. On March 31, in the basement doing my homework in front of the television, I watched as regular programming was interrupted by a special announcement. It was President Johnson declaring, "I shall not seek, and I will not accept, the nomination of my party for another term as your president." I ran upstairs, three steps at a time, to tell my father. Mason looked up over his spectacles, raised one eyebrow, and said, "I know."*

---

*How could he have known? Even though the possibility of Johnson's withdrawal had been anticipated, the announcement had just occurred. Without further comment, I turned and went back downstairs.

But 1968 had only just begun. On April 4, only four days after Johnson's stunning withdrawal from the presidential race, the Reverend Dr. Martin Luther King Jr. was gunned down in Memphis. In the ensuing riots, American cities burned, like Tet, on the evening news.

Rutgers historian Richard McCormick wrote that King's assassination had an "unprecedented impact upon black students at Rutgers," noting their pain, anger, and an inspired sense of urgency.[3]

On the evening after the assassination, Julia heard a knock at the front door at the President's House. She opened the door to find a group of Black students who wanted to speak to Dr. Gross. Julia later recalled that they were neither threatening nor hostile and were courteous yet visibly angry and understandably upset. Although Mason never spoke to me about this episode, Julia later told me that they just wanted to talk and wanted somebody to listen.

Mason's attempts to level the playing field for minorities had started at least a decade previously and would continue through 1971, paralleling nationwide attempts for American Blacks to obtain access to education.

––––––

The first Black graduate of Rutgers had been James Dickson Carr in 1892. In the following fifty years there were "no more than twenty others,"[4] one of whom was famous political activist and virtuoso singer Paul Robeson (Rutgers class of 1919). At Rutgers, Robeson, a minister's son, had been a star athlete, with twelve varsity letters in four sports. Ironically, the Rutgers coach once benched Robeson when an opposing team refused to take the field, having realized that Rutgers had a Black man on the squad. Robeson was on the debating team and sang bass in the glee club. Less well known is that he was the valedictorian speaker at his graduation and was elected to Phi Beta Kappa. In 1922 he earned a law degree from Columbia University, having studied while he was supporting himself playing professional football. Robeson rose to prominence as a singer and a political activist and was branded as a communist agitator. Years later, Mason described Robeson as Rutgers's single "most distinguished graduate."

In the twenty years after becoming New Jersey's own state university, Rutgers awarded twenty-four thousand baccalaureate degrees, less than two hundred of which, less than 1 percent, were awarded to Black graduates. Richard Seclow (Rutgers class of 1951) recalls that of the 750 graduates in his class at Rutgers College, 4 were Black.[5]

One of the many touchstones for those who remember the 1960s was how the escalating struggle for racial equality, whose most recent seeds had been sown with mandatory desegregation both in factories at home and in the U.S. military, found its way onto television's evening news. In 1961 it was the pilgrimage of the Freedom Riders, taking a bus across the South to challenge segregation in public transportation. They were attacked in successive bus stations by white supremacists wielding clubs, blackjacks and tire chains. In Anniston, Alabama, an incendiary bomb was thrown into the bus. In Birmingham, the riders were dragged from the bus and beaten with pipes.

The U.S. Supreme Court's landmark decision *Brown v. Board of Education* had occurred in 1954. But the Supreme Court had no army and no power to enforce its decision. That was up to the executive branch. The integration of schools, now mandated by the Supreme Court, passed through the Eisenhower administration at a glacial pace. After Little Rock in 1957, when nine African American students enrolled in Little Rock Central High School, another opportunity came in 1962.

James Meredith, a nine-year U.S. Air Force veteran, had qualified for admission to the University of Mississippi. In September 1962, after a series of legal battles, the Supreme Court, in the person of Justice Hugo Black, himself an Alabama native, upheld the court of appeals order to admit Meredith. Mississippi governor Ross Barnett refused to allow Meredith to register, citing a defense of "states' rights" and declaring "we will not surrender to the evil and illegal forces of tyranny"; he was referring, of course, to the tyranny of the U.S. Supreme Court. Barnett blockaded Meredith's repeated attempts to register. Finally, President Kennedy mobilized the U.S. infantry at Fort Benning, activated the Mississippi National Guard, and dispatched four hundred federal marshals under the command of Deputy Attorney General Nicholas Katzenbach. Molotov cocktails exploded and rifle fire rang out, killing two bystanders and wounding twenty-eight of the marshals, who kept their sidearms holstered as per Kennedy's specific orders. Barnett later blamed the riot on "trigger happy U.S. Marshals." Forty of the U.S. troops were wounded.

The attacking mob, only a small portion of whom were college students, vanished during the night. The registrar, Robert Ellis, finally admitted Meredith, peacefully, on Monday morning. As Meredith departed the building, a fellow student yelled "Was it worth two lives, nigger?"[6]

As empathetic as northern liberals hoped to be, they could not and cannot still approximate any true depth of understanding or capture the essence of the Black experience in America. Half a century later the force behind the civil rights struggles of the 1960s has slipped so far out of focus that the civil uncertainty and emotional chaos of that era is lost forever. Captured in a few iconic black-and-white still photographs of children attacked with firehoses and police dogs, of Dr. King, James Meredith, and Medgar Evers lying prostrate, bleeding on the ground, what has been lost to history are the countless nameless and faceless others who were on the evening news on so many nights, shot, beaten, bloody, and humiliated.

In 1962, James Baldwin wrote in his famous *New Yorker* essay, "Rope, fire, torture, castration, infanticide, rape; death and humiliation, fear by day and night, fear as deep as the marrow; . . . sorrow for his women, his kin, his children . . . whom he could not protect; rage and hatred . . . so deep that it turned against him and made all love, trust and joy impossible."[7]

The crescendo that had played itself out in Little Rock, Selma, and Oxford arose again in 1963 in Birmingham, Alabama.

On May 2 in Birmingham, Black marchers were met with police dogs and firehoses at the order of Birmingham police commissioner Eugene "Bull" Connor. Bombings of a desegregated hotel and the home of a Black leader followed. After a night of riot and fires, Connor called for assistance from Alabama governor George Wallace. Six weeks later many television viewers first encountered Wallace—who in his January inaugural address had vowed to stand in the doorways to prevent the integration of any Alabama school, stating "Segregation now, segregation tomorrow, and segregation forever"—as he stood in the doorway of a University of Alabama auditorium carrying out his inaugural vow.

On June 3, 1963, Mason addressed the Rutgers commencement, noting that despite unparalleled prosperity and advancements in science, "man's inhumanity to man has never been more vividly revealed.... Read Thucydides on the revolution at Corcyra and you will understand better what is going on in Birmingham." He reminded them of Immanuel Kant's moral philosophy that centered around his categorical imperative, stating the "absolute, ultimate and irreducible dignity of every individual, regardless of color, religion, nationality, achievements, talents, appearance or other qualities." Quoting this principle often in his many addresses, Mason often added the postscript "you do not need to be a disciple of Kant to accept this principle, but you do need to have a strong element of inhumanity in you to reject it."[8]

A court order had authorized three Black students to be admitted to the University of Alabama in Tuscaloosa. President Kennedy and his brother Bobby, the attorney general, wanted to avoid another Oxford. Governor Wallace stood in the doorway.

On the evening of June 11, 1963, President Kennedy spoke to the nation, vowing to submit a civil rights bill to Congress and declaring that civil rights was a moral issue, "as old as the Scriptures and ... as clear as the American constitution."[9]

The speech was heard in Mississippi, where Byron De la Beckwith was a white supremacist and Medgar Evers, a U.S. Army World War II combat veteran, was the NAACP field secretary for Mississippi and a close friend and advisor of James Meredith. On June 12 only hours after Kennedy's speech, Beckwith, lying in ambush, shot Evers in his own driveway; his wife and small children ran outside the house and found him near the door. Grievously wounded yet still alive, when Evers arrived at the local hospital he was denied treatment due to his race and died an hour later. He was buried with full military honors in Arlington Cemetery.

Historian William Manchester wrote that "in the third [and last] year of the Kennedy Presidency, a fundamental change loomed in the character of the civil rights movement."[10] Angrier militant "young Negroes were approaching the end of their patience" and rejected King's nonviolent ideology. On the night of Kennedy's speech, King was pelted with raw eggs in Harlem. The "emergence of an eye for an eye trend foreshadowed a new, darker period in the struggle for integration."[11]

On June 17, Mason received a telegram from President Kennedy requesting his attendance at a meeting in the White House to "discuss aspects of the nation's civil rights problem that relate to our schools at all levels."

The summer of 1963 simmered. In August, I learned of the upcoming March on Washington for Jobs and Freedom. Sara Huntington, the daughter of Mason's oldest Hartford friends Jack and Patsy Huntington, was going with friends and invited me along. I was eleven years old. Mason adamantly refused. There had been enough death that summer, and he was concerned over further threats of violence. President Kennedy had ordered the nearby quartering of federal troops, who had been trained in combat but not in control of civil disturbance. The impending violence never came to pass, and the August 1963 March on Washington became a watershed moment in American history.

An October 1963 headline, dateline Americus, Georgia, in the *Student Voice*, the newspaper of the Student Non-violent Coordinating Committee (SNCC), read "POLICE SMASH DEMONSTRATORS[;] FOUR FACE DEATH PENALTY."[12]

Recent Rutgers graduate Donald Harris (Rutgers class of 1963) had not heard Mason's June commencement address, nor had he marched in Washington, as he was already in the South with SNCC. Majoring in English and physical education, he had played lacrosse and football. The previous year he had joined SNCC. In the summer of 1963, he joined scores of volunteers who headed south to assist with voter registration drives.

On August 8, a meeting was held in the Friendship Baptist Church in Americus, Georgia. Leaving the church, the 250 attendees strode down the street, refusing an order to disperse. The police waded into the crowd, specifically seeking Harris, whom, as SNCC regional field secretary, they perceived to be the leader. Not resisting, Harris went limp. Beaten and then arrested, he was charged with "insurrection, unlawful assembly and rioting," a capital offense for violating a Georgia law against "seditious conspiracy." As conviction on this charge was punishable by death, Harris was held without bail.

While Harris was incarcerated, at yet another church, this one the 16th Street Baptist Church in Birmingham, Alabama, on Sunday, September 15, fifteen sticks of dynamite with a timing device, planted beneath the steps of the church, exploded at 10:00 A.M., killing four girls in the basement about to go to the day's service (Addie Mae Collins, Cynthia Wesley, and Carol Robertson, all age 14, and Carol Denise McNair, age 11) and injuring a score of others in what Dr. King called "one of the most vicious crimes ever perpetrated." The FBI identified in 1965 the four members of the local Ku Klux Klan who had carried out the attack, but no trials took place until 1977, 2001, and 2002.

At Rutgers, stories about Harris's incarceration appeared in the *Daily Targum*, the student daily newspaper. In the fall semester students and faculty rallied, raising funds for Harris's defense. At the fall convocation Mason lent his own support and gave a personal donation to the fund drive.

At an October 1 meeting of the Rutgers Faculty Action Committee in Support of Donald Harris, Mason expressed his support. "Donald Harris, arrested while engaging in peaceful activity designed to enable his fellow citizens to exercise their right to vote, has come to be an inspiring symbol on this campus and throughout the United States . . . of tremendous importance to the preservation of American democracy."[13]

On October 31, a federal court declared that the Georgia law on seditious conspiracy was unconstitutional. Harris and the others were released the next day. A previously scheduled speaking engagement kept Mason from accepting the invitation to Harris's "welcome home" celebration at Rutgers on Wednesday November 20, two days before Kennedy's assassination in Dallas.

Harris's case further elevated Rutgers faculty concerns, which had been brewing since 1960, that minorities were underrepresented in both the faculty and the student body. The Boehm Report, chaired by the dean of the Graduate School of Social Work, supported upcoming civil rights legislation and recommended a multifaceted equal opportunity program. In December 1963, Rutgers initiated the University Committee on Human Rights "to enhance the role of the university in addressing the racial problems of the general community." The committee noted these four areas of concern:

1. Preparation of Negro high school students for college,
2. Scarcity of Negro students at the undergraduate and graduate levels,
3. Scarcity of Negro faculty members, and
4. Scarcity of Negroes employed on University construction projects.

As a result of active recruiting, by 1967 the number of Black undergraduates had risen from less than 100 in 1963 to a still minuscule 400. In 1966 out of a total of 1,500 faculty members at Rutgers, only 9 were Black. The Upward Bound program, sponsored with federal funding from Johnson's Great Society legislation, enrolled another 150 undergraduates. By 1968, Rutgers had added 30 Black faculty members and more Black staff members.

In the summer of 1964 Congress passed Johnson's version of Kennedy's Civil Rights Act, which among other issues addressed equal opportunity in employment. In a letter to U.S. secretary of commerce Luther Hodges, Mason wrote his assurance that Rutgers would carry out both the letter and the spirit of the legislation.

But not all of Mason's civil rights dilemmas were related solely to faculty or student issues. Massive construction was proceeding on all campuses. The construction of the new Rutgers Law School in Newark was hampered by the failure of unions to comply with fairness in hiring practices required by recent federal legislation. Mason noted that the construction of the new law center in Newark must "be built without the taint of racial discrimination in employment." Rutgers, as the initiator of the construction, assumed the responsibility for enforcement of antidiscrimination in employment. In a letter to William Heckel, dean of the law school, Mason noted that at the job site of the Rutgers Newark Law School and the Newark College of

Engineering, the "ironworkers' contractor had no intention of complying with the anti-discrimination clause of the contract." He added later that the "schools must force compliance or stop the job."

Later in his life, Mason noted to a family member that he recalled little difficulty with protesting students, faculty, staff, or state administrators when compared to the contractors and the labor unions, despite his otherwise good relations with both unions and management dating from his previous participation in the New Jersey State Labor Mediation Board and the construction of the new home of the Rutgers Institute for Labor Relations, which had been funded almost exclusively by donations from national labor organizations. The contractors in Newark complained that there were insufficient numbers of qualified Black ironworkers. Since the coveted apprenticeships often went to family members of white union journeymen, there was little possibility for Blacks to be hired or advanced. Rutgers halted several construction contracts due to the failure to comply, which delayed the completion of the projects on the already simmering Newark campus.

SNCC and the Congress of Racial Equality recruited among northern campuses for over a thousand volunteers for Freedom Summer of 1964, with a goal to register as many southern Blacks as possible especially in Mississippi. Within two days of reaching Jackson, Mississippi, three of the volunteers—Michael Schwerner, James Chaney, and Andrew Goodman—were reported missing. They had been murdered. By the end of Freedom Summer, thirty-seven Black churches had been bombed or burned, and 80 volunteers had been beaten.

The Watts riots in 1965 lasted six days, resulting in thirty-four deaths, four hundred arrests, and $40 million in damages. Now on the news were not the faces of children blown up in church but instead soldiers with M16 rifles silhouetted in the smoke and fires of Los Angeles. In that long hot summer, similar riots occurred in New Jersey, in Paterson, Jersey City, and Elizabeth, and also in Rochester (New York), New York City, and other cities throughout the nation.

Conservative white Americans resented what they saw as unnecessary and undeserved handouts, whose increase in payout from Johnson's Great

Society paralleled the increase in urban violence and seemed therefore joined in a causal relationship.

Newark, New Jersey, was next. Newark had the highest percentage of substandard housing of any American city, more than Detroit, Chicago, and even New York City. There were seven thousand units without a flush toilet and twenty-eight thousand units without heat. Black babies died, even in the hospital, of diarrheal illness at rates comparable to a third world country.[14] On a hot summer night in 1967 a riot had started, sparked when a Black cab driver was arrested and beaten. During the subsequent intervention by the state police and the National Guard, twenty-six people died, including children and elderly. It was the worst riot in New Jersey history.

Newark's fires had barely cooled down when seven months later on March 11, 1968, the Newark-based Black Organization of Students officially requested that the university investigate how $100,000 intended for Equal Opportunity projects, financial aid, and assistance for compensatory education had been deleted from Governor Richard Hughes's 1969 budget request. Andrew Dungan, the chancellor of the newly established New Jersey Board of Higher Education, whose office had veto power over the Rutgers budget, went on record saying that Rutgers should not be in the business of providing remedial education to disadvantaged students.

As the Rutgers administration evaluated the request, Martin Luther King was shot in Memphis.

Mason, one of several speakers at a convocation in the College Avenue gymnasium of the day of King's funeral, stated, "The death of Martin Luther King, Jr., has suddenly brought into sharp focus many of the most serious shortcomings of our contemporary society. . . . These problems must be attacked with much more energy and speed than ever before. . . . The ultimate objective must be to wipe out bigotry, prejudice and racism in every shape or form."[15]

Mason addressed some remarks during the May 1968 Rutgers commencement. Referring to the recent chaotic occupation of Columbia by Black Panthers and the activist group Students for a Democratic Society, Mason noted, "We must never allow ourselves to degenerate into a situation where the tremendous emotional power of the students has to be confronted by the physical power of a police force."[16] Alluding to King's assassination, Mason added, "There have been assassins before, but none who have aimed at the heart of the constructive forces in our society so effectively as those who struck down John F. Kennedy and Martin Luther King."[17]

It was a prophetic statement, for another assassin struck only six days later. U.S. senator Robert F. Kennedy, having won the California Democratic primary, was shot in the kitchen of the Ambassador Hotel in Los Angeles shortly after midnight on June 5 and died early the next morning.

———

My sister Ellen's wedding to Mr. Frank Miles took place on a hot and dreadfully humid June afternoon in Hartford's Asylum Hill Congregational Church, in the small chapel that had been built by Mason's father and aunt in memory of their own parents and where Mason had gone to Sunday school fifty years before.

That evening Mason's oldest friends, Jack and Patsy Huntington, held a party at their home. Liquor flowed while Mason and Patsy played duets and everyone sang. One might not have expected the tension of 1968 to erupt during such a festive occasion.

Charlie and I got quite drunk. That happens at weddings. I was sixteen, and Charlie, at twenty-one, had finished his four years at the University of Wisconsin. His II-S student deferment would be revoked, and unknown to the rest of us, he was now about to be reclassified I-A, immediately draftable. On the drive back to Mason's childhood home, where we were staying with his brother and sister, Mason was extremely furious with us; I had never seen him so angry. I suspected that his anger arose because we had been so visibly intoxicated, embarrassing him in front of his best friends. It was a difficult car ride, with six hot and sweaty people in our 1966 Dodge Dart station wagon; Kitty was crying, and Julia sat in the front seat quietly smoking.

It was June 28. The year 1968 was only half over.

CHAPTER 22

Law and Order, 1968

It was getting rather hot in the kitchen.
—MWG, May 11, 1969

Now was the summer of our discontent. In 1968 the world was on fire, with major strikes and riots in many capital cities. In Czechoslovakia, Soviet tanks put an end to the Prague Spring. Lyndon Johnson was not running for reelection. The Democratic challengers to run in his place were predominantly antiwar candidates themselves, but Vice President Hubert Humphrey would not distance himself from the president's current policy. Despite several viable candidates, after Bobby Kennedy's death it was unclear who would win the Democratic nomination.

Richard Nixon rose from the ashes of his previous political defeats, including his 1962 sore-loser promise to the press that "this is my last press conference; you won't have Dick Nixon to kick around anymore." Nixon's star was rising again, as he had carefully calculated his route back into the Republican Party's good graces after Barry Goldwater's humiliating defeat in 1964. The Republicans had taken back Congress and many state houses and legislatures, successfully challenging Johnson's steamroller, which had definitely run out of steam. Nixon ran on a ticket promising a return to "law and order." His big lie of 1968 was that the crime rate in the United States was increasing nine times faster than the population. He cried out that much of this was a result of campus unrest and ghetto riots.

Over thirty thousand American soldiers had died in Vietnam in the three years since Eugene Genovese and the teach-in at Rutgers. Even though there were rumors of peace talks, truly the first conversations between all the parties were about the shape of the conference table.

Nixon's political resurrection was completed when he was nominated in Miami in July. In August, Soviet tanks rolled into Prague. Later that month the Democratic National Convention became a media circus, with riots outside, tear gas drifting into the hotels, and prominent newscasters being assaulted on the convention floor. Live TV coverage caught Chicago Democratic mayor Richard J. Daley calling out to Connecticut delegate U.S. senator Abe Ribicoff, "Fuck you, you Jew son of a bitch." It would be sugarcoating to call this convention anything but a national disgrace.

During his 1968 campaign, Nixon capitalized on the assassinations of Martin Luther King and Robert Kennedy and on the ensuing antiwar protests and urban riots. Nixon accused Humphrey, his Democratic opponent, of being soft on crime. Noting an escalating crime rate, especially on campuses, Nixon claimed crime and disorder as his number one issue.* In fact, "he was obsessed with it."[1]

Mason had seen Nixon at work since the red-baiting days of the House Un-American Activities Committee. Nixon was no friend of Rutgers, having come to New Jersey in 1965 to campaign for Wayne Dumont. But, Mason now tried to stay out of politics. In 1957, he had declined to join a "Meyner for Governor" club, stating, "I doubt whether I, as provost of the state university, should become this active in party politics."[2] Having previously refused to publicly endorse candidates for public office, in 1964 Mason, a self-described "lifelong Democrat" since 1928, had accepted the leadership of a group called the Independent Citizens for Johnson. The pushback had been immediate, mostly from Republican public figures, who claimed that Mason's "backing of Johnson poses ethical questions for Rutgers." Governor Hughes publicly supported Mason's position. In the op-ed pages of New Jersey newspapers, editorials reflected the polarity of the discussion, some stating that

---

* The irony here is too good to pass up. Nixon and Agnew later both left office before the end of their terms, both accused of crimes.

the president of the state university "is not a private citizen" and "should be publicly non-partisan" and others, even including the opinions of moderate Republicans, supporting Mason's right to speak out. Mason himself wrote that his endorsement for the Democratic ticket was similar to his public support for the 1964 New Jersey education bond issue, both of which reflected his opinion of what position served the best interest of the university, "due to the Kennedy and Johnson administrations' continued support for higher education and the flat and unqualified position of the Republicans that no such aid is necessary."[3]

There was another public buildings bond issue on the New Jersey ballot in 1968, this one for $337.5 million. If approved, $62 million would go to Rutgers, with only $6 million going to the Newark Campus and $45 million for the New Brunswick campuses, including $7 million for the construction of a complete second campus at Livingston College. Newark students and staff protested in October 1968 that Newark needed more funding due to its inadequate facilities and implored the Board of Governors to divert funds from the second Livingston campus, where construction had not yet even begun.

Mason was asked if he would be taking a political stand in 1968. He demurred, stating that aside from supporting the bond issue, he had learned his lesson in 1964, recalling that "just once did I indicate a preference for the presidency of the United States, and the roof nearly fell in."[4] In 1968, an election year when over 50 percent of the bond issues failed nationwide, New Jersey voters passed theirs.[5]

In 1968, Ralph A. Dungan was the first commissioner for the nascent New Jersey Board of Higher Education. Born in Pennsylvania, Dungan was a U.S. Navy veteran and served first as an aide and later as a special assistant to President John F. Kennedy and then as U.S. ambassador to Chile during the Johnson administration.

In April 1966, the New Jersey Governor's Conference on Higher Education had asked if "the state's educational administration should remain the responsibility of one agency or is it more efficient for higher education to be separately administered?" On the recommendation of this conference, Governor Hughes and the legislature passed the New Jersey Board of Higher Education Act of 1966, separating the administration of higher education from the Board of Education and establishing the Board of Higher Education to "create a master plan for higher education" in New Jersey.[6] The act was supported by Princeton president Robert Goheen, while five out of six New Jersey state colleges opposed it, as did the state's own Department of Education. Mason was in favor of the concept as long as the board was advisory in nature and did not obstruct the traditional relationship between Rutgers and the governor's office. The exact opposite occurred. Budget requests, which used to go directly from Rutgers to the governor's office, now had to pass through Dungan's office, where they were systematically dissected. The relationship between the university president and the governor now had a go-between.*

In 1968 Mason submitted to the new Board of Higher Education a pro forma request to release the funds, already appropriated in the recent bond issue, for construction of the long-awaited Fine Arts Building on the Douglass campus. He had no reason to expect that his request would be denied. Dungan responded with a laborious review of space utilization at Douglass, noting that that ratio of square footage of classroom space per the number of students was well above the national average. Dungan suggested that some remodeling at Douglass would bring the ratio back down and allow for the redesignation of the surplus space. He sat on the request for two years while the cost of construction went up 20 percent.[7] Mason noted that the "university's operations are being forced into quantitative measurements."[8] He later stated, "We've got to work out more clearly how to work with the Board of Higher Education. That is very bad right now. The Board keeps moving into areas where they have no right to be at all."[9]

---

* Richard L. McCormick, Rutgers president emeritus and son of Rutgers historian Richard P. McCormick, informed me that the single most important professional relationship for running Rutgers is that between the university president and the governor.

Having already deleted funds previously appropriated for Equal Opportunity projects, for Rutgers Dungan had now become one of the chief antagonists in the state government.

———

In late October 1968, ten days before election day, my mother celebrated her fifty-sixth birthday. I came home from boarding school to celebrate, as my birthday was the same day as hers. My parents and I sat down to supper at 7:00 P.M. sharp. Over a most innocuous conversation with Julia over how best to carve a steak, Mason stood up quickly, yelled "Goddammit," grabbed his glasses, and threw them across the room, where they broke against the wall. He stormed up the stairs. The house shook when he slammed the bedroom door.

Julia and I looked at each other quietly. She slid her chair back and walked slowly upstairs. I heard her open the bedroom door and close it with a quiet click. I then heard their muffled voices, his loud and angry, hers soft and conciliatory. I went to the front door, grabbed my coat, and sat outside on the cold ground behind the pump house.

About a half hour later outside in the dark, I heard my dad at the front door call out to me. I did not answer. I had a train ticket in my wallet to get me back to Taft School, so I left that night without going back to the house. When I came home for Thanksgiving there was no mention of that night, as though it had never happened.

Parents argue, and so what? But this was different. I had never seen this kind of outburst before. Julia had a look of resignation on her face indicating that she had seen it a lot. I've searched the Rutgers archives and Mason's daily calendar for any indication of what might have triggered him that day. Finding no scheduled meetings, I wondered what telephone call or message from the legislature or faculty or students had brought him home in such a foul mood. Only now in retrospect as I look at what was going on at Rutgers in the late 1960s, as I see the squeeze that was being placed on everything that Mason was trying to accomplish, do I understand what was going on in his life, one day at a time.

CHAPTER 23

Faith and Reason v.
Law and Order

*There is a grand searchlight playing on us, revealing brilliantly . . . the good
and evil. . . . At the same time man's inhumanity to man has never been more
vividly revealed, . . . the tragic misery of our own citizens, the hopelessly
impoverished. . . . Kant's categorical imperative, describing the irreducible
dignity of all mankind, tells us to reject specious arguments when they are
evoked to justify unequal or inhuman treatment.*   —MWG, June 1963

In 1969, Norman McNatt (Rutgers class of 1964) completed his Fulbright
scholarship in Scotland and returned to Rutgers. After two years abroad, he
and his wife agreed then that they had returned to a different country, angry,
chaotic, divided, and polarized.[1]

The new year of 1969 portended even greater challenges for Mason, as four
separate storms would slowly gather and for the next eighteen months would
make the environment of the president's office significantly more turbulent
than it was ten years earlier when he had been inaugurated.

First, with a promise of law and order, Richard Nixon's 1968 presidential
election climaxed a sharp national political swing to the right, simmering
since 1964, that in the following year would reverberate through New Jersey
politics, resulting in "the bitterest, most vituperative," and most highly contentious gubernatorial election in New Jersey history.[2]

Second, in 1969 at Rutgers, long-simmering racial issues would surface.
Mason would propose solutions to what he perceived as legitimate grievances. But in 1970, a new governor and legislature interpreted these solutions as "caving in" to Black protesters' demands. The legislature pushed

back hard and sought to extract its pound of flesh from the university administration.

Third, the federal budget, squeezed by the inflationary pressure from both the escalating cost of a ground war in Asia and Lyndon Johnson's Great Society, left fewer discretionary funds available for higher education.

Finally, President Nixon's strategy for ending the war, "peace with honor," would not come cheap. American soldiers were dying at a rate approaching five hundred per week. Increasing antiwar resistance resonated through the nation's campuses. Rutgers would not be spared.

Underlying all of these challenges was a rising groundswell, a change in the political landscape. Many Americans, call them "forgotten" or "silent" as Nixon did, or call them middle class, had just about seen enough. Those who had never gone to college began to see college unrest as perpetrated by communist agitators, the big lie promulgated by President Nixon, who was famous for his red-baiting rhetoric. On their televisions, they had seen enough riots. They had seen the Black Panthers openly calling for armed revolution. They went to work every day, but they saw a spiraling increase in their tax dollars spent for programs for the nonworking poor. They had seen enough marches for civil rights, which in their somewhat myopic vision seemed frequently to descend into violence. Many whites had seen the Reverend Marin Luther King Jr. as a troublemaker, a communist, a philanderer, and a rabble-rouser who had reaped a whirlwind of his own creation. The Civil Rights Act of 1964 (outlawing discrimination), the Voting Rights Act of 1965, and the Fair Housing Act of 1968, along with the massively expensive programs of Johnson's Great Society, had paralleled an increase in civil disorder. Nixon's silent majority did not notice that the temporal relationship of these events did not imply causality. There was a large segment of American society, almost exclusively white, that had seen all they wanted of campus unrest, ghetto riots, and antiwar protests. Their heroes were Governors Ronald Reagan, George Wallace, Lester Maddox, and Spiro Agnew. They lauded university presidents such as Father Hesburgh of Notre Dame and S. I. Hayakawa of San Francisco State, who appeared to have drawn a line in the sand and stood up to the protestors.

At Rutgers in the new year 1969, all of these issues, stirred from beneath by this reactionary groundswell, would build a momentum over the next eighteen months. By June 1970 these would prove to be a breaking point for Mason's administration.

———

In his inaugural address in January 1969, President Nixon spoke of a country torn by division, raucous discord, and angry rhetoric but seeking the "decent order that makes . . . our lives secure." His inaugural address advocated "strengthening the justice systems to restore law and order." This was music to the ears of Nixon's "forgotten Americans," from whose safe living rooms they had all watched the televised summer riots and the national disgrace of the chaotic and violent 1968 Democratic National Convention in Chicago.

Rutgers was still growing, or at least trying to, in order to keep up with the postwar baby boom that would see university enrollments peak in 1974. No longer a sleepy private college, there were ninety-five separate construction projects under way simultaneously. Although in 1968 the New Jersey voters did approve yet one more education bond issue, when compared to 1959 the well was definitely drying up. As Andrew Dungan, chancellor of the newly created New Jersey Board of Higher Education, stated to Mason, there are "an increasing number of educational institutions applying for a limited amount of federal aid." In the first meeting of his economic advisors in February 1969, President Nixon immediately called for a decrease in federal aid to education.[3] Even if federal funds had been available, they might not have been as easy to obtain because the 1960s brought a changing view of higher education. The American Council on Education, of which Mason was chairman, is the coordinating agency for higher education in America and includes representatives from 1,500 colleges and universities. In December 1969, the council reported to its membership that "the American public has lost confidence in university governance, . . . manifested in appropriations cutbacks." Noting that cuts in federal grants for education and scientific training reflect the congressional mood toward higher education, the "universities are in crisis with public understanding at a new low."[4]

After World War II and through the 1950s, during the "golden age of public education,"[5] American universities were held up as the nation's future. By 1969, they had "become the whipping boy for all that is wrong in the United States."[6]

———

Only five weeks into Nixon's law-and-order presidency, Newark, New Jersey, was back on the front page. Like Watts and Detroit less than two years previously, Newark's riots had been headline news, as infamous as Selma and Birmingham. Newark's fires had barely cooled when on February 24, 1969, students belonging to the Black Organization of Students (BOS) occupied Conklin Hall on the Newark campus. Citing the university's good intentions but slow progress, they were impatient for reforms that had been promised during the previous two years.

Rutgers was not the first university to be occupied in such a way. Many occupations ended in violence, some with death or permanent injury, such as at Columbia in April 1968. In the autumn of 1968, Black students at San Francisco State had occupied the administration building, presenting demands that would later be echoed in Newark, demands including an ethnic studies program, more Black faculty, and open admissions for Black students. Interim university president S. I. Hayakawa had received accolades from Governor Reagan and the public when he pulled the plug on the protestors' public address system. The half-truth states that Hayakawa was held up as a hero for law and order. The whole truth, not publicized, reveals that in February 1969, Hayakawa quietly acceded to the same demands as those presented later in Newark. Appearance is everything.

The Newark BOS protested the university's apparent lack of commitment to improve admission to minorities, hire minority faculty, and provide a curriculum that was more relevant to students from the inner city. On February 24 in a well-planned operation, the students entered the building and within minutes had chained the entrances. They anticipated a full police response, expecting to be arrested. One student and activist, Vicki Donaldson, accepted that she might be killed in the ensuing violence.[7]

Mr. Robert Ochs (Rutgers class of 1949), director of the Rutgers University Police, traveled to Newark as soon as he heard of the occupation. Upon his arrival, he discovered that President Mason Gross and the university secretary, Mr. Karl Metzger (Rutgers class of 1933), were already there to meet with the protestors. Mason rejected Ochs's proposed solution to evict the students by force, recalling that in many cases these confrontations had led to violence, physical injury, and further disorder.[8] Mason believed that "many of the extremists want more than anything else to be photographed and if possible televised being carried out of the building by police."[9] Realizing that some of the students wanted a confrontation, Mason was adamantly unwilling to provide that for them.

But Mason also recognized that the protestors, underneath all their rhetoric, had legitimate grievances. The university had not followed up on promises made the previous year to expand enrollments, promises that had been vetoed by Chancellor Dungan. Mason's goal was to treat the cause and not just the symptom.

Meanwhile, white students, including members of Young Americans for Freedom, a nationwide ideologically conservative group founded in 1960, protested outside, calling for law and order, and threatened to break down the doors and storm the building.

Even for his mere willingness to negotiate, Mason was immediately vilified in the press and in numerous letters from irate citizens. Many letters were firm and some were even respectful, but a large number resorted to racial epithets.[10] Many criticisms sharply contrasted his action with that of Father Theodore Hesburgh, the president of Notre Dame University, who one week earlier had given his occupying students exactly fifteen minutes to vacate the premises or face immediate expulsion. Predictably, President Nixon publicly praised Hesburgh's ultimatum. Nixon did not address specifically the incident at Rutgers but did enjoy the opportunity later in May to state that "university presidents have no backbone."

Karl Metzger (Rutgers class of 1933), onetime mayor of nearby Metuchen, was the secretary of the university. He was Mason's executive officer. One of Mason's closest friends, Karl often came to Rumson with his wife Ellie to swim in the ocean. Long after Mason passed away, Karl continued to come to Kirkpatrick Chapel every Sunday. He loved the music. (Photo credit: Rutgers University Library Special Collections and University Archives)

As a result of tense negotiations, the student protestors vacated Conklin Hall in triumph, believing that they had won concessions from the university. As the devil is always in the details, discussion of these details stalled, and by early March tensions in Newark were rising again.

The campus had been in turmoil for a month. Despite the absence of violence, the avowed militancy of the BOS was a threatening posture, as was the possibility that local community supporters of the BOS, including the Black Panthers, would intervene.[11]

The Board of Governors met in executive session on March 14. From this meeting there arose a separate and experimental admissions program for economically and educationally disadvantaged students to be admitted to Rutgers, anticipating that with assistance these students could eventually meet the standard admissions criteria for full matriculation. The program, called the Urban University Program (UUP), was doomed from the outset and would last only two years.

Critics ignited a firestorm of dissent, decrying a lowering of Rutgers's standards or admitting poor-quality students when fully qualified students would be rejected. They accused Mason of capitulating swiftly and overwhelmingly under duress. Again, some of the letters of protest were abusive and blatantly racist. The Achilles' heel of this program would be, as always, funding.

Voices in the legislature protested that this program had not been submitted for legislative approval, which obviously would not have been forthcoming. Mason and the Board of Governors sought funding elsewhere, unsuccessfully, and finally decided initially to fund the program with small reserve funds maintained by the Board of Governors and the Board of Trustees. The state's issue of funding and fiscal autonomy was a smoke screen that cloaked the reactionary and racist response to Mason's attempt to provide "opportunity without artificial barriers denying all people their right to full development."[12]

The UUP was being widely excoriated. Chancellor Dungan had been bypassed in the development of the program and stated that Rutgers should not "provide remedial education for disadvantaged students."[13] Mason attempted to provide damage control. His responses fell on deaf ears. To answer the charge that Rutgers was lowering its admissions standards, Mason noted that the UUP was not an open door but rather an experimental program that would attempt to raise applicants to current standards. To the claim that qualified white students would be denied admission, he added that this was a program separate from regular admissions and that no otherwise qualified student would be denied admission because of the UUP.[14] Asked how he would address the claim that he had been blackmailed by the protestors, Mason responded curtly, "I would ignore it."[15]

The 1969 New Jersey gubernatorial race heated up, with Rutgers already a major campaign issue. New Jersey Democratic governor Richard Hughes was nearing the end of his second term in office and was constitutionally ineligible for re-election to a consecutive third term. The state Republicans remembered their drubbing in the 1965 gubernatorial election, which had centered on Rutgers and Mason's refusal to fire Professor Eugene Genovese for welcoming a pending Viet Cong victory in Vietnam. Now, after Newark, in an election year in New Jersey, Mason's "surrender" to the Black students "brought indignation from gubernatorial candidates and state senators."[16] Early in 1969, falling in line with a national conservative swing to the right, New Jersey Republican challengers lined up. Charles Sandman, the most conservative of these challengers, led the pack early on. He refused to consider raising taxes in spite of a $300 million state budget shortfall and fully supported President Nixon's call for law and order. Sandman was especially critical of the university administration. He "promised to clamp down on campus disorder."[17]

All Republican candidates opposed the Rutgers experimental UUP to admit disadvantaged students. Sandman was especially critical of Mason's concessions concerning the UUP. "The plan stinks," Sandman stated bluntly.[18]

In the June primary after a close race, New Jersey Republicans chose former FBI agent Congressman William Cahill, who favored an expeditious end to the Vietnam War and saw the need for tax reform in New Jersey, reform that included a state income tax. After an equally contentious primary, the state Democrats chose former governor Robert Meyner, who campaigned based on his experience.

In his 1969 Rutgers commencement speech, Mason spoke about some recent struggles, alluding to events at Berkeley when protestors on campus were met with tear gas fired from military helicopters. Describing current national priorities such as "the continued slaughter in Vietnam," he noted the low priority given to "the misery of our cities, ... the very slow movement towards elimination of segregation, the continuing denial of education to those who may need it most, and the acquiescence to brutality, and the almost hysterical anxiety to punish dissenters."[19]

As the political and fiscal landscape was shifting underfoot, so was Rutgers itself. Recall that upon his arrival at Rutgers in the fall of 1945, Mason had quickly met most of the faculty. At that time he was one of two professors of philosophy, whereas Columbia had several dozen. He knew all the coaches. He knew the groundkeepers by first name and chatted with them as he walked to class.[20] Mason's classes were eagerly attended. He knew many of the students, who would shout out "Hey, Mase" to him across the Neilson campus.

Mason "served in an era when the American people and their elected officials regarded higher education as the foundation for America's future."[21] Despite this enthusiasm, New Jersey voters in 1948 and 1954 had rejected bond issues drafted in support of higher education.

From 1959 to 1970, total Rutgers University enrollment increased from nine thousand students to thirty thousand. By 1970, the university's operating budget had grown fourfold, from $28.2 million in 1959 to $115 million.* During this period, New Jersey voters altered course and passed three out of four large bond issues. But the era of easy fund-raising was over. The 1958 National Defense Education Act and bond issues under a supportive state government were history, replaced by decreased aid to higher education from a federal government that was trying unsuccessfully to balance the fiscal

---

* Estimates vary depending on the source, but clearly the change was significant. I have chosen to use Clemens, *Rutgers since 1945*, for student numbers and McCormick and Schlatter, *The Selected Speeches of Mason Welch Gross*, for the budgets.

requirements of a Great Society program, a costly strategic arms race, and an even costlier war in Asia.

The role of a university president had also changed dramatically. A college president had once been an academic, temporarily assigned as an administrator mostly dealing with faculty and student issues, and was expected to return to teaching after his tenure as president was over.* University presidents were now becoming chief executive officers of multibillion-dollar corporations, with increasing amounts of their time spent scrambling for funding and less time to deal with details within their administrations. Heaven forbid there would be time to teach a class. But Mason continued throughout the late 1960s to teach, sometimes two classes each semester. He was not solely a university administrator, "a title he disliked as being akin to 'bureaucrat.'"[22] Karl Metzger (Rutgers class of 1933), secretary of the university and Mason's close friend ever since he came to Rutgers, urged Mason to consider paying attention to the New Jersey voices who were suggesting that he run for governor. Mason answered, "Karl, what do you think is more important, the governorship of New Jersey or the presidency of the state university?"[23] Mason later also answered this question, stating that the only problem with his running for governor was that "I'm afraid I might get elected."[24] Karl once suggested that Mason could even be president. "Karl," Mason quipped, "why in hell would I want to be President of the United States?"[25]

———

Amid the squeeze from funding battles and the controversy over Mason's management of the racial tensions, yet another situation was developing. By the summer of 1969, President Nixon's plan to end the war in Vietnam was not going as smoothly as planned. For those in the Oval Office, Vietnam was rapidly becoming the same quagmire that it had been for Johnson's administration.

---

*Rutgers's most recent presidents, Richard L. McCormick and Robert Barchi, have both returned to teaching.

Back in July 1959, two months after Mason's inauguration at Rutgers, the first two American soldiers had died in Vietnam. Ten years later, by the time of Nixon's inauguration, the number of American dead had steadily climbed above thirty thousand. Over half of those American combat deaths had occurred in 1968 alone. This total would almost double again before Nixon's goal of "peace with honor" would be attained. For Mason, the term "peace with honor" would have been too reminiscent of British prime minister Neville Chamberlain's similar claim at Munich in 1938, the ultimate sellout in a series of appeasements that led to war and the loss of the best friends Mason ever had.*

In the summer of 1969 Julia's nephew Dev Kernan, an enlisted U.S. Army combat photographer, was safely home from Vietnam and was physically uninjured. Mason took Dev aside one summer afternoon. He closed the French doors to the living room, shutting out the rest of the family and the outside world. They spoke, as one veteran to another. Dev spoke about Vietnam; Mason listened. Fifty years later Dev could recall little of the details of their conversation, but he recalled that Mason asked few questions and sat leaning forward in his chair, the smoke from his cigarette curling upward in the hot humid air, and just let him talk.[26] Mason had always preferred firsthand accounts to secondary sources. Dev had been a witness with a front-row seat and a U.S. Army camera, and Mason wanted to hear every word.

On June 27, 1969, as I graduated from high school, *Life* magazine published a pictorial essay titled "The Faces of the American Dead: One Week's Toll" that, using a high school yearbook format, revealed the faces and names of the 242 American soldiers who had perished during *one single week*, May 28 through June 3.[27] Many of the soldiers were not yet nineteen years old, only slightly older than me.

In the summer of 1969, antiwar activists began to campaign for a day of peaceful protest titled the Moratorium to End the War in Vietnam. On Octo-

---

* Colin Cotteril, the wild hard-drinking Irishman with whom Mason played darts and read Kant, and Lambert Shepard, who rowed at both Cambridge and Dunkirk.

ber 15, 1969, in countless communities there occurred peaceful marches and gatherings. Surprisingly, many businesses, both large and small, complied with the Vietnam Moratorium Committee's request to suspend business as usual on that day so that employees could participate in marches or in other gatherings that were intended to increase awareness of the issues surrounding the war.

The Vietnam Moratorium Committee originally intended that there would be one Moratorium Day in October and then two in November, increasing by one day each subsequent month. A November moratorium did occur, although fewer businesses were willing to participate for two full days. By December, support for the moratoriums, as originally conceived, had run out of momentum.

At Rutgers, Mason addressed the upcoming October moratorium as a time "to go beyond protest to a critical examination of basic issues affecting the nation." He suggested an investigation into the "role of the university as a guardian of civilized values, as a critical and moral intelligence which compels the community to ponder its course of action" during difficult times.[28] Although Mason and the remainder of the university administration neither cancelled classes nor took an active stand on the war itself, some faculty did cancel their classes. The various meetings to discuss Vietnam were well attended and remained peaceful.

In October, the New Jersey gubernatorial election, which was being characterized as the most acrimonious contest in state history, even more so than in 1965, was drawing to a close. The race between Cahill and Meyner was too close to call.[29] In October, President Nixon came to New Jersey to campaign in support of Cahill, the Republican candidate, as he had done for Dumont in 1965.

In a televised speech on November 3, Nixon outlined his plan for ending the American involvement in Vietnam, closing with a request for support from "the great silent majority." In the era before personal computers, the phrase went viral.

On November 4, New Jersey voters elected Cahill, the first Republican governor in sixteen years.

On Veterans' Day, November 11, 1969, supporters of Nixon's policies gathered at the Washington Monument in part to advocate for an increased combat presence in pursuit of total victory in Vietnam.

Also early in November, soon after my eighteenth birthday, as required by law, I climbed a dirty, narrow, and poorly lit stairway on a side street in downtown New Brunswick to the decrepit office of the New Brunswick Draft Board. Barely mature enough to shave and not yet old enough to vote or buy myself a cold beer, I registered, unceremoniously, for the draft.* Not certain whether Mason was even aware of this key moment in my life, I never mentioned it to him, and he never brought it up. The distance between us grew steadily larger.

On November 12, 1969, a story broke via the Associated Press of a massacre by American soldiers in a small Vietnamese hamlet that had occurred in March 1968, soon after that year's infamous Tet Offensive. By the following week, most news media were hot on the story of the My Lai Massacre. Details varied, but it was clear that a U.S. Army company had descended upon My Lai with reports that it was a Viet Cong stronghold. Unarmed civilians, mostly women, children, and elderly, were gathered into groups. There were no males close to military age in the village. The company commander ordered his soldiers to open fire with their automatic weapons at point-blank range into the groups, executing mothers attempting to shield their own children. Although totals vary, the very lowest estimates state that over 350 bodies were later counted.

All wars descend inevitably into cycles of unspeakable violence perpetrated by all sides. At its best, if there is such a state, war is a maelstrom of chaos, revenge, and unimaginable inhumanity that defies description and the depths of which are understood only by those who have personally experienced it. Describing a "systematic massacre" of wounded U.S. marines by the Viet Cong, Phil Caputo wrote of his tour as a U.S. Marine Corps lieutenant. "Both we and the Viet Cong began to make a habit of atrocities. . . .

---

*The Twenty-Sixth Amendment to the U.S. Constitution, authorizing eighteen-year-olds to vote in national elections, did not go into effect until July 1971.

We paid the enemy back, sometimes with interest."[30] The combat veteran knows how quickly it becomes pointless to ask which side committed the greatest outrage first. The news of the My Lai Massacre was first broken not by the so-called liberal media but instead by a U.S. Army press release in September 1969 from Fort Benning, Georgia, stating that a company commander was to be court-martialed for directing the massacre and for personally executing several dozen unarmed captives. Many Americans believed the reactionary White House response that the photos were faked and that American soldiers could never commit such acts. The My Lai Massacre was the largest of many similar atrocities attributed not only to the U.S. Army and the Army of the Republic of Vietnam but also to the Viet Cong, the North Vietnamese Army, and the South Korean Army, which had been sent to Vietnam at President Johnson's request and had a well-deserved reputation for unparalleled brutality.

On many occasions, Mason reminded his audiences to read Thucydides on the civil war in Corcyra as a reminder from twenty-five centuries ago about how war brings out the extremes in human behavior.* To Lieutenant Caputo in Vietnam, the discussions of "ethics seemed to be a matter of distance" from a "war of survival in a wilderness without rules or laws."[31] But arguments over who committed what atrocities first, whose massacre was most justified, or who was the most savage all miss the point; namely, regardless of what really happened in that tiny hamlet, the My Lai incident created a firestorm of outrage that resonates more than fifty years later. If the My Lai story had broken when it occurred, on the heels of the Tet Offensive in 1968, who can say if it would have generated such an effect? But when the My Lai story broke in the autumn of 1969, hundreds of flag-draped caskets and crippled soldiers were coming home weekly to many more American neighborhoods, no longer just to the poor inner cities, bringing the true cost of the war home to the great silent majority in Middle America. More and more people, not just on university campuses and in large cities, conservatives

---

* On the Corcyraean revolution, I suggest Thucydides, *The History of the Peloponnesian War*, book 3, chap. 81, 198.

as well as liberals, were starting to ask "What are we doing there?" Although revisionist historical accounts may seek to promote the fairy tale that Vietnam was "lost" because of lies published by the liberal media,[32] after My Lai the cat was really out of the bag, forever.

By the end of 1969, my brother Charlie and I were both classified I-A and eligible to be drafted. Around this time, Charlie received his draft notice. Torn between accepting the draft or considering refusing and going to jail, he went to Mason for guidance. Mason, who had volunteered for military duty after Pearl Harbor, would soon publicly denounce the "sheer utter horrible immorality"[33] of the war in Vietnam. But he had never been one to offer advice to his sons, maintaining an emotional distance that we would repeatedly misinterpret as indifference or even antipathy. On this occasion, however, confessing ambivalence, Mason confided to Charlie that he was not sure what action he would take in his situation.[34] Charlie boarded the bus to the U.S. Army induction center in Newark, at that moment not knowing which option he would select.

The Vietnam War, well covered by local print media including the Rutgers *Daily Targum*, affected the campus on a daily basis as protests arose over such issues as Reserve Officers' Training Corp (ROTC) on campus and the rumors that Rutgers was performing research directly funded by the Department of Defense. However, other issues that were less noticeable publicly were also bearing down on Mason's administration.

———

By now, New Jersey state government was struggling financially. Early in 1970, New Jersey governor-elect William Cahill described a "major state fiscal crisis."[35] In 1965 New Jersey had been one of only three states, including Nebraska and New Hampshire, that levied neither income tax nor a statewide sales tax. Property taxes were rising precipitously. Governor Hughes had campaigned for re-election in 1965 proposing an income tax in order to support his state budget of $876 million. He had won re-election, but in the biggest tax battle in New Jersey history his measure had quickly failed to garner sufficient legislative support and was withdrawn. Hughes compromised and agreed to a 3 percent sales tax that went into effect July 1, 1966.[36]

Governor Cahill took office in January 1970, noting a "serious law enforcement problem" and recognizing New Jersey's impending fiscal emergency. His $1.6 billion budget, growing rapidly due to "mandated rises in continuing state programs," was almost twice that of Hughes's budget only four years earlier and faced a $300 million shortfall. Cahill stated one week prior to his own inauguration that "we are going to cut, to squeeze and to trim the present cost of government."[37]

In a shrinking fiscal environment, Rutgers had already been vilified in the most acrimonious gubernatorial election in New Jersey history. To a new Republican governor and legislature "crying for blood,"[38] by early 1970 Rutgers University was clearly an easy target.

In January, Chancellor Andrew Dungan prohibited all out-of-state travel for Rutgers personnel without his prior approval. This included travel across the river to New York or Philadelphia. He also stated that all vacancies would remain unfilled until further notice.[39] This was problematic, as all teaching assistants were rehired every semester, and assistant professors were all on three-year contracts.*

In April 1970, the Republican majority in the New Jersey Senate, "goaded by simmering resentment over an open enrollment program primarily for black students at Rutgers, overwhelmingly voted final legislative approval to a measure giving tight control over Rutgers fiscal affairs."[40] Approved by Governor Cahill, this unprecedented measure, already approved by the state legislature, ended the "relative fiscal autonomy that Rutgers had enjoyed since it became a state university in 1947." Spokesmen for the legislature stated that this was the "price Rutgers must pay for continuing its controversial Urban University Program," which provided Rutgers admission for disadvantaged students and had been adopted "in the wake of demonstrations

---

* Mason's successor at Rutgers, Dr. Edward Bloustein, later stated that Commissioner Ralph A. Dungan "does not understand the nature of universities."

by black students" in the previous year.[41] Governor Cahill and the Republican Senate were angry that Mason and the Board of Governors had initiated the new UUP program without first seeking the state's approval and the fiscal authorization to proceed. All of Rutgers spending and all budget requests that used to go directly to the governor's office would henceforth be managed through Andrew Dungan, commissioner of the Board of Higher Education. One interviewer suggested that there was still a good relationship between Rutgers and the state government, to which Mason, ever articulate, responded, "That's bullshit."

Mason was busy dealing with the assault on Rutgers's fiscal autonomy. Also in April, Nixon had already "secretly" resumed the bombing of North Vietnam, which President Johnson had stopped eighteen months previously. On April 30, 1970, having watched the newly released biographic feature film *Patton* no less than four times,[42] Nixon announced that he had ordered an American "incursion" into the "Parrot Beak" region of Cambodia's border with South Vietnam. This invasion was initiated in response to North Vietnamese forces that were using officially neutral Cambodia as a safe refuge from which to conduct raids into South Vietnam. (They had been using Laos for years.) Sensing an escalation of the war, student protests erupted around the country. Despite violence at many colleges, most campuses across the country maintained peaceful but well-attended demonstrations.

On Friday, May 1, at Rutgers and at many other campuses across the nation, student organizations gathered momentum in support of student strikes, that is, the end of classes for the remainder of the year so students could concentrate on activities to stop the war. Many of these organizations had different agendas so that a singular antiwar platform often morphed into other issues.

On Saturday, May 2, Rutgers hosted the annual military field day at the football stadium in Piscataway. This spring event had been held here for decades, with both static and active displays by active army and reserve units, including the Rutgers ROTC contingent. This year, members of the Youth

International Party, or "Yippies," protested the event. Present at the ceremony, Mason stated later that the antiwar demonstration had been orderly.
The records do reveal that it was an orderly demonstration, albeit loud, dis-
ruptive, disrespectful, and significantly inflammatory, as antiwar protestors
performed a "goose step" march around the track. At one point, thirty angry
spectators left their seats and entered the field, attacking and beating the anti-
ROTC demonstrators. On this same day there was a firebombing to the
outside of the ROTC building on the Livingston campus that was rapidly
extinguished without structural damage.

In New Brunswick, on May 4 demonstrators gathered outside Old Queens,
the main administration building, having previously announced their plans
to occupy it in protest. After some speeches, at 9:30 A.M. they entered the
building.

Although most of the protestors had left by noon, a small cadre remained,
vowing not to leave until their demands were met even up to the point of
violence. Their demands were an end to ROTC at Rutgers, an end to Rutgers's contracts with the Department of Defense, and that any university
workers who had been displaced by the student strike would receive full pay.

One student who had entered Queens recalled the situation. "During the
event, the New Brunswick tactical police arrived in their blue bus, decked
out in blue riot helmets, tapping their batons against black leather gloves.
Dr. Gross went outside and told the police that we were his guests and that
he would call them if he needed them."[43]

Remembering that it takes two sides to fight, Mason called upon Campus Police superintendent Robert Ochs to establish a police line around
Queens. Ochs believed that this action was intended to keep further protestors out of Queens while his officers could forcefully evict the trespassers.
Ochs had misunderstood Mason's intention.

Mason and Chief Ochs had known each other for more than twenty years.
Ochs had been an undergraduate in 1948, one of many new students who
were World War II veterans attending college on the G.I. Bill. Ochs later
credited Mason's intervention in an unpleasant incident involving a professor

with saving Ochs from expulsion. After graduation, Ochs completed a master's degree in education at Rutgers. In 1963 Mason insisted that Ochs accept the position of director of the newly established Rutgers University Police Department and Division of Public Safety, a position Ochs would hold until his retirement in 1988.

On the morning of May 4, 1970, as the antiwar protestors occupied Queens, Mason, having ordered the police barrier, then surprised Ochs by also ordering not only the remaining protestors but also the police to remain outside the police line, effectively establishing a boundary between two groups, both of which were itching for a confrontation. "I didn't agree with him," Ochs recalled years later, "but, Mason and I had a history, and I owed him one. And, in retrospect, he was right."[44]

One student recalled, "My friends and I were aware that the only thing that stood between us and our (relatively) peaceful campus and the tender mercies of the New Brunswick riot police was Dr. Gross' insistence that they keep off the property. . . . The legislature in Trenton was crying for blood but Dr. Gross would have none of it."[45] Yet another student echoed a similar sentiment. "Unlike many of his presidential contemporaries, Dr. Gross did not flee the building or threaten the students with arrest. Instead he spoke to the students in sympathetic tones and had punch and cookies sent in for his 'captors.'"[46]

Actually, anticipating that the occupants would remain overnight, Mason sent to the University Commons for trays of sandwiches and coffee. Arnold Grobman, dean of Rutgers College, noted that during the occupation of Queens, "the place was a mess, with soft drink cans and sandwich wrappers." Grobman recalls that once the faculty had agreed to the occupiers' terms, he ordered the protesters to vacate the building.

"Please leave immediately!" Grobman demanded.

The protesters refused.

"We'll be out by noon," they replied. "We have to clean up." Grobman says the place was "spotless when they left."[47] Nothing had been disturbed. There was no damage. After the protestors left the building, voluntarily and peacefully, Mason later noted that they had taken out the trash and scrubbed "the desks with some furniture polish"[48] as they departed.*

———

Protests at Kent State University in Kent, Ohio, had been escalating all weekend, with vandalism even off campus in the city itself. A fire started by a burning American flag soon spread and destroyed the ROTC building. The mayor had requested assistance from the governor. The Ohio National Guard had arrived in Kent on Saturday and then on Sunday had been involved in dispersing the crowds.

Shortly after noon on Monday, May 4, a student demonstration at Kent State degenerated into violence. While National Guard troops, sent to quell the disturbance, were maneuvering back to their starting point, they were followed by demonstrators. The guardsmen turned and opened fire, killing four and wounding others. Student strikes spread across the country, with injuries on many campuses due to conflicts with law enforcement or National Guard units. Governor Reagan closed all twenty-seven campuses of the California state university system and declared that any students remaining on campus were trespassing. Although only 5 percent of college campuses experienced demonstrations that descended into violence, those that did were heavily hit.

At Rutgers, classes continued on May 5. Mason resisted the protestors' demand that the university cancel all classes, but he did not refuse the option of faculty members to cancel a class if they so desired.

———

There is a moment from that day that everyone who was there remembers. Several thousand people crowded shoulder to shoulder onto the lawn at Queens. The Kent State shootings had been a tragic misjudgment, but to many

---

* This did not happen at Columbia, Cornell, Berkeley, San Francisco State, or any other campus that I know of.

people they also represented an escalation against the antiwar movement. On campuses all over the United States, students paused in remembrance and, in shock, then picked up their banners and marched, louder than before.

At Rutgers, Mason came outside to address the crowd. Conversely, some university presidents, when their offices were occupied, had escaped out the back door. Mason had no prepared speech. The transcript of this address states that these were "impromptu remarks."

For a moment Mason stopped being the university administrator, instead revealing his real self, the teacher and a student of philosophy and history, the superior philosopher at the top of his game, the master of the dialectic, doing what he loved most.

Mason spoke not of protests or rights. Other than expressing "grave regret and deep sorrow" for the Kent State "martyrs," he barely mentioned Vietnam. Instead, recalling Abraham Lincoln and a nation dedicated to liberty, Mason talked about government secrecy as a threat to the preservation of liberty for the American citizen. He added "we have to stop fighting wars that are none of our damn business."[49]

Here Mason was Socrates in the marketplace, and like Socrates, was being condemned by the powers that be for corrupting the youth.

Socrates had stated that "there was an objective standard of what is right." Just like Socrates before him, both military officers in their youth, Mason had developed a low tolerance for bullshit. Specifically recalling Adolf Hitler's 1938 invasion of Czechoslovakia, in his impromptu remarks Mason noted that you cannot invade another country and do it in the name of peace. He said that you cannot bomb another country's capital and call it "defensive." He alluded to Julius Caesar's crossing of the Rubicon, suggesting that those who perpetrated such acts also justified them as defensive maneuvers made in the name of peace. Having once stated that if "you read Thucydides on Corcyra you will understand true human nature,"[50] today Mason again showed that knowledge of history matters.

Mason spoke in a way that showed how he lived. He showed that Plato matters, that Kant matters, Leviticus, Spinoza, and Whitehead matter. Mason cared about his audience in the way that Socrates cared about the youth of

Athens. Mason later spoke of the protesting students as an "honest, sincere, concerned group of young men and women, who have been shocked into the realization that all is not well."[51]

Then Mason tasked the audience. He described a public that had grown increasingly "suspicious of university students," sometimes suspicious of a "mode of dress, language or unconventional ideas." But, he stated, citing the youth effort that had made itself so well noticed during the 1968 New Hampshire Democratic primary campaign, that "this is the public that . . . we've got to bring over to our side." He cautioned the audience to avoid distracting the public with quarrels within the university but stated that we must "keep our eye on the ball" and "bring this country back to peace."

"More power to you," Mason said in closing as he sent the audience out to convince the American people that this was the most important issue facing our country. He tasked his audience to show "that we are all united in our efforts to bring peace."[52]

Mason turned and walked away. Two thousand people loudly applauded in a way that Hesburgh, president of Notre Dame University, and Hayakawa, president of San Francisco State University, were never applauded. Provost Richard Schlatter, one of Mason's closest friends, was there and later wrote that "no one has ever been more widely respected and revered."[53] The ovation was an eruption. Mason had hit a grand-slam home run.

In the depth of Mason's greatest struggle, it was also his finest hour.

———

But Governor Cahill still had one more item on his Rutgers agenda, one more shoe to drop.

By the middle of May amid the chaos after Kent State, the new legislature had completed its hijacking of Rutgers's traditional fiscal autonomy. This top-down control would not only manifest in tighter budgets and significantly less autonomy but would also soon result in a significant evisceration of the university.

As the tempers following Kent State were starting to cool, in a hearing in Trenton on Tuesday, May 12, 1970, the New Jersey legislature opened discussion on Assembly Bill A-1059, which would separate the eight-year-old Rutgers Medical School from Rutgers University and join it to the New Jersey College of Medicine in Newark under the auspices of a brand-new university with a new and separate Board of Trustees, conveniently to be appointed by the new governor who created it.

Mason traveled to Trenton to speak to the hearing on Assembly Bill A-1059. But, he was bringing a knife to a gunfight. Mason argued that A-1059 was a threat to the university's autonomy, that if the legislature could separate out a medical school, it could also do so to any program that did not meet with the governor's favor, such as a Black studies program. Mason stated that "this destruction of the University is something too horrible to contemplate." Yet despite some cursory assurance that this was only a preliminary hearing, the atmosphere prevailed that this was a "done deal."[54]

A stormy three-hour debate followed in which the opposition crossed party lines. High-pressure arm twisting included personal summons for reluctant Republican legislators to come to the governor's office. Republican assemblyman Robert Haelig called the measure "ill advised, inappropriate and ill conceived" and added that this measure was actually intended "to get back at Mason Gross," in reference to the running public battle between Mason, some legislators, and members of the Cahill administration.[55]

At the closure of the debate, A-1059 narrowly passed in the Assembly and awaited Senate action. Haelig stated that "no member of the assembly offered a single valid reason for the passage of that bill and yet it passed because the governor wanted it passed."[56]

Some news reports suggested that Mason looked tired. A close friend later described him during this period as "edgy as a wounded bear." His calm demeanor on campus was not always evident at home. Never abusive or intoxicated, he was increasingly short-tempered. He barked at a family friend for taking a candid photo during a festive supper, complaining that "a man shouldn't have a camera shoved in his face in his own home." It is not known how much Mason confided to Julia, but his children, now all living out of state, were in the dark as to the depth of his struggles, which throughout his life he had always kept to himself and would continue to do in the future as his struggles intensified and became even more personal and threatening.

———

What did Mason reveal of himself in the storms of these last eighteen months? We saw a man who had once undertaken an intense study of philosophy and then lived according to its dictates, directing his actions from Socrates's "grand searchlight revealing brilliantly the good and the evil" and from Kant's categorical imperative that commanded respect for the "principle of the absolute and irreducible dignity of mankind, regardless of color or religion."[57]

In words that could apply equally to Mason, Socrates has been described as "a man of singular character and intelligence, imbued with a passion for intellectual honesty and moral integrity rare for his or any other age.... His personal character was full of paradoxical contrasts ... presumptuously confident, ... witty yet morally urgent, engaging ... yet solitary.... Socrates was ... consumed by a passion for truth."[58] Socrates had found his way to a morality that, unlike that of his Sophist predecessors, was grounded in something much more fundamental than mere convention: absolute good, absolute truth, and absolute beauty.

We saw in Mason a man who, like Socrates, saw the secrecy and the blatant lies of the autocrats, from Pericles and Caesar, Hitler and Stalin, to Johnson and Nixon, as the true danger to a democracy. As in 1965 with the Genovese controversy, Mason had refused to give in to the forces of mere convention that would find an enemy in every closet and strip away the dignity of the individual.

We saw a philosopher who had demanded at Newark "freedom for opportunity without artificial barriers denying all people their right to full development." Mason did not see the admissions of poorly prepared Black or Latino students as being a lowering of university standards of admission. He saw that the university's glass was half full, not half empty. He saw that the new groups entering the university were enriching the culture of the university.

Mason's best friend and colleague, Provost Dick Schlatter, later stated that Mason was "the philosopher-teacher of Rutgers."[59]

———

In twenty-four years at Rutgers, even before he was president, Mason never missed a commencement. As president, every year he had provided the commencement address. This year was no different.

But in this year's address, from the dais on the one-yard line in Rutgers Stadium, Mason could not speak solely of the students' accomplishments and their confidence in beginning a new stage of their lives. He compared this commencement to others, such as in 1861 "amid the echoes of the attack on Fort Sumter," in 1918 after "a war declared only two months earlier," in 1932 during the Great Depression, and in 1942 after Pearl Harbor, that cast a long shadow over graduates' futures.

Mason emphasized his "belief in the absolute distinction between right and wrong" as a "fundamental tenet of religion." He spoke of the violent kickback and backlash, the attack on the concept of the university itself, as universities were "becoming the whipping boy for all the unrest in our society." He said, "Like Socrates, we are found guilty of corrupting the young."

Here Mason was again no longer solely the administrator but also Socrates speaking in the marketplace, the scholar, the teacher, the student of philosophy, fully engaged in the battle of faith and reason versus law and order.

Mason's final words hovered in the long shadows of an early summer evening and settled in the soft humid air. He closed his address to the graduates by asking that their accomplishments at Rutgers "always provide you with joy and enable you to contribute to the benefit of your fellow men in a world at peace."[60]

CHAPTER 24

June 1970

Commencement 1970 cannot be classified with those utterly peaceful days when there were no doubts, no uncertainties. . . . I need not elaborate on the main problems; we all know them only too well—war and peace, poverty, abject miserable poverty amidst such abundant plenty, the apparently invincible forces of racism and the willful spoiling of our environment.
—MWG, June 3, 1970

The spring of 1970 had wrought a succession of disasters at Rutgers. First, antiwar protests accelerated in the wake of the shootings at Kent State and later at Jackson State, Mississippi, in that state where so many shootings had occurred in the previous decade that they had stopped being front-page national news. Second, at Rutgers Medical School, as the large classroom and laboratory sciences building was about to be dedicated, the swift passage of New Jersey Assembly Bill A-1059 and its subsequent rapid passage in the Senate tore the Rutgers Medical School away from Rutgers and created the new College of Medicine and Dentistry of New Jersey, administratively and, confusingly, separate but obviously still colocated with the Rutgers Science campus in the University Heights. Those medical school faculty who had joint appointments in both life sciences departments and medicine struggled to determine if the short-sighted A-1059 had set them adrift. Dr. Walter Schlesinger, assistant dean of the medical school, wrote that most of the medical school faculty wished to remain with Rutgers University and not transfer to the College of Medicine and Dentistry of New Jersey. Dean DeWitt Stetten announced his resignation, effective that September.

Third, the legislature was pounding the final nails into the coffin of the Urban University Program, initiated in the wake of the Conklin Hall occupation in February 1969. Finally, Rutgers's long-standing fiscal autonomy was being dismantled, as the new governor's administration sought to punish Rutgers, in the person of Mason himself, for his unyielding support of education for minorities.

In mid-June Mason stormed nervously around the house for several days, visibly frustrated, impatient, and angry that he could not reach my brother Charlie, who was living on a dairy farm outside of Madison, Wisconsin. Nobody was answering the phone, and in the era before voice recorders, Mason could not leave a message.

Finally, he reached Charlie. From another room, I eavesdropped as Mason spoke with him quietly from a sunroom at the President's House.

"I am going to announce my retirement from Rutgers," he told Charlie, "and I wanted you to hear it from me." I had sat several evenings with my parents in the living room, but this was the first I had heard of it. Ever secretive, Mason never actually mentioned it to me himself.

Mason had discussed this with a few members of the Board of Governors, most likely Archie Alexander and Charlie Brower, as they were also good friends. Certainly Mason would have told Dick Schlatter and Karl Metzger, longtime colleagues but also close friends. One assumes that Mason would have discussed it with Julia.

Mason prepared a letter to the Board of Governors to be read into the minutes at its July meeting, proposing a retirement date in a year, on September 1, 1971, commemorating that Mason would have spent exactly twenty-five years at Rutgers, with exactly twelve and a half years as president. He wrote that the job "needed some new blood."[1] He specifically stated that his decision was not based on recent events, nor was he planning employment elsewhere.

After the July meeting when Mason announced his retirement, the Board of Governors held a press conference. Due to the antiwar protests and the administration's adverse relations with the new governor, the press conference was packed with reporters not only from New Jersey newspapers but also those from the greater Philadelphia and New York metropolitan areas.

Ron Reisman (Rutgers class of 1971), reporting for WRSU, the student radio station, was in the Rutgers library waiting for the press conference to begin. "When Dr. Gross walked into the room," Reisman later wrote, "the entire press corps stood up and applauded him. I've never seen anything like that."

As Mason walked to the front of the room, Reisman recalled, "he saw me, put his hand on my shoulder and said, 'Hi, Ron, how are you?' I absolutely went to pieces. . . . Can you imagine? This was one of the biggest events of his life, and he still found time to say hello to a student reporter."[2]

Mason had drafted a letter to Governor William Cahill announcing his retirement. Mason purposefully mailed it only on the eve of the press conference so Cahill would learn of the retirement only after the press knew and would not have time to draft a response before the reporters told him.

There was much speculation as to the real reason behind Mason's decision to retire. He continued to claim that he was "feeling stale" and that Rutgers needed someone with fresh ideas to come to the job. Rutgers historian Paul Clemens concludes that "the frustrations in negotiating with the state for support and autonomy probably influenced his decision."[3] The Philadelphia *Evening Bulletin* later reported that Mason retired in 1971 "exhausted from student strikes, sit-ins, skirmishes with the legislature and Governor Cahill's own merger of Rutgers Medical School into the New Jersey College of Medicine and Dentistry."[4]

On September 14, *Daily Targum* editor Tony Mauro (Rutgers class of 1971) offered his summary of Mason's decision to retire, adding that although it was no surprise to many who had seen him struggling with the politics of the presidency, the reality of his pending departure was a shock. Some proposed that Mason had made his decision as early as the previous fall, though I have found no evidence to support that claim. Only two years previously, he had cautioned that Rutgers must never degenerate to a situation "where the tremendous emotional power of the students has to be confronted by the physical power of a police force."[5] However, following the Vietnam moratorium in December 1969, Mason called for the New Brunswick police

Against the background of constant protests opposing the Vietnam War and the underrepresentation of minorities at the university, Mason was dealing with a student body that increasingly viewed those in power as conservative "fascists" and with a state government and citizenry that saw him as excessively liberal. A turning point came in December 1969, when Mason first allowed the police to intervene, arresting protestors who had insisted on disrupting a Board of Governors' meeting. Mason was tired, short-tempered, and "edgy as a wounded bear." (Photo credit: Rutgers University Library Special Collections and University Archives)

to intervene during a disruption by Students for a Democratic Society of a Board of Governors meeting. This had been "the first use of police on the Rutgers campus to end a demonstration."[6] In his September 1970 editorial Mauro added, "There were clearly many times that Mason Gross enjoyed being president of Rutgers, when that flash of love and rapport for his students and colleagues crossed his face, but it was just as clear that those times were becoming fewer and further between in the last two years. . . . What had scarred him perhaps for the longest time was the incredible insensitivity of the state, its legislature and its citizens towards the needs of the university."[7]

Some later articles published after Mason's retirement reflect incorrectly that his decision to retire had come due to illness, but his hospitalization and surgery for colon cancer did not occur until January 1971, a full six months after his announcement. Although one reporter did state that Mason "looked tired," there was no evidence at that time that he was ill. Referring to the recent events at Rutgers, Mason's colleague Dick McCormick later concluded that after 1968, Mason had "changed tremendously. . . . These things weakened him, no question about it."[8]

CHAPTER 25

Complicated, 1971

Mason is complicated.
—Dr. Gabriel Pickar, April 1972

Back in 1965, when Mason and Julia had returned from their Carnegie-sponsored trip through Africa, the Middle East, and Eastern Europe, Mason wanted to look at the photos he had taken. Not wanting to bother with a heavy camera, which he had no interest in learning to use anyway, he had taken along a new point-and-shoot Kodak Instamatic camera, which instead of film rolls used film cartridges that could be popped in quickly. I had also purchased for him some prepaid mailers so he could send the film straight to Kodak for developing, so the slides would be ready for him to view when he got home.

I set Mason up with a slide viewer. He was terribly disappointed. Unbeknownst to Mason, the camera had a fixed extremely wide-angle lens, so when he took a photo of an elephant that was practically standing on his shoe, it appeared to be tiny, over a hundred yards away.

Mason never wanted to see the photos again. But there was a lone picture that had caught his eye. It was a photograph of him and Julia, standing on the equator. Mason looked huge. He was embarrassed at the weight that he had gained over the years, up to almost three hundred pounds. Immediately upon their return, he sought advice from our local physician, Dr. Gabriel Pickar.

Born in Brooklyn in 1913, Gabe Pickar was an internist, a graduate of Edinburgh's Royal College of Surgeons and a combat veteran with the

U.S Army during World War II.* A contemporary of Mason's, Dr. Pickar had started his own practice in 1946, the same year Mason had come to Rutgers, on Second Avenue in Highland Park, around the corner and four blocks up the street from our home on Grant Avenue. Pickar had occasionally seen Mason as a patient, but Mason went to the doctor extremely rarely. Pickar had been the chief of internal medicine at Middlesex General Hospital when Mason was chairman of the board, and he also was a founding adjunct faculty member of the new Rutgers Medical School.

Pickar started Mason on the 1960s version of a low-carbohydrate diet, then called the Royal Canadian Air Force diet, avoiding starches such as pasta, rice, potatoes, and toast. Known also as "the drinking man's diet," the diet called for a voluntary moderate but unquantified limitation of alcohol consumption.

Low-carbohydrate diets work well, and Mason was disciplined and dedicated enough to make it work spectacularly. Within a few years, he had shed much of his excess weight and was pleased when people noticed.

Unfortunately, one of the first signs of cancer is weight loss.

Mason had remained a heavy smoker, to which the brown nicotine stains on his fingers and on the overhead liner of his old Oldsmobile would attest. He had always noted, even in his undergraduate correspondence to his parents forty years earlier, persistent gastrointestinal difficulties, mostly chronic heartburn, which is now called "gastric reflux" of stomach acid into the esophagus.

Mason and Julia took a trip to California in January 1971 for meetings with the Rutgers Alumni Association in Los Angeles and San Francisco. They took the occasion to visit me, then in my freshman year at Berkeley.† As we walked through Sather Gate and around the Life Sciences Building where I spent most of my time, Mason did not seem especially weakened, certainly

---

* At Casablanca in 1943, Pickar attended to British prime minister Winston Churchill, extremely ill with a severe case of pneumonia.
† The reader may recall that Mason had been on the campus once before, forty years previously in the late summer of 1928.

no different than he had been the previous summer, but I admit that I had seen so little of him in recent years that I had not noticed his weight loss and growing frailty. I remember feeling uneasy around him, but I cannot remember whether I was being distant or he was.

In the early summer of 1971, I came home from Berkeley to help with my parents' transition into retirement and their move from the Rutgers President's House back to their home in Rumson. Since winter they had planned the first modifications to their old house, which had not even seen a new coat of paint in over a decade. They rebuilt the kitchen and built shelves for Mason's study and his record collection.

I arrived in mid-June. Mason and Julia were away for a few days, so our nearest neighbors, Skip and Harriet Wilver, invited me over for supper. During the meal, Skip reflected on my dad's last year as president of Rutgers.

"We sure were worried about your dad last winter," Skip said. "For a while, we thought we were going to lose him."

Pausing with a mouthful, I asked, "What are you talking about?"

Skip and Harriet exchanged an embarrassed glance. "His cancer," Harriet said.

I set my fork down and sat back in my chair. "I'm sorry," I said, "what cancer?"

Harriet's words were exactly "You mean you don't know?" I then learned the story of Mason's cancer not from my family but instead from our neighbors. It seemed that everyone knew except me.

Soon after my parents' return from San Francisco, Mason had begun to experience abdominal pain and vomiting. One day he was unable to get out of bed. Dr. Pickar, a physician of the old school, made a house call and found Mason "collapsed secondary to complications from continuing diarrhea."[1] Pickar immediately arranged for Mason to go to Middlesex Hospital. Pickar suspected a bowel obstruction, a classic finding in advanced colon cancer.

Mason was diagnosed with disseminated colorectal cancer. Surgery was performed the same day, resulting in a complete colectomy, or removal of the entire large intestine, and the placement of a colostomy, an opening in the right lower anterior abdomen, a new outlet for the gastrointestinal tract but without the normal anatomical sphincter that would allow one to have some control over the timing of bowel moments. A patient with a colostomy wears a plastic bag over the stoma (the hole), and the liquid stool collects spontaneously in the bag. In 1971 the bag was held in place by straps hung from a garter belt around the waist, which gurgled, leaked, and smelled like one would expect bowel contents to smell. Mason was anemic and exhausted. Although the surgeons had successfully removed the malignant tumor, there was evidence that the cancer had spread to the interior wall of the pelvis and the surrounding structures.

Mason remained in the hospital for several weeks. Dick Schlatter, Rutgers's provost and Mason's closest friend, took over as acting president for several months as Mason recovered. Dick knew about the cancer. After a while, everyone at Rutgers knew. Mason recovered slowly. He had not expected to be out for the entire semester. Houston Peterson, then seventy-four, came out of retirement to pick up Mason's teaching load for the remainder of the year.

Looking back, one of the early signs of colorectal cancer can be rectal bleeding, at first occasional and annoying, later persistent, often mistaken by patients as a bleeding hemorrhoid. This can be followed by bloody diarrhea. Typically, early colon cancer can cause some lower abdominal discomfort and difficulty with bowel movements due to partial obstruction by the growing tumor but for a long time may be free of disabling symptoms. It is impossible to know how long Mason experienced these early signs and symptoms, but Pickar stated that they had "continued with increasing intensity."

But we know that Mason did discuss them with Pickar sometime early in 1970, *over a year* before his collapse.[2] Despite the absence of technologies such as the CT scan and the colonoscopy that we rely on today, sometime in the busy spring of 1970 Pickar had easily and quickly made the diagnosis of colorectal cancer, still in its early stage. But in the midst of struggles with the new governor, campus unrest, the pushback over his Urban University Program, and the loss of the medical school and Rutgers's own fiscal autonomy, Mason chose to do nothing about it. Dr. Pickar wrote later to my sister

Ellen that "Mason is complicated and so is his response to this severe illness, all its complications and implications. It is unfortunate that Mason chose, for whatever reason, to neglect and disregard these disturbing symptoms until he collapsed."

Gabe's son, David Pickar, MD (Rutgers class of 1969), recalls how heartbroken Gabe was over Mason's cancer. There is no evidence to suggest that Gabe's and Mason's relationship was less than extremely cordial, so it is difficult to attribute Mason's reluctance solely to stereotypical poor doctor-patient communication. When he made the diagnosis sometime around early 1970, Pickar believed that Mason understood the seriousness of this condition and the nature of malignancy but wished not to discuss it further. It is not clear that Mason had informed Julia either.

Mason was no stranger to medical professionals and could have reached out to any of several at a moment's notice for advice. Having been chairman of the board at Middlesex Hospital during much of his presidency as the medical school was first in planning and then in discussion and early operation, he had been in constant discussion with Dr. DeWitt Stetten and other early faculty members such as Drs. Walter Schlesinger and Richard Cross. But Mason chose to keep his symptoms a secret, to the detriment of his own future. As Pickar had speculated, "Mason could have had an excellent result if the operation had been performed a year earlier."

Julia later told me that Mason had sworn her to secrecy after his surgery. She was to tell the children that he'd been hospitalized with the flu. Kitty was seven months pregnant, and Mason claimed that he did not want to upset her. Ellen learned that Mason had been hospitalized and visited him there, but neither she nor Charlie recall how they learned of his cancer. Ellen states that once she learned of his operation, she contacted Dr. Pickar because neither Mason nor Julia was willing to discuss it. As previously mentioned, I learned about it from the neighbors, much to their embarrassment that my family had not told me themselves.

Although one can never state with assurance that his ultimate outcome would have been any different, Dr. Pickar was certain that Mason's choice to delay treatment contributed to his poor outcome. But I must wonder what factors impeded Mason's full understanding of the seriousness of this illness when it was in its earliest stages. Was it simply denial? Fifty years ago, the word "cancer" was often spoken in hushed tones. People were afraid of the C-word. Cancer was widely perceived, correctly so in many cases, as a death sentence. The treatments were often as barbaric and painful as the symptoms themselves, and public perception was that they did no good anyway. Patients often met a diagnosis of cancer with a fatalistic shrug of the shoulders and kept on smoking.

Was this merely fatalism? It seems so out of character for a person such as Mason who had rushed headlong into so many battles, both literally and figuratively.

Throughout his life, Mason had been dismissive of people whose opinions he did not share. As a young man, he acted this way with his father and with ministers whose sermons he disagreed with. To what degree did this dismissive nature contribute to Mason's failure to take this threat seriously? To what degree did he misunderstand the seriousness of this condition even in its earliest stages? Pickar pointed out clearly in his letter to Ellen that both Mason and Julla minimized any discussion of any specifics of his illness.

For a man who proposed that "the unexamined life is not worth living," his failure to examine this crucial aspect of his own health presents a contradiction. But as his own colleague Richard McCormick stated, "Mason never took care of himself."[3]

What kept Mason from sharing the important aspects of his life, those both positive and negative, with his family? It would be easy to claim that he was just another taciturn and stoic New Englander, but that still does not address why. He was neither taciturn nor stoic in public or in class.

Family can get too close. Family can see past the veil. Family members know you for real, when you come in the door and the public persona goes away. Family knows if you curse, rage, or drink too much. As I've mentioned previously, Mason clearly personifies historian William Manchester's assessment of Winston Churchill: "Most public men have one personality for the world and another in private."[4]

Upon Mason's retirement, he and Julia moved back to their home in Rumson, New Jersey. Caring for a husband with stage IV cancer, Julia's workload now increased. (Photo credit: Rutgers University Library Special Collections and University Archives)

But Mason's friends barely knew him either. They did sometimes see him at his most raw, occasionally verbally abusive. But I am grasping at straws here, trying to uncover Mason's reasons for his failure to take action in the face of serious cancer. Maybe it was simple denial. There were no outward signs of depression. And maybe he did decide simply to retire just because he had "gone stale." Knowing Mason as well as I do, now anyway, I do know that there was nothing simple about him.

In the spring, with Mason still weak from surgery, he and Julia flew to Atlanta to see Kitty and their first grandchild, Julia Kernan Farnham. The colostomy bag, held in place with straps like a girdle, leaked and stank. He had no control over noisy passage of bowel contents into the bag.

The summer of 1971 was eventful. First, Mason and Julia moved from the President's House back to Rumson. Julia was now managing a household on her own, preparing three meals a day with no help. Ellen had completed her graduate studies in art history at Yale. In June, she was en route to her new job at the National Portrait Gallery in Washington, D.C. Her stormy three-year marriage to Frank Miles would not survive the stress of the move.

Also in June, Julia's brother Reg, who had lived in Paris since 1954, survived a heart attack. She never told us about it. On August 19, Julia's beloved youngest brother Walter, who had taken her for her first airplane flight in a J-3 Piper Cub in 1938, perished in the crash of a commuter plane in a thunderstorm in Maine, leaving behind a wife and five children. His sudden loss devastated our entire family.

And Mason was retiring, officially on September 1, exactly twenty-five years to the day from his first day at Rutgers in 1946.

Julia withdrew. Dr. Pickar expressed in a letter to Ellen that "I hear that she does not leave the house very much." He expressed concern over the possibility of depression. In one year, Julia's husband had retired with widespread cancer, one brother had died violently, her only other brother had suffered a heart attack, and one daughter was in the midst of a contentious divorce.

But Julia had suffered quietly for many years. In the President's House she had gone to bed late, an hour after Mason, staying up drinking scotch, smoking, and reading. She slept in. When I was still a teenager living at home, she would be in bed when Mason left for work and I left for school. She had seen Dr. Pickar on several occasions in the past to deal with the stress of her required public life. Publicly, as Pickar noted, she was genuinely "sweet, charming and pleasant" but had expressed to him that she would occasionally explode, only when alone, throwing objects across the room in anger and frustration. As private as Mason was, Julia was even more secretive.

Once an avid painter, Julia had always painted people, often dancing, sailing, or playing at the beach. She never touched a canvas again after the summer of 1971. Now that Mason's workload was decreasing subsequent to his retirement, with his illness her workload was increasing.

CHAPTER 26

Guggenheim, 1972

Never was there a time when the causes and effects of man's basic behavior,
especially his tendencies to violence, aggression and dominance, stood more
in need of explanation and exploration.   *—MWG, January 1972*

In 1959, Harry Frank Guggenheim, a former naval aviator, publisher, and scion of the Guggenheim family, gathered two close friends,* also aviators, to redirect the efforts of his forty-year-old Harry Frank Guggenheim (HFG) Foundation specifically toward research in the fields of human aggression and violence, under the heading "Man's Relation to Man."

In January 1971, upon Guggenheim's death, his heir, Peter Lawson-Johnston, a former Rhodes Scholar and the grandson of industrialist Solomon R. Guggenheim, succeeded him as a chairman of the board. Soon after this, Dr. Henry Allen Moe, president of the HFG Foundation, retired due to disability secondary to multiple surgeries. Living in Princeton, New Jersey, Lawson-Johnston was well acquainted with Mason Gross's reputation at Rutgers as both an administrator and a scholar. Lawson-Johnston knew that in 1967 Mason had been instrumental in obtaining three graduate fellowships from the foundation for the new Rutgers Anthropology Department. In December 1971, Lawson-Johnston invited Mason to be the next president of the HFG Foundation.

Still recovering from his colectomy earlier that year, Mason was now fully retired. He had accepted a position as chairman of a funding drive for the new Monmouth County Museum, but the academic life that he had loved for over forty years was gone. He had courteously chosen not to remain in

---

* His aviator friends were General James H. Doolittle and Charles A. Lindbergh.

any capacity at Rutgers, as that would have shackled the new president, who would be trying to develop his own style of leadership and needed to be out of the shadow of the previous administration. Interestingly enough, the new stereo system that Julius Bloom had helped Mason choose to listen to his favorite music went unused. Mason had needed the music to relax and escape from the stresses of Rutgers. No longer needing the escape, he rarely listened to the music. The stereo and his records, like his grandmother's unused piano in the corner, quietly gathered dust.

In other words, for the first time in his life, Mason was bored stiff.

This next chapter of Mason's life had begun in 1966 as Rutgers was developing the curriculum for the new Livingston College. A poll of Rutgers students revealed that the students wanted more anthropology. Rutgers had no anthropology department at the time, but Mason had long recognized this discipline's value. "The development of the science of anthropology has revealed to us the different ways in which cultures have evolved, and have taught us to be more objective about our own as well as less superior about others."[1]

On the basis of several recommendations, including Robert Ardrey, author of *African Genesis* and *The Territorial Imperative*, Ernest Linton, the first dean of Livingston College, hired Robin Fox to become the first chairman of anthropology at Rutgers. Fox agreed as long as Lionel Tiger also be brought on board. Fox came from the London School of Economics in 1967, and Tiger came a year later from the University of British Columbia. Collaborating at Rutgers since then, Tiger and Fox had each "achieved considerable prominence in the study of the evolution of human behavior."[2]

Tiger credits Mason with the development of the Rutgers Anthropology Department in 1967. To help kick-start the department, Mason found funding for three graduate fellowships and obtained three more from the HFG Foundation. Additionally, he obtained a $500,000 National Institutes of Health fellowship to create a joint program in medicine, biology, and anthropology with the Rutgers Medical School, which was also in its infancy at the time. "This wonderful program involving Rutgers and Guggenheim and several primate field sites flourished under Mason and the others until New

Jersey politics dismantled it."[3] Fox credits Mason's oversight as instrumental in the establishment of the "tremendously effective Rutgers Center for
Human Evolutionary Studies, now ranked in the top ten in the country."[4]

In late 1971, it was not clear what Mason's initial reaction was to the invitation to become president of the HFG Foundation. However, we know that,
encouraged by a favorable *New York Times* book review, Mason went to his
favorite bookstore to purchase B. F. Skinner's newest publication, *Beyond
Freedom and Dignity*, which denied the existence of free will and moral
autonomy. In the bookstore, Mason was not impressed with his first perusal
of Skinner's book. His eye drifted on the same shelf to the newly published
The Imperial Animal, coauthored by Rutgers anthropologists Lionel Tiger
and Robin Fox.

Mason read *The Imperial Animal* and decided that this was the right
direction for himself and for the HFG Foundation. He accepted the position of president of the foundation. Mason suggested that Fox and Tiger
could write a proposal to the HFG Foundation to support their work. Instead,
they submitted a design for a whole program of research involving human
and animal behavior whose researchers were contributing to the development of ethology and related subjects. Mason successfully proposed that
Tiger and Fox become the foundation's first research directors.

In January 1972, Tiger and Fox proposed a detailed five-year plan emphasizing the universal factors behind the cultural manifestations of dominance and its accompanying violence. With Mason, they brought something
new to the HFG Foundation, namely a research proposal with a set of con-
crete goals and objectives and specifics for funding research fellowships,
symposia, and publications.

Mason's desk at Rumson was stacked with books by Tiger and Fox and
also by Robert Ardrey, Robert Jay Lifton, and sociobiologist E. O. Wilson.
There were research proposals from anthropologists and behavioral scientists, such as Drs. Louis S. B., Mary, and Richard Leakey.

Twice weekly, Mason drove to the HFG Foundation's offices in midtown
Manhattan. According to Fox, Mason was a "hands-off" boss. Mason chaired
many of the successful conferences and seminars that resulted from their

collaboration. His strictest criterion was that all afternoon meetings had to conclude prior to five o'clock "so that we could hit the martinis before dinner."

Refreshingly freed from the endless politics of running a state university, Mason was back in the world he loved. His mind was sharp as ever, but he was physically weakening. Fox's wife Lin still remembers those occasions when Mason had to lean "upon her arm as he grew shakier over the years."

The cancer was catching up with him.

CHAPTER 27

The Door Opens, Then Closes Tight, 1975–1977

The same thing happened to me in Miami in 1942. I got the flag caught in a telephone line.
                                                                    —*MWG, May 1975*

I had been the tallest guy in my company in basic training. As such, I was assigned the honor of carrying the American flag with a color guard on a cold, rainy, and windy April day in the 1975 bicentennial parade in Massachusetts that commemorated the Battles of Lexington and Concord. During the parade, right "by the rude bridge that arched the flood,"[1] I got the American flag caught in a tree.

Home on leave, I sat in my parent's kitchen and told this story to my mother and sister. Mason had been mixing himself a scotch and water in the pantry and came in and sat at the kitchen table. Ellen and Julia were astonished; he had never come in to sit with us before.

"I bet you were the tallest guy in your company," he laughed.

"Yes, how did you know?"

"The same thing happened to me in Miami in 1942," he answered. "I was the tallest one also, and we were having a parade for a visiting general. A thunderstorm came up, and I got the tip of the flag staff caught in a low-hanging telephone line."

There it was, finally, a moment and a common experience for us to share.

The following summer, I was stationed in Alaska but was sent back to Connecticut to the Sikorsky factory for six weeks of training on helicopter maintenance. My time there coincided with Mason's sixty-fifth birthday. I

Mason had dark eyebrows that moved independently of each other, like those of a border collie, and could corroborate his full range of emotions, from playful inquiry (shown here) to arctic glare. This was Julia's favorite photograph of him. (Photo credit: Rutgers University Library Special Collections and University Archives)

asked my mom to keep the secret that I would take an afternoon train to New Jersey and arrive in time for Mason's birthday supper.

Trains and connections being what they are, I arrived to their home in Rumson just after supper. Julia and her friends were in the kitchen cleaning up and talking. When I walked in the backdoor, they all crowed and said their greetings and gestured for me to sit at the table and have some supper.

Julia interrupted, "Go say hello to your father." I rose from the table and headed toward the living room, where all the men were smoking, drinking, and laughing. I was backlit by the setting sun, shining through the tall windows, so that when I walked into the room, Mason at first thought I was Charlie. But when he realized it was me he called out in surprise "Tommy!" and stood to embrace me. I could not believe his smile and the glow in his eyes. He was glad to see me.

That had never occurred before.

Mason sat me down next to him, and the men, all of whom I had known since I was a child, gathered around to hear what I had been doing in Alaska. Finally, Mason asked if I had eaten yet. When I answered "no" he told me to go get some supper and then come back.

I walked back to the kitchen, shaking my head in disbelief. He was so warm and outgoing, like a different person.

I wrote home, typically every month or so. There was not much else to do in Alaska at night in the winter. Mason sent me a letter on my birthday in Alaska. He had done that only once before, on the occasion of my twenty-first birthday. He did not speak of his colostomy, only that his feet were tingling and numb from diabetes. He did add that he suspected that my time was mostly boredom interspersed with moments of sheer terror, which was absolutely correct.

He was reaching out again.

————

Mason was growing weaker. A frame that at its athletic peak was 173 pounds had ballooned during the good life at Rutgers. With lunch daily at the faculty club and considerable calories from alcohol, he had once weighed to close to 280 but now was below 150 pounds. His barrel torso was barely supported by legs so thin they looked like stilts.

Mason needed help going up the winding wooden stairs to the bedroom. Julia, herself also frail from mild emphysema due to forty years of smoking, was afraid to walk behind him, worried that if he fell backwards on the stairs they would both go down. Charlie was living in Freehold, a thirty-minute drive from Rumson. Every evening after work, he came in the late evening, enjoying a home-cooked meal and his parents' company. When Mason said he was going to bed, Charlie followed him on his slow climb up the eighteen hardwood steps and helped him into bed. As private as he had ever been, Mason allowed only Julia to help him with changing out the colostomy bag, always full of liquid stool.

The bag would burst if Mason rolled over on it. It would sometimes come loose, always embarrassing during social situations or flying to see his grandchildren in Atlanta.

There is no record of when his esophageal symptoms began. However, he had written home since he was a graduate student in 1935 requesting more antacid for his indigestion. He had written Julia during the war with the same request. As a child, I remember that he carried a tin of Bisodol with him everywhere, taking a small pill from it regularly throughout the day. The medical profession had not yet identified the major risks for esophageal cancer, now known to be hard liquor, cigarettes, and chronic esophageal reflux (i.e., indigestion) requiring constant antacid use. Mason had all three risk factors and had been symptomatic for decades.

Mason began to have trouble swallowing. At first, solid foods would intermittently get caught in his esophagus, then softer foods and more frequently. By Christmas 1976, he could not hide that his food was getting caught. He sat at the head of the table, turning red. He wasn't choking; he could breathe, but his food had gotten stuck. To what extent he blew off these symptoms is unknown, but we know that Mason was not one to run to the doctor all the time. He was getting a regular follow-up every month with his private physician. It is very difficult to imagine that an experienced internist would not have done something about these symptoms if Mason had mentioned them. Every time he came home from his doctor's visit he told Julia, "The doctor says I'm doing great!" He did not seek medical attention for another six months.

In May, Mason and Julia traveled to New Haven to witness Ellen awarded her PhD in art history. It was his last pleasure trip.

In June 1977, Mason was admitted to Middlesex General Hospital in New Brunswick. This county hospital, of which he had once been chairman of the board, was preparing to become the main teaching hospital for Rutgers Medical School, no longer a part of Rutgers but now with the University of Medicine and Dentistry of New Jersey. There, Mason was diagnosed with primary esophageal cancer, primary in that it was an original cancer and not a metastasis, or spread from his original bowel cancer. This was a brand-new plague.

I visited Mason there in July before his surgery. He was standing by the window smoking. I told him that I had recently been assigned to assist in the diving operations for an archaeological expedition searching for under-water evidence of Etruscan ruins on the Italian coast, north of Rome.

"Exactly where will you be?" he asked.

I tried to pronounce the city. "Kee-vee, Kivvee . . . ?"

"Civitavecchia," he interrupted with great clarity. "I was there in 1944."*

Mason continued. "I want you to go into my library. On the shelves clos-est to the door, on the third shelf up from the bottom, the fourth book in from the left is a blue book, by T. E. Lawrence, titled *The Etruscans.* Take it with you."

That evening, I went to Mason's library and pulled the book out. The bind-ing, which had been exposed for three decades on that shelf, had bleached to gray, but the cover itself, protected from the sun, was robin's-egg blue. As I had his permission to borrow the book, I removed it from its rightful place and took it with me to Italy. I replaced it when I got home.

---

*Mason volunteered no further details at that time, but I later discovered from his let-ters home during the war that Civitavecchia was where he and his army colleagues had gotten lost and had inadvertently crossed behind enemy lines in search of the road to Rome.

Esophageal surgery is very difficult to perform, so Mason was transferred to New York Hospital, where the surgery was a success, as is often claimed, but the patient was not doing well. He suffered considerable hallucinations for several weeks after the surgery, impatient with the nursing staff and, once in his delusion, barking that "what this place needs is a good sergeant." He ordered Julia's brother Reg, himself by now a retired physician, to find his shoes so they could go out and get a drink.

This was the longest period Mason had gone without alcohol or tobacco in many decades. It was unclear if he was hallucinating from alcohol withdrawal or due to the now well-described effects of general anesthesia among the elderly. There was no mention of it in the hospital record.

Mason's rehabilitation from surgery required slow and careful advancing of his diet from liquids to soft solids and finally to a normal diet. Mason was transferred from New York back to Middlesex General Hospital and finally released home in September, after three months in the hospital.

One Friday in early October, Ellen called home saying she was coming up that weekend from D.C. for a visit. Mason's last words to her on the phone were prophetic and ominous. "Please come quickly," he said.[2]

Back at my Coast Guard base in Massachusetts, on Sunday, October 9, I received a phone message that my father was ill. I called home, and Julia informed me that Mason was back in the local hospital because he had been vomiting, unable to keep anything down.

Mason had been diagnosed with a life-threatening small bowel obstruction, most likely secondary to adhesions and scarring from his original surgery. The doctors recommended immediate surgery to relieve the obstruction. Already comatose, Mason could not communicate his consent, but Julia agreed to the procedure on his behalf. I later found out that the surgeons opened him up, took one look, and closed him right away. His entire abdominal contents were rigid, fused into one large metastatic tumor. There were hardly any individual organs left to identify.

Mason never awoke. Julia sat with him, stroking the back of his hand and, in a one-sided conversation, recalling their good times together. She got up on the bed and lay down next to him for a short while.

The next day, Monday, October 10, I took the Peter Pan Bus lines to Providence and Amtrak to New York. I sat in the café car, drinking Ballantine Ale. I wrote in my journal that day "I think he's going to give up." I took the North Jersey Coast local to Red Bank and walked from there a mile or so along the Navesink River to Riverview Hospital.

In the calm of the early evening, with the red hues of sunset reflected in the still water, I saw rowers out on the river.

At Riverview, I was informed that visiting hours were over. I was instructed to return in the morning. I took a cab home. Julia knew I was en route, but I had not communicated when I would be arriving. Somewhere along the way, I had learned to keep the details of my life to myself. So, Julia had left me a plate of supper in the oven. Charlie and Ellen were there and had visited him in the hospital that day. Kitty was flying up from Atlanta in the morning.

"He's in a coma," Charlie said. "They have a machine breathing for him." Charlie also noted that in order to keep a nasogastric tube in place in his nose, the nurses had shaved his gray mustache. Charlie said that he hardly recognized Mason without it.

At 7:30 A.M. as we were preparing to go visit Mason, the hospital called to say that he had just passed away. The death certificate would read "pneumonia," also known as the "old man's friend," but would not mention his recent three months in the hospital for cancer.

Mason was buried in Hartford on a cold and gray autumn afternoon. I rode from New Jersey with Dick and Suzanne Schlatter. That night, I sat in Bill and Jane Robinson's hotel room. We drank scotch and watched the Yankees win the third game of the World Series against the Dodgers. Mason had been an ardent Yankees fan, and they hadn't won the World Series since 1962.

Their victory seemed appropriate.

CHAPTER 28

The Last Post, 1977

Loyal sons of Rutgers battling
'Mid the shadows of twilight.
For the prestige of old Rutgers
On the gridiron now they fight.
Ring the bell of old Queens College,
Paint the town as ne'er before,
Play the game, boys, play together,
Score once more,
> *Oh, score once more.*
> *— "Loyal Sons"*

Ellen, my oldest sister, recalls that she could not believe Mason was really gone. Before she arrived on his last days, he had gone into a coma and then slipped away without a word. She noted in her journal, "I have lost my leader, my guide."

Already very slender, Julia lost a lot of weight and was drinking heavily in the evenings, crying at night in the ambivalence of his absence versus the final relief of his recent suffering. She kept humming the old hymn that she had chosen for Mason's funeral in Hartford:

The strife is o'er, the battle done

Now is the Victor's triumph won . . .

On Thursday, November 3, 1977, Rutgers held a memorial service in the Kirkpatrick Chapel, with music by organist David Drinkwater, the Rutgers Men's Glee Club, and the Kirkpatrick Chapel Choir. President Edward Bloustein, Mason's successor, spoke no words of eulogy, as "none are needed," but asked everyone "to remember and to celebrate a fulfilled life."[1]

Mason's closest friends and colleagues read selections from his speeches, some of which Rutgers University Press published three years later as *The Selected Speeches of Mason Welch Gross*, edited by Mason's colleagues Richard P. McCormick and Richard Schlatter. Houston Peterson, long retired and still living in his Greenwich Village apartment, did not attend. His colleagues later told me that the saddest days of his life were after the death of Mason Gross.

Under "Soup" Walter's direction, the Rutgers Glee Club sang "A Hymn to Queens":

The evening shadows soft are falling,
The twilight glows from out the west.
The charm of darkness gently falling
Brings all the world to peace and rest.[2]

Drinkwater's Kirkpatrick Chapel Choir sang one of Handel's Chandos anthems:

Let the whole earth stand in awe.
Let the heavens rejoice and let the earth be glad.

The speakers described a man I hadn't known. But during the service, I remember thinking that in his last few years Mason had reached out to me, telling me about Civitavecchia, sharing a story about basic training in Miami, and expressing his clear joy at seeing me when I wandered in unannounced on his sixty-fifth birthday.

During the readings, my mind wandered and I recalled a summer morning when I was fifteen, not yet driving. Mason was impatient to get to an appointment, and his big gray Oldsmobile would not start. He loathed being late. He came back in the front door, furious, and slammed it so hard that the house shook. He called to Julia to phone a mechanic to come help him start his car. He growled at me when I suggested that we try it again.

We went outside, and Mason sat in the driver's seat. I popped the hood and unscrewed the top of the air filter.

"Try it again," I said. Mason cranked the starter. The automatic choke was closed, and the engine had flooded. I stuck my index finger into the carburetor and flipped open the choke. The engine started with a roar. I screwed the air filter cover back in place and closed the hood.

I stood by the side of the car as Mason cranked his window down. I think that I expected him to mutter "Thanks." He didn't. He couldn't.

Mason didn't ask me how I had done that, because he couldn't give a damn to know the inner workings of an Oldsmobile's automatic choke or the ideal stoichiometric ratio of gasoline and air necessary to support combustion. But ever the philosopher, searching for the origin of knowledge, he did look up at me with a look of wonder and asked, "How did you *know* how to do that?" I shrugged my shoulders; I didn't have an answer. I guess it was part logic and part flash of insight, the essence of the human experience, maybe also part faith and part reason.

At the memorial service, Rutgers historian and Mason's friend Richard P. McCormick was reading from Mason's 1959 Kirkpatrick sermon "Faith and Reason": "The hypothesis of the power and goodness of a loving god has enabled us to deduce that life is meaningful and purposeful; that personal and social morality are not merely conventions of the moment; that human beings can hope to grasp, by reason, and understand the significance of both the moral and the physical order of the universe."[3]

In an ancient Rutgers tradition, at the close of every football game, win or lose, the Rutgers fans always stood and sang "Loyal Sons." Mason's baritone had always been as loud as anyone's. The Rutgers Glee Club chose it to close the ceremony this day as well.

After the memorial, President Bloustein had offered his office for a small gathering and refreshments. But it was a beautiful autumn morning, and everyone stayed outside, feeling the warmth of the sun on our shoulders, milling about and talking. I ran into old neighbors and friends, including my eighth-grade English teacher, James Burke (Rutgers class of 1962), whom I had not seen in twelve years.

Ellen recalls that during the memorial, hearing Mason's own words read by his closest friends, she could feel him still living in those words, and at the close of the service she was able to say goodbye.

Music professor Scott Whitener described a very moving service, offering "the deepest reverence" for Mason. Standing outside after the service, Scott tried to offer his condolences to Julia, but walking up to her on that exquisite autumn morning, he found himself unable to speak because he was "so choked with tears." Julia had to comfort him instead. Scott later added, "I was but a small dot on the tapestry that he wove, but he was the guiding light of my life."[4]

CHAPTER 29

The Hope That Lies within You, 2020

So, my friends, I have a maxim for you: Trust your instinctive sense of joy.
—MWG, June 1961

In any biography, chronology is not the critical issue and is at best a matrix, or a scaffold, upon which the author can drape the real stories of a person's life, stories that weave through the times in which he or she lived. Mason's chronology ended on October 11, 1977, but his story does not end with his interment. There are recollections, but those too will fade and finally self-extinguish as his chronology moves from memory into history. So, what remains except for a collection of archives, speeches, handwritten letters, and a bronze relief on the Voorhees Mall* only yards away from where Mason took his oath of office and read his inaugural address over sixty years ago in the spring of 1959?

Several years ago, Jim Shokoff (Rutgers class of 1962) was driving through New Brunswick with his granddaughter Meghan, who was then a student at Rutgers. When they passed the Mason Gross School of the Arts, she asked Jim, "Who was Mason Gross, anyway?"

Jim answered that he had known Mason and that Mason had been one of his teachers. Meghan was astonished.

"You *knew* him?" she asked. Meghan asked Jim to tell her about Mason, because she had heard the name many times and not many people knew much about him.

---

* Previously known as the Nielson campus.

The reader may recall that Mason had first proposed a school for the performing and visual arts in 1954 and that for many decades he had struggled trying to build a proper concert hall at Rutgers. Although money appeared plentiful for classroom construction, especially so for science and technology departments, he was never able to generate widespread enthusiasm for a proper auditorium. He applauded Eugene Ormandy for his annual concerts in the Rutgers gymnasium but understood when Ormandy said he could no longer bring his orchestra there. Mason's colleague Julius Bloom, executive director of Carnegie Hall and Rutgers's coordinator of concerts and lectures, had noted how so many large state universities had built auditoriums for this purpose, but Mason could never get funding for a concert hall. Repeated requests through the 1960s fell on deaf ears.

Definitive commitment to a separate school of the arts did not come until June 1975, four years after Mason's retirement, when Rutgers president Edward Bloustein appointed a small committee to plan the development of the School for the Creative and Performing Arts. On February 13, 1976, although noting that funding had not yet been obtained for the school's formation, the Board of Governors committed Rutgers to the creation of the School for the Creative and Performing Arts and appointed Douglass theater arts professor Jack Bettenbender as its first acting dean.

On Friday, October 14, 1977, as Mason was being interred into the family plot in Hartford, Connecticut, the Rutgers Board of Governors, at its regularly scheduled monthly meeting, moved to rename the new school from Rutgers School for the Creative and Performing Arts to the Mason Gross School of the Arts.

The new Mason Gross School of the Arts moved into temporary quarters in the former P. J. Young's department store in downtown New Brunswick, reminding us of the previous temporary quarters for the veterans in 1946; for the Institute of Alcohol Studies; for the Institute for Labor and Management; for the Newark Law School, which had started in an abandoned brewery; and for the Rutgers Medical School, which had held its first classes in an old army barracks that caught fire after being struck by lightning.

We must remember that nothing at Rutgers has ever been easy.

In time, with the eventual construction of its own facilities, the Mason Gross School of the Arts became the center that exists today, with its own auditoria. For two decades Mason had unknowingly advocated for his own legacy, namely a school that has since become a world-class center of excellence in the arts and a public university that, not merely regional, has joined the ranks of the truly great American universities.

In addition to the Mason Gross School of the Arts, what else remains?

———

I promised to the reader more for your trouble than the mere chronology of a long-deceased Rutgers philosophy professor. I promised something that we could all take forward into our lives, as Mason himself once stated. "In a well-done biography, one can enter into the very soul of great individuals and expand one's own soul along with them. . . . The identification of one's self with the great men and women of history is the surest way of arousing the imagination to a sense of the possibilities of one's spiritual growth and to a . . . realization of one's own potential."[1]

I cannot read Greek, and I am not half the musician Mason was. But I have learned a great deal in this adventure. I never took one of Mason's classes, but in the last two years I've studied Plato, Aristotle, Thucydides, Saint Augustine, Spinoza, Kant, and Whitehead. I've learned that the study of philosophy, both Western and Eastern, is not just an esoteric subject for the smart guys in the ivory tower but instead is "the self-critique of one's values."[2]

I've read about the value of courtesy and how mutual respect even for those who disagree with us can help with difficult negotiations. Noting the value of expertise in any given field, I now recognize that expertise alone can yield for us judgment of facts but that we need also to examine our judgment of values.

Thinking back to the Rutgers class of 1951 in which there were four black graduates, one can see how the face of Rutgers has changed. Rutgers president emeritus Richard L. McCormick has stated that Rutgers has become "one of the most culturally and racially diverse universities in the world."

He added that "although these achievements are the result of decades of hard work by Rutgers men and women, that work unquestionably began during the presidency of Mason Gross, who stood strongly with black students and supported the university's positive responses to their demands," even at the risk of his own reputation with the state government and with the public at large.[3] As we have learned from his own words, Mason believed that including students and faculty from different backgrounds enhanced everyone's experience at a university and would help break down the artificial barriers that keep certain groups forever consigned to poverty.

———

From Mason's combat experience and from that of his students who were veterans, I recall that the true nature of war can never be fully appreciated except by those who have experienced its horror firsthand, reminding me to highly suspect the motives of those who advocate war but have never been to war themselves. I've seen from Mason's example how true patriotism can take many forms beyond mere flag-waving. As Adlai Stevenson once stated, patriotism is "not short, frenzied outbursts of emotion, but the tranquil and steady dedication of a lifetime," adding in the same address that it is "easier to fight for principles than it is to live up to them."[4]

I've learned what excellence feels like, as Mason once described to the 1961 graduating class of Milton Academy: "Excellence in an object or an idea, an activity or a person, is that quality which evokes in you directly a sense of tremendous excitement and joy. . . . Times are serious, yes. But surely the issue before us in these serious times is the preservation and enhancement of freedom, and freedom is a joyous notion. We will never know what the freedom is that we are fighting for if we lose our sense of joy in the beauty and goodness which is around us."[5]

I've read about education and that real education is self-education, and I've learned to develop a sense of truth that will not be deceived by half-truth. "A half-truth is a statement which purports to be true and offers some evidence of the truth, but which is such that the whole truth would either prove it to be false or would radically change its meaning. It appeals to people who have been taught to demand evidence but are not critical about the quality of the evidence provided."[6]

In his "impromptu remarks" in front of Old Queens in May 1970, Mason spoke of the need to "go out and persuade." Persuasion is not the same as marching in passionate protest. Persuasion involves deliberate and cogent conversation, with respect for those whose opinions differ from yours. Mason's constant message was how fear and anger could yield to facts and ideas. I've learned that if I care about my country and my democracy, I must help persuade the public, sometimes one person at a time, that the value of literature, art, music, history, and philosophy lies not merely in the subject matter, but rather in the transformation, which affects the human soul, to a broader and richer understanding of what is worthwhile in this world.

Mason's life shows the importance of being involved in one's community and not just by voting every four years. It means volunteering for the PTA, even if your children are all grown. It means supporting the local library, going to town council meetings, volunteering at the food bank, helping to count absentee ballots, or vocally backing local candidates who support public education. It means looking inside oneself and asking how in the most prosperous country on Earth we have come to acquiesce to such miserable, abject poverty of our own citizens.

Most of all, I have learned about hope in troubled times, and we certainly do now live in troubled times. Mason once said that hope is "the steady and settled habit of soul which makes us constantly move towards achieving the things which we believe in. . . . Our sure hope rests upon our faith in a divine purpose, motivated by divine love. With this firm belief, hope can still remake the world."[7]

In a sermon at the Kirkpatrick Chapel in 1960, Mason reminded us that within the Bible there is an underlying "theme of hope casting out fear," most often quoted from Paul's First Epistle to the Corinthians: "and now abideth these three: faith, hope and charity."*

---

* This is from I Corinthians 13:13 in the King James version, Mason's favorite. The Greek word *agápē* is here translated as "charity" but is seen in other translations as "love."

Spinoza has pointed out that "hope and fear are counterparts, and both relate to the future outcome which is currently in doubt."[8] We do not have to hope that the sun will rise tomorrow, neither do we fear that it will not. Individually or sometimes collectively, we may hope that we will be here to see it or may fear that we may not be, but the physics of the sunrise itself is, for now, never in doubt. Mason said, "Hope, like fear, involves uncertainty, but differs from fear in that it anticipates a good rather than a bad result. . . . The habit or state of character which we call hope is more than that of an optimist," who says "don't worry," or that difficult situations will resolve on their own. Mason believed that "hope is not satisfied with the cheap assurance that everything is going to be all right" and "is not merely a vision of a better order of things, nor can it wait patiently until some better order works itself out."[9]

In this sermon, Mason said that love is often manifested in works of love, to which we can ascribe the translation of the Greek word *agápē* as "charity." Just as love is often expressed in works of charity and as faith is also expressed in good works, so too hope does not sit still; it moves forward. He added that the truly hopeful person will not sit and hope, but will bend "every energy to bring the goal nearer."[10] As we can recall from Reverend Willis Howard Butler's sermons from a hundred years ago, "we are the means by which the will of God is accomplished."[11]

What kinds of actions should we expect would be the "inevitable expression of hope"? Like true virtue, true courage, true faith, and true love, true hope manifests itself in a life of confident action. Hope does not sit quietly, waiting for things to turn out well. "As Spinoza points out, hope calls upon us to do something to bring the desired goals about."[12]

In the Rutgers commencement address in the turbulent spring of 1970, Mason said that "universities are established to train and develop the intellect and to put it to use for the benefit of mankind." Mason's own hope for us was manifested in the creation of a great state university, with "hope for our future generations, . . . hope in so many ways that gives meaning to all that we are trying to do."[13] "Love, our love of God for us and our love for our fellow men, paints a picture of the goal to be achieved. Faith causes us to believe in this goal, rejecting all attempts to view the world as a series of meaningless accidents. And Hope provides us with the energy to move toward that goal. Without faith, we would have nothing to hope for. Without love we would have no comprehension of the values to be achieved. And hope is necessary to keep us driving forward."[14]

Retiring twenty-five years to the day from his arrival on the banks of the Old Raritan, Mason closed his career at Rutgers suggesting to all a renewed contemplation of a few basic concepts. As he stood for his last commencement address in June 1971, his body wracked with cancer, he spoke a few last words. These were not the last words in his life but rather his last official words to his students, now graduates of his legacy, his beloved Rutgers, a truly great state university.

These last words from a philosophy professor, who in the distant past had considered a career in the ministry, were not from Plato or Augustine or Spinoza or Kant or even Whitehead. The words were from St. Paul's letter to the Corinthians. Mason, the philosopher, spoke again of faith, hope, and love. "Faith has broad theological implications, but in a simpler sense, it can mean faith in ourselves. . . . Hope has to be based on the belief that life is meaningful and that therefore the evils by which we are surrounded can be overcome. But the most meaningful of all is the concept of love."[15]

So, like Socrates who brought philosophy down from the clouds and into the marketplace, the agora, so did Mason Gross endeavor to bring it down from the ivory tower and translate it into a life not of speculation but instead of action. His solution to life's inevitable struggles is summarized in these few simple actions for us forever to remember:

> These three principles, or what really
> are commandments, I leave with you:
> To respect the dignity of man,
> to reject the unexamined life as not worth living,
> and to love thy neighbor as thyself.[16]

Appendix

Omer Brown II (Rutgers class of 1969)

W. David ("Bill") Burns

Forrest Clark (Rutgers class of 1949)

Dennis Dalton (Rutgers class of 1960)

Lewis deSchweinitz (U.S. Army Air Force, 1942–1945)

Mary deSchweinitz Parrish

David Drinkwater (U.S. Air Force, 1953–1955)

Katherine (Kitty) Gross Farnham

Marion Freeman (Princeton class of 1973)

Monte Gaffin (Rutgers class of 1945, also 98th Bomb Group, 15th Air Force)

David Gars (Rutgers class of 1949)

James Gerstenzang (Rutgers class of 1969)

Phillip "Sandy" Greene

Charles Welles Gross (Mason's older son)

Cornelia Gross (Mason's sister)

Julia Kernan Gross

Clifford Hemphill (Rutgers class of 1966)

John Huntington

Michael Illuzzi

A. D. "Dev" Kernan (U.S. Army, 1966–1968)

B. Robert Kreiser

Everett Landers (Rutgers class of 1950)

Richard Levao (Rutgers class of 1970)

Tony Mauro (Rutgers class of 1971)

Richard L. McCormick

Norman McNatt (Rutgers class of 1964)

Karl Metzger (Rutgers class of 1933)

Ellen Gross Miles

Dolly and Philip Minis

Bob Ochs (Rutgers class of 1948, also platoon sergeant, 6th Marines, Okinawa)

Lance Odden

Sara Huntington Ohly

Houston and Mitzi Peterson

David Pickar (Rutgers class of 1969)

Ron Reisman (Rutgers class of 1971)

William Robinson (Princeton class of 1939, also U.S. Navy, 1941–1945)

D. W. Rogers (Rutgers class of 1954)

Richard Schlatter

Richard Seclow (Rutgers class of 1951)

James Shokoff (Rutgers class of 1960)

Mark Singley

Stu Smith (Rutgers class of 1964)

Lionel Tiger

Jackson Toby

James Ulsamer ((Rutgers class of 1972)

Ed Vincz (Rutgers class of 1947)

Steve Wagner

F. Austin "Soup" Walter (Rutgers class of 1933)

Scott Whitener

Roland Winter

Acknowledgments

As any mission is rarely accomplished by one person alone, so I must acknowledge my gratitude to so many who assisted in this project. Mr. Peter Mickulas, senior editor at Rutgers University Press, provided much guidance along the way. Professor Susan Hertz, Professor Thomas Payne, and other English Department faculty members at the University of New Hampshire added valuable input.

This biography would not have been possible without Mason Gross's own words, which more than any interpretations of my own have led us into the depth of his character. As Mason himself never kept a journal or wrote a memoir, the two most important sources of his own words were the hundreds of letters, addresses, and speeches now in the Rutgers University Special Collections and University Archives and also over a thousand letters than Mason wrote either to his parents or to my mother Julia from 1924 to 1950. I owe a debt of thanks to Ms. Erika Gorder and her staff at the Rutgers University archive. Aside from putting in many hours, including workarounds, assisting me in my research while the facilities were undergoing extensive repair, the staff was enthusiastic for the project, for which I am indebted. As to Mason's own personal correspondence, I must humbly thank three generations of the women in my family, namely my grandmother Hilda Welch Gross, my mother Julia, and my older sisters Ellen and Kitty, who kept these archives safe and (mostly) dry for decades.

I must thank the scores of "Loyal Sons of Rutgers," namely the Rutgers alumni, retired staff, and emeritus faculty, listed below, who consented to be interviewed or corresponded with me and with my sisters. I wish specifically to thank Professor David Drinkwater (emeritus), Mr. Steve Wagner (Rutgers crew coach), and Professor Richard L. McCormick, president emeritus of Rutgers University.

My greatest appreciation goes to my two sisters, Ellen and Kitty, both professional historians, and to my brother Charlie, the research librarian, whose recollections were essential but whose support, encouragement, and assistance made this biography possible. My partner Suzanne Cornelius was instrumental in finding addresses and telephone numbers of Rutgers alumni whose contact information had been lost.

Inevitably, as in all biography, this story would be very different if it had been written by somebody else. I can only hope that I have appropriately honored everyone's affection for Mason's legacy and their memory of a wonderful man and a wonderful time to have been at Rutgers.

Notes

ABBREVIATIONS

CWG   Charles Welles Gross, Mason's father
EGM   Ellen Gross Miles, Mason's eldest daughter
HDT   Horace Dutton Taft, founder of the Taft School
JKG   Julia Kernan Gross, Mason's wife
KGF   Katharine Gross Farnham, Mason's second daughter
MWG   Mason Welch Gross
RAM   *Rutgers Alumni Monthly*
SC/UA   Special Collections and University Archives, in Rutgers Univer-
            sity Library
SC/UA MWG   Special Collections and University Archives, in Rutgers Univer-
            sity Library, Mason Gross Presidential Records, RG 04/ A16

AUTHOR'S NOTE

Epigraph: SC/UA MWG, Box 120, Folder 28, November 12, 1954, 14.

1. SC/UA MWG, Box 3, Folder 2, Letter to Miss DiGiacomantonio, January 1968.
2. SC/UA MWG, Box 123, Folder 1, May 5, 1970.
3. SC/UA MWG, Box 121, Folder 35, November 1962.
4. SC/UA MWG, Box 120, Folder 42, June 13, 1958.

CHAPTER 1 — PROLOGUE: THE INAUGURATION, 1959

Epigraph: Mason Gross, Inaugural Address, May 6, 1959, SC/UA MWG, Box 120, Folder 45.

1. *Daily Home News* [New Brunswick], May 6, 1959.
2. Clemens, *Rutgers since 1945*, 1.
3. Halberstam, *The Fifties*, 624.

4. *RAM* 51, no. 1 (September 1971): 10.

5. McCormick and Schlatter, *The Selected Speeches of Mason Welch* Gross, x.

CHAPTER 2 — POSTMARK: WILLCOX, ARIZONA, 1928

Except as noted, the quotations in this chapter are from numerous letters that Mason wrote to his family from 1926 through 1928, now in the Gross family archives.

Epigraph: SC/UA MWG, Box 122, Folder 12, April 23, 1964, 18.

1. *RAM* 51, no. 1 (September 1971): 3.

2. Gross family archives, as recorded in nineteenth-century Gross family Bibles.

3. Correspondence between CWG and principal of Hartford High School, in Gross family archives.

4. Taft School report cards 1926–1929, in Gross family archives.

5. Letter from HDT to CWG, in Gross family archives.

6. Correspondence between CWG and Yale admissions director, in Gross family archives.

7. Wilson et al., *Harrison's Principles of Internal Medicine*, 564.

8. Isaacson, "Deming Welch Isaacson, the Hot Springs Ranch, and the Muleshoe Cattle Company."

9. The Thacher School, https://www.thacher.org/.

10. MWG letter to his parents, May 1928, in Gross family archives.

11. SC/UA MWG, Box 122, Folder 12, April 23, 1964, 18.

12. MWG letter to his parents, June 1928, in Gross family archives.

13. *RAM* 51, no. 1 (September 1971): 4.

CHAPTER 3 — POSTMARK: CAMBRIDGE, ENGLAND, 1930

Except as noted, the quotations in this chapter came from numerous letters that Mason wrote to his family from 1929 through 1934, now in the Gross family archives.

Epigraph: SC/UA MWG, Box 122, Folder 1, Rutgers Commencement Address, June 5, 1963, 2.

1. MWG letter to his parents, 1934.

2. MWG letter to his parents, 1930.

3. Taft yearbook, class of 1929.

4. Correspondence between CWG and Yale admissions director, 1929, in Gross family archives.

5. Letter from HDT to Cambridge University, June 12, 1929, in Gross family archives.

6. Letter from HDT to CWG, 1929, in Gross family archives.

7. MWG letter to his parents, October 1929, in Gross family archives.

8. *RAM* 51, no. 1 (September 1971): 4.

9. Correspondence between CWG and Professor Souter, 1930, Gross family archives.

10. Taft yearbook, class of 1929.

11. MWG letter to his parents, April 1931, in Gross family archives.

12. *RAM* 51, no. 1 (September 1971): 4.

13. Letter from Rutgers dean Samuel McCullough to MWG, SC/UA.

14. Cunard Entertainment Program, RMS *Mauretania*, September 17, 1932, in Gross family archives.

15. Mansfield, *The History of the Asylum Hill Congregational Church, 1865–1965.*

16. Ibid.

17. McCormick and Schlatter, *The Selected Speeches of Mason Welch Gross*, 27.

18. Reverend Willis H. Butler, circa 1924, in Mansfield, *The History of the Asylum Hill Congregational Church, 1865–1965.*

19. McCormick and Schlatter, *The Selected Speeches of Mason Welch Gross*, 135.

20. Reverend Willis H. Butler, circa 1925, in Mansfield, *The History of the Asylum Hill Congregational Church, 1865–1965.*

21. Brown, *The Boys in the Boat*, 161.

22. McCormick and Schlatter, "On Excellence," June 9, 1961, in *The Selected Speeches of Mason Welch Gross*, 76.

23. MWG, personal anecdote.

24. Mason Gross to his parents, November 1933, Gross family archives.

CHAPTER 4 — THE BLIND DATE, 1939

Except as noted, the quotations in this chapter came from numerous letters that Mason wrote to his family, contained in the Gross family archives. Sources for the information on the rise of Nazism and the pathway to war derive from several sources, including William Manchester's three-volume biography of Winston Churchill, *The Last Lion*, as well as Manchester's summary of U.S. history in *The Glory and the Dream* and Churchill's own 1949 six-volume *The Second World War.*

Epigraph: MWG to his parents, April 1940.

1. Author's discussion with Phil and Dolly Minis, West Tisbury, MA, July, 1978.

2. K. C. Kernan and J. D. Kernan, *Francis Kernan*, 199.

3. Various news clippings from Thomas Wood family archives.

4. Author's discussion with JKG.

5. Chadis, "National Register of Historic Places Continuation Sheet: Johnny Seesaw's Historic District," 7.

6. "Seesaw's Lodge History," Seesaw's Lodge, www.seesawslodge.com/history.

7. MWG letter to his parents, October 1934.

8. SC/UA MWG, Box 122, Folder 8, address at Brooklyn College, October 15, 1963.

9. Tarnas, *The Passion of the Western Mind*, 354.

10. Mason Gross, "Contemporary Philosophy," 212.

11. Tarnas, *The Passion of the Western Mind*, 354.

12. Ibid.

13. Gross, "Contemporary Philosophy," 213.

14. Ibid., 222.

15. Gross, "Whitehead's Philosophy of Adventure."

16. Gross, "Contemporary Philosophy," 221.

17. MWG correspondence with William Welch, in Gross family archives.

18. Manchester, *The Last Lion*, 177.

19. MWG letter to JKG, 1943.

20. MWG correspondence with William Welch, in Gross family archives.

21. Letter to MWG from Lambert Shepard, in Gross family archives.

22. Personal recollection, JKG to author.

23. Letter to MWG from Lambert Shepard, in Gross family archives.

CHAPTER 5 — POSTMARK: SOMEWHERE IN ITALY, 1944

Except as noted, the quotations in this chapter came from 120 letters that Mason wrote during the war to Julia (JKG) or to his parents from 1942 to 1945, in Gross family archives.

Epigraph: MWG in a letter to JKG, October 1944, in Gross family archives.

1. Letter to MWG from Lambert Shepard, April 1941, in Gross family archives.

2. Letter to MWG from Iris Shepard, July 1941, in Gross family archives.

3. Letter to MWG from Peggy Cotteril, February 1942, in Gross family archives.

4. Manchester, *Goodbye, Darkness*, 167.

5. Atkinson, *The Day of Battle*. 467.

6. Birdsall, *The Log of the Liberators*.

7. Personal recollection, JKG to author.

CHAPTER 6 — THE HOMECOMING, 1945

Epigraph: SC/UA MWG, Box 120, Folder 13, Bennett Junior College, June 1950, 11.

1. Manchester, *The Glory and the Dream*, 430.

2. SC/UA MWG, Box 120, Folder 13, Bennett Junior College, June 1950, 11.

3. Reverend Willis Butler, circa 1925, in Mansfield, *The History of the Asylum Hill Congregational Church, 1865–1965*.

CHAPTER 7 — GOODBYE TO NEW YORK, 1946

Once settled at Rutgers, Mason wrote fewer letters. Except as noted, the quotations in this chapter came from letters that Mason wrote to his parents, almost every Sunday afternoon, from 1945 to 1948, in Gross family archives.

Epigraph: MWG in a letter to JKG, April 1945.

1. Personal communication with Houston and Mitzi Peterson, Dennis, MA, June 1977.

2. Cooper Union, www.cooper.edu.

3. MWG letters to his parents, 1946.

4. Personal recollection, JKG to author.

5. SC/UA MWG, Box 123, Folder 5, June 10, 1970, 5.

6. Richard Seclow (Rutgers class of 1950), interview with author, April 2019.

7. Letter to KGF from Forrest Clark (Rutgers class of 1949), in Gross family archives.

8. Letter to KGF from Ed Vincz (Rutgers class of 1947), in Gross family archives.

9. Letter to KGF from Monte Gaffin (Rutgers class of 1945), in Gross family archives.

10. Letter to KGF from Roland Winter (Rutgers class of 1949), in Gross family archives.

11. Letter to KGF from Robert Ochs (Rutgers class of 1949), in Gross family archives.

12. David Drinkwater, interview with author, June 2019.

13. "On Excellence," June 9, 1961, in McCormick and Schlatter, *The Selected Speeches of Mason Welch Gross*, 75.

14. Letter to KGF from Robert Ochs, 1998, in Gross family archives.

15 MWG letter to his parents, September 1948, in Gross family archives.

CHAPTER 8 — IN THE SECOND CHAIR, 1949

Epigraph: MWG in a letter to the Taft School headmaster, November 1948, in the Gross family archives.

1. SC/UA MWG, Box 28, Folder 8, letter to President Clothier.

2. SC/UA MWG, Box 21, Folder 14.

3. Letter to MWG from Charles P. Taft, in Gross family archives.

4. MWG reply to Charles P. Taft, in Gross family archives.

5. Robinson and Bliss, *A Life to Measure By*, 3.

CHAPTER 9 — RUTGERS V. THE RED SCARE, 1954

Epigraph: MWG in a letter to Julia from Italy, 1945.

1. Manchester, *The Glory and the Dream*, 425.

2. MWG in a letter to his parents from Aberdeen, 1930.

3. MWG in a letter to Julia from Italy, 1945.

4. Kreiser, "Championing Academic Freedom at Rutgers," 5.

5. Schlatter, "On Being a Communist at Harvard."

6. Kreiser, "Championing Academic Freedom at Rutgers," 6. See also McCormick, *Rutgers: A Bicentennial History*, 293–296.

7. SC/UA MWG, Box 57, Folder 7.

8. Kreiser, "Championing Academic Freedom at Rutgers," 6.

CHAPTER 10 — PHILOSOPHY OF EDUCATION V. THE "BIG LIE"

Much of Alfred North Whitehead's personal history comes from the autobiograph-
ical notes in his *Essays in Science and Philosophy*. Many of Mason's speeches discuss objective versus subjective education, but much of this chapter derives from
just a few, including his November 1962 lecture not to philosophy students but
instead to a senior class in the School of Business (SC/UA MWG Box 121, Folder 38)
in which he discusses Plato, Aristotle, Augustine, Aquinas, Descartes, Kant, and
Whitehead.

Epigraph: SC/UA MWG, Box 120, Folder 42, June 13, 1958.

1. SC/UA MWG, Box 3, Folder 2, letter to Miss Giacomantonio, January 1968.

2. SC/UA MWG, Box 4, Folder 4, letter to Green Knoll Elementary, May 1968.

3. Reverend Willis Howard Butler in Mansfield, *The History of the Asylum Hill Congregational Church, 1865–1965*.

4. Whitehead, *Essays in Science and Philosophy*, 3.

5. Ibid., 14.

6. Gross, "Contemporary Philosophy," 222.

7. MWG in letter to Julia from Italy 1945.

8. Whitehead, *The Aims of Education and Other Essays*, 3.

9. Whitehead, *Essays in Science and Philosophy*, 12.

10. KWG personal correspondence with author, 2019.

11. Whitehead, *The Aims of Education and Other Essays*, 16.

12. SC/UA MWG, Box 120, Folder 38, to the Am. Council of Education, Octo-
ber 1957, 11. Also in McCormick and Schlatter, *The Selected Speeches of Mason Welch Gross*, 8.

13. Whitehead, *The Aims of Education and Other Essays*, 18.

14. SC/UA MWG, Box 120, Folder 8, 1.

15. Ibid., 6.

16. Ibid., 8.

17. Letter to KGF from David Mars, 1998.

18. SC/UA MWG, Box 120, Folder 27, Address to the Pennsylvania Society of
Newspaper Editors, May 20, 1954, 5.

19. SC/UA MWG, Box 121, Folder 38, 6.

20. Whitehead, *The Aims of Education and Other Essays*, 3.

21. SC/UA MWG, Box 121, Folder 38, 5.

22. Ibid., 9.

23. Gross, "Whitehead's Philosophy of Adventure," 362.

24. Gross, "Contemporary Philosophy," 222.

25. SC/UA MWG, Box 121, Folder 38, 19.

26. SC/UA MWG, Box 120, Folder 48, 4.

27. SC/UA MWG, Box 121, Folder 38, 19.

28. Ibid., 22.

29. SC/UA MWG, Box 122, Folder 12, April 23, 1964, 18.

30. SC/UA MWG, Box 120, Folder 31.

31. Letter to KGF from D. W. Rogers, 1998.

32. SC/UA MWG, Box 120, Folder 14, New Jersey Welfare Conference in November 1950, 1.

CHAPTER 11 — THE INAUGURATION, 1959

Epigraph: SC/UA MWG, Box 120, Folder 46, Inaugural Address, May 6, 1959, 12.

1. McCormick, *Rutgers: A Bicentennial History*, 3–8.

2. Shorto, *The Island at the Center of the World*, 98.

3. David Drinkwater, interview with author, June 2019.

4. *RAM* 51, no. 1 (September 1971): 18.

5. Schlatter, in McCormick and Schlatter, *The Selected Speeches of Mason Welch Gross*, i.

6. SC/UA MWG, Box 120, Folder 46, Inaugural Address, May 6, 1959, 2.

7. Ibid., 7.

8. Ibid., 9.

9. Ibid., 12.

10. McCormick and Schlatter, *The Selected Speeches of Mason Welch Gross*, 61.

11. MWG, letter to Hon. Wayne Dumont, October 13, 1965.

12. *New York Times*, July 10, 1959.

CHAPTER 12 — INTO THE FISHBOWL, 1959

Epigraph: Mason Gross in a letter to his parents, Cambridge, 1932.

1. KGF to author, 2020.

2. Ibid.

3. Clayton H. Farnham (MWG's son-in-law), conversation with author, circa 2012.

4. Schlatter, in McCormick and Schlatter, *The Selected Speeches of Mason Welch Gross*, iii.

5. Ibid.

6. Shokoff, communication with author, 2019.

7. Schlatter, in McCormick and Schlatter, *The Selected Speeches of Mason Welch Gross*, iii.

8. Ibid., i.

9. McNatt, communication with author, 2019.

10. Singley, letter to KGF in 1998.

11. Shokoff, communication with author, 2019.

12. McNatt, communication with author, 2019.

13. Manchester, *The Last Lion*, 384.

14. EGM to author, 2019.

15. Robinson, letter to author, 1995.

CHAPTER 13 — THE CULTURAL WASTELAND, 1959

Epigraph: SC/UA MWG, Box 121, Folder 43, April 1963, 9–10.

1. Letter to CWG from HDT, June 1929.

2. SC/UA MWG, Box 120, Folder 48, September 12, 1959, 2.

3. *New York Times*, September 13, 1959.

4. SC/UA MWG, Box 120, Folder 48, September 12, 1959, 3.

5. Ibid.

6. Schlatter, in McCormick and Schlatter, *The Selected Speeches of Mason Welch Gross*, vii.

7. Krober and Kluckhohn, *Culture*.

8. SC/UA MWG, Box 120, Folder 49, 2.

9. Louis Menand, "The Looking Glass," *New Yorker*, August 26, 2019.

10. JKG to author, circa 1995.

11. SC/UA MWG, Box 120, Folder 49, 2.

12. SC/UA MWG, Box 120, Folder 47, 4.

13. Ibid., 5.

14. Ibid.

CHAPTER 14 — NOTHING AT RUTGERS WAS EVER EASY

Epigraph: SC/UA MWG, Box 121, Folder 13, October 31, 1960, 11.

1. Fuentes and White, *Scarlet and Black*, 154.

2. McCormick, *Rutgers: A Bicentennial History*, 226.

3. Ibid., 283.

4. Ibid., 307.

5. Birkner, *McCormick of Rutgers*, 138.

6. Halberstam, *The Fifties*, 624.

7. McCormick, *Rutgers: A Bicentennial History*, 312.

8. Perlstein, *Nixonland*, 162.

CHAPTER 15 — CRISIS, 1961

Epigraph: SC/UA MWG, Box 61, Folder 1, 1961.

1. Manchester, *The Glory and the Dream*, 890.

2. Kempe, *Berlin 1961*, xv.

3. Ibid.

4. SC/UA MWG, Box 120, Folder 48, September 12, 1959, 1.

5. SC/UA MWG, Box 15, Folder 8, Institute for Alcohol Studies.

6. *New York Times*, April 18, 1965.

7. SC/UA MWG, Box 62, Folder 1.

CHAPTER 16 — FAITH AND REASON

Epigraph: "Faith and Reason," in McCormick and Schlatter, *The Selected Speeches of Mason Welch Gross*, 27.

1. Ibid.

2. Ibid., 28.

3. MWG letter to JKG from Italy, January 1945.

4. "Faith and Reason," in McCormick and Schlatter, *The Selected Speeches of Mason Welch Gross*, 27.

5. SC/UA MWG, Box 123, Folder 4, June 3, 1970.

6. Tarnas, *The Passion of the Western Mind*, 474.

7. Ibid., 112. Mason translated this as "Believe in order that ye may understand."

8. "Faith and Reason," in McCormick and Schlatter, *The Selected Speeches of Mason Welch Gross*, 30.

9. SC/UA MWG, Box 120, Folder 26, April 21, 1954, 6.

10. SC/UA MWG, Box 121, Folder 11, June 5, 1963, 4.

11. Ibid., 5.

12. Ibid., 7.

13. "Faith and Reason," in McCormick and Schlatter, *The Selected Speeches of Mason Welch Gross*, 32.

14. Ibid.

15. SC/UA MWG, Box 121, Folder 35, November 1962.

16. Gross, "Contemporary Philosophy," 220.

CHAPTER 17 — SCORE ONCE MORE, 1965

Epigraph: "How to Frame an Athletic Policy," December 8, 1960, in McCormick and Schlatter, *The Selected Speeches of Mason Welch Gross*, 69.

1. Dowling, *Confessions of a Spoilsport*, 51.

2. Anecdote provided by Steve Wagner, Rutgers crew coach, personal communication with author.

3. SC/UA MWG, Box 83, Folder 12, Correspondence with Comptroller M. A. Johnson.

4. Ibid.

5. Dowling, *Confessions of a Spoilsport*, 35.

6. Ibid., 34.

7. McNatt, communication with author, 2019.

8. Dowling, *Confessions of a Spoilsport*, 36.

9. Clemens, *Rutgers since 1945*, 319.

10. Dowling, *Confessions of a Spoilsport*, 157.

11. Clemens, *Rutgers since 1945*, 322. A letter to this effect from Mark Singley is in the Gross family archives.

CHAPTER 18 — THE INFLECTION POINT, 1965

For the best summary of the entire Genovese episode and its backstory, I am indebted to B. Robert Kreiser, "Championing Academic Freedom at Rutgers: The Genovese Affair and the Teach-In of April 1965." For the details of the history of the Vietnam War, the author referred to Kahin and Lewis, *The United States in Vietnam*, and former U.S. Marine Corps lieutenant Philip Caputo's *A Rumor of War*.

Epigraph: Mason Gross on WOR-TV, August 8, 1965.

1. Kahin and Lewis, *The United States in Vietnam*, 419.

2. Leebaert, *Grand Improvisation*, 407.

3. Caputo, *A Rumor of War*, 53.

4. Kreiser, "Championing Academic Freedom at Rutgers," 7.

5. Ibid., 11.

6. Ibid.

7. Ibid., 12.

8. Ibid., 22.

9. Perlstein, *Nixonland*, 68.

10. SC/UA MWG, Box 120 (Misc. correspondence), MWG letter to Hon. Wayne Dumont, candidate for governor, October 13, 1965, 2.

11. SC/UA MWG, Box 120, Folder 23, January 31, 1953.

12. Manchester, *The Glory and the Dream*, 1039.

13. Birkner, *McCormick of Rutgers*, 140.

14. Birkner, "The Turbulent Sixties at Rutgers," 48.

15. SC/UA MWG, Box 33, Folder 7.

CHAPTER 19 — THE SILENT STEINWAY, 1965

Epigraph: McCormick and Schlatter, *The Selected Speeches of Mason Welch Gross*, 79.

1. MWG in a letter to his parents from college, 1931.

2. David Drinkwater, interview with author, June 2019.

3. Ibid.

4. KGF, interview with author, December 2019.

5. JKG recollection.

6. SC/UA MWG, Box 31, Folder 2.

7. SC/UA MWG, Box 16, Folder 15.

8. David Drinkwater, interview with author, June 2019.

9. McCormick and Schlatter, *The Selected Speeches of Mason Welch Gross*, 103.

10. SC/UA MWG, Box 77, Folder 3, Letter from NJ citizen.

11. SC/UA MWG, Box 120, Folder 38, October 31, 1957, 3.

12. SC/UA, records of Provost Richard Schlatter.

CHAPTER 20 — THE JEWEL IN THE CROWN

Epigraph: SC/UA MWG, Box 122, Folder 44, Rutgers Commencement Address, May 29, 1968.

1. SC/UA MWG, Box 16, Folder 11.

2. SC/UA MWG, Box 16, Folder 11, PHS Publication 709.

3. SC/UA MWG, Stetten letter to MWG, October 4, 1965.

CHAPTER 21 — THE YEAR EVERYTHING WENT WRONG, 1968

Major sources for this chapter include Bowden, *Hue 1968*; McCormick, *The Black Student Protest Movement at Rutgers*; Perlstein, *Nixonland*; and Manchester, *The Glory and the Dream*. Donald Harris's story is documented in SC/UA, MWG papers (Harris).

Epigraph: SC/UA MWG, Mason Gross, June 3, 1963.

1. Manchester, *The Glory and the Dream*, 1122.

2. Bowden, *Hue 1968*, 40.

3. McCormick, *The Black Student Protest Movement at Rutgers*, 24.

4. Ibid., 7.

5. Richard Seclow, interview with author, 2019.

6. Manchester, *The Glory and the Dream*, 1156.

7. Baldwin, "A Letter from a Region in My Mind." See also Manchester, *The Glory and the Dream*, 1204.

8. SC/UA MWG, Box 122, Folder 1, Rutgers Commencement Address, June 1963.

9. Manchester, *The Glory and the Dream*, 981.

10. Ibid., 1195.

11. Ibid., 1201.

12. *Student Voice* 4, no. 3 (October 1963).

13. SC/UA MWG, Box 28, Folder 4, Letter to faculty committee for Donald Harris.

14. Perlstein, *Nixonland*, 190.

15. SC/UA MWG, Box 122, Folder 41, April 9, 1968.

16. SC/UA MWG, Box 122, Folder 44, May 29, 1968, 9.

17. Ibid., 11.

CHAPTER 22 — LAW AND ORDER, 1968

Epigraph: SC/UA MWG, Box 33, Folder 7, NBC interview with Frank McGee, May 11, 1969.

1. Perlstein, *Nixonland*, 363.
2. SC/UA MWG, Box 77, Folder 3.
3. *Newark Star Ledger*, November 23, 1968, 1.
4. SC/UA MWG, Box 61, Folder 4.
5. SC/UA MWG, Box 77, Folder 8.
6. SC/UA MWG, Box 76.
7. *RAM* 51, no. 1 (September 1971): 22.
8. SC/UA MWG, Box 120, Folder 40.
9. *RAM* 51, no. 1 (September 1971): 22.

CHAPTER 23 — FAITH AND REASON V. LAW AND ORDER

Summaries of the Newark occupation and subsequent events are provided in McCormick, *The Black Student Protest Movement at Rutgers*. The Rutgers College student strike, occupation of Old Queens, and antiwar protests are summarized in Tony Mauro, "The Strike at Rutgers." See also Clemens, *Rutgers since 1945*. The Gross family archives have a great deal of correspondence from Rutgers alumni recalling this period.

Epigraph: SC/UA MWG, Box 122, Folder 1, June 1963.

1. Norman McNatt, interview with author, 2019.
2. Ronald Sullivan, "Cahill Beats Meyner in New Jersey," *New York Times*, November 5, 1969, 35.
3. Perlstein, *Nixonland*, 361.
4. SC/UA MWG, Box 16, Folder 8, American Council on Education letter, December 12, 1969.
5. Clemens, *Rutgers since 1945*, 16.
6. SC/UA MWG, Box 123, Folder 13.
7. McCormick, *The Black Student Protest Movement at Rutgers*, 40.
8. Letter from Robt. Ochs to KGF, January 19, 1998, Gross family archives.
9. SC/UA, MWG, Box 30, Folder 13, MWG's answer to a letter critical of his handling of campus protest.
10. SC/UA MWG, Box 33, Folder 7. Statements included those such as "giving in to these niggers . . . was a disgrace."
11. McCormick, *The Black Student Protest Movement at Rutgers*, 45.
12. SC/UA MWG, Box 122, Folder 47, unpublished draft, 6.
13. SC/UA MWG, Box 61, Folder 4.
14. Walter Wagonner, "Open Entry Started at Rutgers," *New York Times*, September 12, 1969, 45.

15. SC/UA MWG, Box 33, Folder 7, transcript of NBC interview with Frank McGee, May 11, 1969.

16. SC/UA MWG, Box 33, Folder 7, *Philadelphia Inquirer*, March 10, 1969.

17. Ronald Sullivan, "Meyner and Cahill Victors in Jersey Primary Races," *New York Times*, June 4, 1969, 1.

18. Ronald Sullivan, "Candidates Split on Rutgers Plan," *New York Times*, May 28, 1969, 31.

19. SC/UA MWG, Box 122, Folder 46, Rutgers Commencement Address, June 4, 1969.

20. David Drinkwater, interview with author, June 2019.

21. Clemens, *Rutgers since 1945*, 16.

22. Schlatter, in McCormick and Schlatter, *The Selected Speeches of Mason Welch Gross*, i.

23. *RAM* 57, no. 2 (December 1977): 6.

24. *RAM* 51, no. 1 (September 1971): 20.

25. *RAM* 57, no. 2 (December 1977): 7.

26. A. Devereux Kernan, interview with author, July 2018.

27. *Life*, June 27, 1969.

28. SC/UA, MWG, Box 115, Folder 10, Letter to the Rutgers Community.

29. Ronald Sullivan, "New Jersey Gubernatorial Election Too Close for Experts to Call," *New York Times*, November 2, 1969, 84.

30. Caputo, *A Rumor of War*, 228.

31. Ibid., 229.

32. David Greenberg, "A Half Century of 'Liberal Media Bias,'" *Wall Street Journal*, August 25, 2018, C4.

33. SC/UA MWG, Box 123, Folder 3.

34. Charles W. Gross, personal communication, 2018.

35. Ronald Sullivan, "Cahill Proposes 5% Sales Levy in Fiscal Crisis," *New York Times*, January 13, 1970, 34.

36. Ibid.

37. Ibid.

38. Letter from Peter Johnson (Rutgers class of 1971), December 13, 1997, in Gross family archives.

39. SC/UA MWG, Box 76, Folder 7.

40. Ronald Sullivan, "Passed in Jersey," *New York Times*, April 14, 1970, 1.

41. Ibid.

42. Perlstein, *Before the Storm*, 472, 478, 482.

43. Letter to KGF from J. Fromkin, February 10, 1998, Gross family archives.

44. Robert Ochs, personal communication, November 1977, standing outside MWG's memorial service at Kirkpatrick Chapel, New Brunswick.

45. Letter from Peter Johnson (Rutgers class of 1971), December 13, 1997, Gross family archives.

46. Michael Illuzzi (Rutgers class of 1977), in *1766: The Magazine of the Rutgers Alumni Association*, Fall 1987, 27.

47. Dean Arnold Grobman, letter to KGF, 1998, Gross family archives.

48. "Student Unrest and Educational Change," June 3, 1970, in McCormick and Schlatter, *The Selected Speeches of Mason Welch Gross*, 137.

49. "Remarks to Student Strike Rally," May 4, 1970, in McCormick and Schlatter, *The Selected Speeches of Mason Welch Gross*, 133.

50. SC/UA MWG, Box 122, Folder 1, Rutgers Commencement Address, June 1963.

51. "Student Unrest and Educational Change," June 3, 1970, in McCormick and Schlatter, *The Selected Speeches of Mason Welch Gross*, 136.

52. "Remarks to Student Strike Rally," May 4, 1970, in McCormick and Schlatter, *The Selected Speeches of Mason Welch Gross*, 133.

53. Schlatter, in McCormick and Schlatter, *The Selected Speeches of Mason Welch Gross*, x.

54. SC/UA MWG, Box 123, Folder 2.

55. Richard J. H. Johnston, "New Brunswick Weighs Future," *New York Times*, June 1, 1970.

56. Ibid.

57. SC/UA MWG, Box 123, Folder 1.

58. Tarnas, *The Passion of the Western Mind*, 31–32.

59. Schlatter, in McCormick and Schlatter, *The Selected Speeches of Mason Welch Gross*, x.

60. "Student Unrest and Educational Change," June 3, 1970, in McCormick and Schlatter, *The Selected Speeches of Mason Welch Gross*, 142.

CHAPTER 24 — JUNE 1970

Epigraph: "Student Unrest and Educational Change," June 3, 1970, in McCormick and Schlatter, *The Selected Speeches of Mason Welch Gross*, 134.

1. MWG letter to Board of Governors, July 1970.

2. Ron Reisman, interview with author, August 2020.

3. Clemens, *Rutgers since 1945*, 30.

4. SC/UA MWG, Box 51, Folder 15, September 20, 1973.

5. SC/UA MWG, Box 122, Folder 44, Rutgers Commencement Address, May 29, 1968, 9.

6. *Daily Targum*, December 15, 1969.

7. Tony Mauro, *Daily Targum*, September 14, 1970.

8. Birkner, *McCormick of Rutgers*, 151.

CHAPTER 25 — COMPLICATED, 1971

Epigraph: Letter from Dr. Gabriel Pickar to EGM, April 1972, in Gross family archives.

1. Ibid.
2. Ibid.
3. Birkner, *McCormick of Rutgers*, 151.
4. Manchester, *The Last Lion*, 384.

CHAPTER 26 — GUGGENHEIM, 1972

Information about Mason's role with the Harry Frank Guggenheim (HFG) Foundation comes from documents provided to the author by the foundation and correspondence with Rutgers professors emeriti Lionel Tiger and Robin Fox.

Epigraph: Mason Gross, in the Report of the HFG Foundation, January 1972.

1. SC/UA MWG, Box 122, Folder 34, May 1962.
2. Mason Gross, in the Report of the HFG Foundation, January 1972, 11.
3. Robin Fox, personal communication, 2020.
4. Ibid.

CHAPTER 27 — THE DOOR OPENS, THEN CLOSES TIGHT, 1975–1977

Epigraph: MWG, recalling a story about army basic training, May 1975.

1. Ralph Waldo Emerson, "Concord Hymn," in Ferguson, Salter, and Stallworthy (eds.), *The Norton Anthology of Poetry*, 515.
2. MWG to his daughter EGM, October 1977.

CHAPTER 28 — THE LAST POST, 1977

Epigraph: McKinney, *Songs of Rutgers*, 12.

1. In the program for the Mason Gross memorial, Kirkpatrick Chapel, November 1977.
2. McKinney, *Songs of Rutgers*, 16.
3. "Faith and Reason," in McCormick and Schlatter, *The Selected Speeches of Mason Welch Gross*, 32.
4. Author correspondence with Scott Whitener, professor of music emeritus.

CHAPTER 29 — THE HOPE THAT LIES WITHIN YOU, 2020

Epigraph: "On Excellence," June 1961, in McCormick and Schlatter, *The Selected Speeches of Mason Welch Gross*, 79.

1. SC/UA MWG, Box 120, Folder 28, November 12, 1954.
2. SC/UA MWG, Box 120, Folder 11.
3. Richard L. McCormick, personal communication, 2020.

4. Adlai Stevenson, "The Nature of Patriotism," Speech to the American Legion, August 27, 1952.

5. "On Excellence," in McCormick and Schlatter, *The Selected Speeches of Mason Welch Gross*, 79.

6. SC/UA MWG, Box 120, Folder 27, May 20, 1954.

7. "The Hope That Is within You," in McCormick and Schlatter, *The Selected Speeches of Mason Welch Gross*, 58.

8. Ibid., 56.

9. Ibid., 58.

10. Ibid.

11. Reverend Willis H. Butler, circa 1924, in Mansfield, *The History of the Asylum Hill Congregational Church, 1865–1965*.

12. "The Hope That Is within You," in McCormick and Schlatter, *The Selected Speeches of Mason Welch Gross*, 58.

13. Ibid., 59.

14. Ibid., 58.

15. SC/UA MWG, Box 123, Folder 6, Rutgers Commencement Address, June 4, 1971.

16. SC/UA MWG, Box 121, Folder 41, Rutgers Commencement Address, June 5, 1963, 7.

Bibliography

Ambrose, Stephen E. *The Wild Blue*. New York: Simon and Schuster, 2001.

Atkinson, Rick. *The Day of Battle: The War in Sicily and Italy, 1943–1944*. New York: Henry Holt, 2007.

Baldwin, James. "A Letter from a Region in My Mind." *New Yorker*, November 17, 1962, 59–144.

Birdsall, Steve. *The Log of the Liberators: An Illustrated History of the B-24*. New York: Doubleday, 1973.

Birkner, Michael J. *McCormick of Rutgers: Scholar, Teacher, Public Historian*. Westport, CT: Greenwood, 2001.

———. "The Turbulent Sixties at Rutgers: An Interview with Richard P. McCormick." *Journal of the Rutgers University Libraries* 58 (1997): 42–61.

Bowden, Mark. *Hue 1968*. New York: Grove, 2017.

Brown, James D. *The Boys in the Boat*. New York: Penguin, 2013.

Caputo, Philip. *A Rumor of War*. New York: Holt, Rinehart and Winston, 1977.

Chadis, Paula I. "National Register of Historic Places Continuation Sheet: Johnny Seesaw's Historic District." National Registry of Historic Places, NRIS 08000686, July 18, 2008, https://npgallery.nps.gov/GetAsset/ef4bfc0d-5c3c-47a1-84b5-2fae495879d9.

Clemens, Paul G. E. *Rutgers since 1945: A History of the State University of New Jersey*. New Brunswick, NJ: Rutgers University Press, 2015.

Dowling, William C. *Confessions of a Spoilsport*. University Park: Penn State University Press, 2007.

Fairbairn, Steve. *Chats on Rowing*. Cambridge, UK: W. Heffer and Sons, 1934.

Ferguson, Margaret, Mary Jo Salter, and Jon Stallworthy, eds. *The Norton Anthology of Poetry*. Shorter 4th ed. New York: W. W. Norton, 1997.

Frank, Richard. *Downfall: The End of the Japanese Empire*. New York: Random House, 1999.

Fuentes, Marisa J., and Deborah Gray White, eds. *Scarlet and Black*, Vol. 1, *Slavery and Dispossession in Rutgers History*. New Brunswick, NJ: Rutgers University Press, 2016.

Gross, Mason. "Contemporary Philosophy." *Columbia University Quarterly* 32, no. 3 (1940): 210–222.

———. "Whitehead's Philosophy of Adventure." *American Scholar* 9, no. 3 (1940): 361–371.

Guthrie, W.K.C. *The History of Greek Philosophy*, Vol. 3. Cambridge: Cambridge University Press, 1961.

Halberstam, David. *The Fifties*. New York: Random House, 1993.

Illuzzi, Michael. "Mason Gross: A Fond Remembrance of Rutgers' 16th President." *1766, The Magazine of the Rutgers Alumni Association*, Fall 1987.

Isaacson, Robert. "Deming Welch Isaacson, the Hot Springs Ranch, and the Muleshoe Cattle Company." Bob Isaacson Blog, August 12, 2010, http://bisaacson .blogspot.com/2010/08/deming-welch-isaacson-hot-springs-ranch.html.

Kahin, George M., and John W. Lewis. *The United States in Vietnam*. New York: Dell, 1967.

Kempe, Frederick. *Berlin 1961*. New York: Putnam, 2011.

Kernan, Karen C., and John D. Kernan. *Francis Kernan*. Utica, NY: Oneida County Historical Society, 1999.

Kreiser, B. Robert. "Championing Academic Freedom at Rutgers: The Genovese Affair and the Teach-In of April 1965." *AAUP Journal of Academic Freedom* 7 (2016), https://www.aaup.org/sites/default/files/Kreiser_0.pdf.

Kroeber, A. L., and C. Kluckhohn. *Culture: A Critical Review of Concepts and Definitions*. Cambridge, MA: Peabody Museum, 1952.

Laney, Matthew. *Faith Forward*. Hartford, CT: Asylum Hill Congregational Church, 2016.

Leebaert, Derek. *Grand Improvisation: America Confronts the British Superpower, 1945–1957*. New York: Farrah, Strauss and Giroux, 2018.

Manchester, William. *The Glory and the Dream*. Boston: Little, Brown, 1973.

———. *Goodbye, Darkness: A Memoir of the Pacific War*. Boston: Little, Brown, 1979.

———. *The Last Lion: Winston Spencer Churchill Alone, 1932–1940*. Boston: Little, Brown, 1988.

Manchester, William, and Paul Reid. *The Last Lion: Winston Spencer Churchill, Defender of the Faith*. Boston: Little, Brown, 2012.

Mansfield, Lillian. *The History of the Asylum Hill Congregational Church, 1865–1965*. Hartford, CT: Asylum Hill Congregational Church, 1993.

Massing, Michael. *Fatal Discord*. New York: HarperCollins, 2018.

Mauro, Tony. "The Strike at Rutgers." Unpublished manuscript, used with permission of the author.

McCormick, Richard L. *Raised at Rutgers*. New Brunswick, NJ: Rutgers University Press, 2014.

McCormick, Richard P. *The Black Student Protest Movement at Rutgers*. New Brunswick, NJ: Rutgers University Press, 1990.

———. *Rutgers: A Bicentennial History*. New Brunswick, NJ: Rutgers University Press, 1966.

McCormick, Richard P., and Richard Schlatter, eds. *The Selected Speeches of Mason Welch Gross*. New Brunswick, NJ: Rutgers University Press, 1980.

McKinney, Howard D., ed. *Songs of Rutgers*. New York: J. Fischer and Bros., 1920.

Menand, Louis. "The Looking Glass." *New Yorker*, August 26, 2019, 81–86.

Morehead, James. *In My Sights: The Memoir of a P-40 Ace*. Novato, CA: Presidio, 1998.

Nature Conservancy. "Muleshoe Ranch CMA." Accessed October 2019. https://www.nature.org/en-us/get-involved/how-to-help/places-we-protect/muleshoe-ranch-cma/.

Northrop, F.S.C., and Mason W. Gross, eds. *Alfred North Whitehead: An Anthology*. New York: Cambridge University Press, 1947.

Perlstein, Rick. *Before the Storm: Barry Goldwater and the Unmaking of the American Consensus*. New York: Farrar, Straus and Giroux, 2001.

———. *Nixonland: The Rise of a President and the Fracturing of America*. New York: Scribner, 2008.

Robinson, William, and Martha Bliss. *A Life to Measure By: Bill Robinson, 1918–2007*. n.p.: Imprint Communications, 2007.

Russell, Bertrand. *A History of Western Philosophy*. New York: Simon and Schuster, 1945.

Schlatter, Richard. "On Being a Communist at Harvard." *Partisan Review* 44, no. 4 (1977): 605–615.

Shorto, Russell. *The Island at the Center of the World*. New York: Random House, 2004.

Tarnas, Richard. *The Passion of the Western Mind*. New York: Ballantine, 1991.

Thucydides. *The History of the Peloponnesian War*. Edited by Donald Lateiner. New York: Barnes and Noble Books, 2006.

Whitehead, Alfred North. *The Aims of Education and Other Essays*. New York: Macmillan, 1929.

———. *Essays in Science and Philosophy*. New York. Philosophical Library, 1947.

————. *Science and the Modern World: Lowell Lectures, 1925.* New York: Mentor, 1931.

Wiener, Jonathan. "Radical Historians and the Crisis in American History, 1959–1980." *Journal of American History* 76, no. 2 (1989): 399–434.

Wilson, Jean D., Eugene Braunwald, Kurt J. Isselbacher, Robert G. Petersdorf, Joseph B. Martin, Anthony S. Fauci, and Richard K. Root. *Harrison's Principles of Internal Medicine.* 12th ed. New York: McGraw-Hill, 1991.

Index

Page numbers in *italics* indicate information in photographs and captions. Mason Welch Gross is abbreviated as MWG.

About the Author

Dr. Thomas W. Gross is a retired firefighter, emergency physician, and military officer. He is a graduate of the University of California, Berkeley (AB in zoology, 1981) and Rutgers Medical School (MD, 1985). Gross is a previously published essayist, and this is his first full-length book. As a pilot, he volunteers to fly his aircraft, taking severely ill children and veterans to health care facilities. In the summer he captains a research vessel for the Shoals Marine Laboratory of the University of New Hampshire. Gross currently has four brilliant and creative granddaughters whom he doesn't get to see anywhere near enough.